OCCULT
GERMANY

"Christopher McIntosh has written the first 'hierohistory' of the German-speaking world: a history of its sacred task among the family of nations. Its essence, simply stated, is to assert the inseparability of matter and spirit. Thanks to enlightened monarchs, mystics, alchemists, poets, painters, and polymaths both famous and obscure, this truth has survived all hazards. Even the best-informed reader will find surprises here and benefit from the author's involvement both as spectator and actor in a never-ending process."

JOSCELYN GODWIN, AUTHOR OF
ATHANASIUS KIRCHER'S THEATRE OF THE WORLD

"Christopher McIntosh, a skilled storyteller and pioneer in the study of esotericism, takes readers on a captivating journey through the hidden realms of German culture, exploring the esoteric traditions that have shaped the nation's identity. From enigmatic secret societies to influential figures who walked the fine line between the seen and unseen, McIntosh delivers a compelling personal account of his exploration of the many facets of Germany's occult history while not shying away from the 'Nazi elephant in the room.' Engaging and enlightening, this book is a must-read for anyone seeking to understand the occult dimensions of one of Europe's most intriguing cultural landscapes."

HENRIK BOGDAN, PROFESSOR OF RELIGIOUS STUDIES
AT THE UNIVERSITY OF GOTHENBURG

"This is a deeply absorbing book that brings alive the hugely rich spiritual and philosophical world of German esotericism. It ranges from the mythology and archeological traces of the ancient Germanic tribes through profound medieval and Renaissance mystics to the modern world of Goethe and Rudolf Steiner. Through it all, Christopher McIntosh blends his customarily vast range of scholarship with a charming personal narrative of his own wide experiences in the German-speaking world. Among the numerous places and eras he evokes are the mysteriously atmospheric Externsteine stones and the romance and alchemical magic of Heidelberg Castle. He identifies an especially Germanic emphasis on the presence of spirit within matter that has given so much insight and wisdom to the world. The time has come for the German cultural sphere to reclaim its place as the home of one of the world's great esoteric traditions. This book is an important contribution to its welcome reemergence."

RALPH WHITE, AUTHOR OF *THE JEWELED HIGHWAY* AND COFOUNDER OF THE NEW YORK OPEN CENTER

"The strange and poetic world of the German occult imagination has for understandable reasons been something of a third rail for readers who know that reality is itself an enchantment. There is no better guide to that twilight world than Christopher McIntosh, who combines the erudition of the scholar, the curiosity of the explorer, and the sensibility of the poet. There are dark places in that vast mythic landscape of belief, practice, and speculation. But there are places of beauty and light as well: to read this book is to have a glimpse of the cultural dreamlife of such giants as Mozart, Goethe, Jung, and the great Teutonic philosophers."

FREDERICK TURNER, PROFESSOR EMERITUS, THE BASS SCHOOL OF ARTS, HUMANITIES, AND TECHNOLOGY, UNIVERSITY OF TEXAS AT DALLAS

"Christopher McIntosh's detailed and enlightening occult history of the German-speaking people takes the reader on an illuminating journey through the world of the spirits of the Earth, its early mythic heritage, and its many groups, artists, composers, and authors that have arisen to maintain this heritage."

NICHOLAS E. BRINK, PH.D., AUTHOR OF *THE POWER OF ECSTATIC TRANCE, BALDR'S MAGIC,* AND *BEOWULF'S ECSTATIC TRANCE MAGIC*

OCCULT GERMANY

OLD GODS, MYSTICS, AND MAGICIANS

CHRISTOPHER McINTOSH

Inner Traditions
Rochester, Vermont

Inner Traditions
One Park Street
Rochester, Vermont 05767
www.InnerTraditions.com

Cataloging-in-Publication Data for this title is available from the Library of Congress

ISBN 978-1-64411-734-7 (print)
ISBN 978-1-64411-735-4 (ebook)

Printed and bound in the United States by Lake Book Manufacturing, LLC
The text stock is SFI certified. The Sustainable Forestry Initiative® program promotes sustainable forest management.

10 9 8 7 6 5 4 3 2 1

Text design by Virginia Scott Bowman and layout by Priscilla Harris Baker
This book was typeset in Garamond Premier Pro with Frutiger, Gill Sans, Pineforest, and The Folman used as display typefaces

To send correspondence to the author of this book, mail a first-class letter to the author c/o Inner Traditions • Bear & Company, One Park Street, Rochester, VT 05767, and we will forward the communication. Contact information is also included on the author's website: **www.ozgard.net.**

Scan the QR code and save 25% at InnerTraditions.com. Browse over 2,000 titles on spirituality, the occult, ancient mysteries, new science, holistic health, and natural medicine.

To Donate

CONTENTS

Preface   ix

Acknowledgments   xiii

INTRODUCTION
Sky-God Land   1

1   Heidelberg: An Enchanted Gateway   16

2   Places of Power   25

3   Following Ancient Footprints   34

4   Fall and Rise of the Old Gods   48

5   Mystics, Magicians, and Witches   65

6   Rosicrucians, Freemasons, and Alchemists   77

7   Symbol-Strewn Spaces   94

8   Seers and Somnambulists   106

9   Seekers of the Light   114

10 Journey to the Self   130

11 Interbellum and Armageddon   148

12 Postwar Perspectives   166

13 Pagan Pathways   178

14 Spirit and Matter   193

15 Soul of the Landscape   199

16 Occult Germany Today   207

    Notes   218

    Bibliography   226

    Index   233

PREFACE

In this book I would like to take the reader on a magical journey through the enchanted land of Germany, which has been my home for what feels like half my life. Unlike most of the books I have written in the past, this one represents a personal quest, an itinerary, a history, a narrative, a journey of discovery, and a meditation.

Given the wide range of the subject matter, any attempt to be comprehensive would not have made sense, so I have adopted a selective and somewhat random approach to the places, people, events, and topics that are covered within the overall theme of occult, mystical, and esoteric Germany. To a considerable extent I have based my accounts on personal experience. The time frame extends from prehistory up to modern times, but not strictly in chronological order, and past and present are often interwoven. As for the geographical parameters, until relatively recently Germany was not a nation-state but a cultural and linguistic entity, extending far beyond the borders of present-day Germany. Therefore the book will include sorties into Austria, German-speaking Switzerland, and places such as Prague, where in former times there were sizeable German communities.

In this book, as in much of my earlier writing, I explore the connection between history and myth and how the one is constantly turning into the other. In my previous book, *Occult Russia,* I argued that Russian history since the late nineteenth century can be seen as the acting out of an epic scenario involving the notion of three successive ages, based on a prophetic tradition going back to biblical times. First comes the age of the Emperor of the Last Days (the Tsar), then the age of the Antichrist (the Bolshevik government), and finally the age of Christ returned (present-day Russia and the resurgence of the Orthodox Church).

What might be the corresponding scenario for Germany? One thinks of Karl Marx's dialectical process (taken over from Hegel), ending in the final triumph of the proletariat and perfect communism, but this never really put down deep roots in Germany as it did in Russia, apart from the relatively brief period of the German Democratic Republic. Whereas Russia can see itself as having reached the grand final stage of a historic drama, Germany is still engaged in an existential search for which the quest for the Holy Grail is an apt metaphor. Germany is the wounded king and his ailing country, waiting for the knight Parsifal to come and bring healing.

In Germany there is, of course, a big elephant in the room—namely, the memory of the Third Reich. The elephant either tends to dominate the conversation or is studiously ignored in such a way that he dominates it anyway. Even when he is invisible, the people in the room uneasily skirt around an elephant-shaped space. Then there are those who insist on seeing elephant footprints everywhere and are always ready to blast away with their rifles, even at the shadow or the phantom of an elephant. There are even some who persist in treating the elephant as a fetish.

In an insightful book called *Die deutsche Seele* (The German Soul) the coauthors Thea Dorn and Richard Wagner write, "We are not worried that Germany will abolish itself. We just observe that it is running itself down, losing its memory." While some, they write, are overcome with shame at the crimes of Nazism, "others are content as long as the television works and there is enough beer in the refrigerator." And yet these authors discern a growing longing for that which is essentially German.[1]

Something profoundly German is the element of the mystical, magical, occult, and esoteric that runs through German history, going right back to the ancient Germanic tribes in their deep forests, with their shamans and their sacred groves. The same spirit is there in the great mystics like Hildegard of Bingen, Meister Eckhart, and Jakob Boehme, in the strivings of the alchemists and Rosicrucians, in the poetry of Goethe, in the music of Wagner, in the Masonic lodges and esoteric orders, and in the religious counterculture of recent times. All these things are part of a great current that has run a partly underground course for many centuries but whose time has now perhaps arrived. I have spent much of my life exploring various aspects of that current. It has been a fascinating and richly rewarding journey. I now share with my readers the German phase of that journey.

ACKNOWLEDGMENTS

As regards acknowledgments it is hard to know where to start, as my German odyssey has been a long one. It began when I was a small child growing up in Edinburgh, and a young German woman named Ingrid Koch (later Pickhardt after her marriage) came to stay with us as an au pair. She instilled in me a love of her country and taught me my first German words. We remained in contact intermittently and then more regularly after I moved to Germany and until her death in 2021. Without her I might never have written this book.

Deep gratitude, as always, goes to my wife, Donate, especially as she is an important part of the story told here. Posthumous thanks and a tribute go to my dear friend the late Nicholas Goodrick-Clarke, author of the classic work *The Occult Roots of Nazism*. Together we explored many interesting byways of German esoteric history. Another dear friend, also sadly deceased, was Jörg Rohfeld, a fellow explorer of the Northern mysteries, from whose richly stored mind I learned much. Like many other scholars and researchers, I must pay a debt of gratitude to my friend Hans Thomas Hakl of Graz, Austria, creator of one of the finest libraries of esoterica in the world. He also features in this book. Another friend, Elisabeth Pahnke, a naturopath and Anthroposophist of Bremen, gave me much valuable information about Anthroposophical and Paracelsian medicine. On the latter I am also grateful to Karin Proeller and Christoph Proeller of the Soluna Laboraties and Heike Kretschmer of the firm of Phylak for their help and for photographs provided. For other photographs and permissions, I must thank Axel Seiler and the directorate of the Meiningen City Museums. In the domain of geomancy and sacred space I am grateful to the landscape architect Christiane Fink for useful information; to the late Harald Jordan for giving me the benefit of his wide-ranging knowledge of geomancy, earth energies and more; and to Reinhard Wolf for sharing his own knowledge in these areas and providing me with valuable contacts. Thanks also to Dieter Stephan for checking part of the book; and to Ronald Engert, editor in chief of the magazine *Tattva Viveka,* for sharing his experience as someone closely involved in the esoteric scene in Germany; and also to Gudrun Pannier for sharing her insights into the German pagan scene. And once again, many thanks to Jon Graham, acquisitions editor of Inner Traditions, for taking on the book; as well as to vice president and editor in chief, Jeanie Levitan; the book's project editor, Renée Heitman; the copy editor, Elizabeth Wilson; the publicity manager, Ashley Kolesnik; the publicist, Manzanita Carpenter Sanz; and to all others at Inner Traditions who have been involved in bringing it to fruition.

INTRODUCTION

SKY-GOD LAND

No country is richer in occult and esoteric traditions than Germany. The German lands have been enchanted territory since remote times, as shown by numerous prehistoric sites and archaeological discoveries pointing to long-buried ancient cultures. This belies a widespread historical narrative about Germany, which goes back to when the Roman historian Tacitus wrote his treatise *Germania* in the first century CE. Tacitus, while admiring the Germanic tribes for their virtues, such as courage and monogamy, essentially portrays them as backward, unwashed, and uncivilized. This image has persisted over the centuries. In the early nineteenth century the French author Madame de Staël wrote, "The Germanic nations have almost always resisted the Roman yoke; they were civilized later and only by Christianity; they passed almost directly from a sort of barbarism to a Christian society."[1] And just over a century later the Anglo-French writer Hilaire Belloc penned the following verse about the Nordic/Germanic type:

> *Behold, my child, the Nordic man,*
> *And be as like him as you can;*
> *His legs are long, his mind is slow,*
> *His hair is lank and made of tow.*[2]

1

Stereotypes die hard, but it is time to put this one to rest and offer a more differentiated picture. First a clarification about what we mean by Germany. For many centuries Germany was a collection of various principalities, dukedoms, bishoprics, and city-states loosely forming what was called the Holy Roman Empire of the German Nation, which saw itself in some sense as the successor to the original Roman Empire. The Holy Roman Empire in effect came to an end in the wake of the Napoleonic wars. A few decades later in 1871 came the creation of Bismarck's Reich, in which the German states, excluding Austria, were unified, and the king of Prussia became kaiser. This empire lasted until the First World War. Then, when the Nazis came to power, they proclaimed their regime to be the Third Empire (Drittes Reich). Following the Second World War came the years of the divided Germany and finally the united Federal Republic that we know today. Thus, for most of its history, Germany has not been a single nation-state but rather a linguistic, ethnic, and cultural entity extending far beyond the borders of the present-day Federal Republic. Furthermore, a large part of the territory that we think of as Germanic was in fact occupied by Celtic tribes, who had their own myths, traditions, and customs.

Another question is how far back we need to go in time. According to Tacitus it all began with a sky god named Teut (alternatively Tius or Tiwaz), the grandfather of the German peoples. Changing the initial T to the voiced consonant D we get the name Deut, hence Deutschland and also the related adjective Teutonic. Teut or Tius in turn comes from the name of an Indo-European sky god called Dyaus, who reappeared in Latin as *deus,* the generic Latin name for a god. So you could say that the root meaning of Deutschland is something like "Sky-God Land." Teut is said to have had a human son called Mannus, after whom the city of Mannheim is named, and Mannus in turn had three sons who became the progenitors of three Germanic tribes—the Ingaevones, Istiones, and Hermiones—that came to occupy, respectively, the northern, western, and eastern parts of the German heartland. The name that Tacitus used for this heartland was Germania, hence the English name for the country: Germany.

Both the Germanic and the Celtic tribes belonged to the Indo-European peoples, who are believed to have originated somewhere in the region that is now southern Russia and Kirgistan and then migrated outward from about the second millennium BCE, one group going east to India, others going north and west into Europe and Scandinavia. But long before the Indo-Europeans arrived there was a much older population living in central Europe. We know little about them, but the evidence of archaeology shows them to have had a rich culture.

In 2008 archaeologists exploring a complex of caves known as the Hohle Fels (Hollow Cliff) in the mountains of Baden-Württemberg, near the town of Schelklingen, found a series of remarkable objects from the Stone Age. One of these was a flute made from the bone of a vulture and estimated to be at least 35,000 years old. This object tells us quite a lot about the people who made it. Clearly they felt the impulse to make music and had enough leisure to do so, as well as the technical skill required to create instruments. Other bone artifacts found in the caves included a small figure of a large-breasted woman, dubbed the Venus of the Hohle Fels, similar in form to the Venus of Willendorf, found in Lower Austria in 1908.

Fast forward about thirty millennia and we are in what is called the New Stone Age, when megalithic circles, dolmens, and passage graves appeared all over Europe from the Hebrides to the Mediterranean islands and from Spain to the Caucasus. There is reason to believe that these sites were carefully placed in accordance with a network of lines and nodes of earth energy. Proponents of this theory often refer to the lines as "ley lines," a term coined by the British researcher Alfred Watkins in the 1920s. While the ley line theory is controversial among archaeologists, many people have reported feeling a charged atmosphere emanating from megalithic sites. This may be due to a variety of factors: ley lines, underground water courses, the construction of the sites themselves, or possibly the accumulated collective energy of the people who have used them. In Germany in prehistoric times there were innumerable such sites. Many have since been destroyed or plundered for building materials, but there are still thousands left.

We fast forward again to the Bronze Age (roughly fourth to second millennium BCE), which has also yielded many remarkable finds. Some of the finest specimens are to be found in the Museum for Pre- and Early History on the Museum Island in Berlin. One of them is a magnificent headpiece in the form of a tall, narrow cone about 29 inches high, made of a gold alloy, and intricately wrought with a pattern of bands and parallel rows of bosses. Three other similar objects have also been found. The markings are believed to be a calendar marking the solar and lunar months over a cycle of four and a half years.[3] This object, found in southern Germany, or Switzerland, is not the work of primitive barbarians. It has a high aesthetic quality, shows superb craftsmanship, and underlines the importance of the lunar cycle for the people who made it. Why the lunar cycle? For one thing, because optimum conditions for planting and harvesting vary according to the moon's phases.

An equally sensational Bronze Age find was the Nebra Sky Disk, discovered in 1999 by illegal treasure seekers in the hills near Nebra, in Saxony-Anhalt, along with two swords, two axes, two bracelets, and a chisel, and now displayed in the State Museum of Prehistory in Halle. The objects, dating from about 1600 BCE, all evince high-quality craftsmanship, especially the disk, measuring about 12 inches in diameter; made of copper with a gold inlay of stars, new moon, full moon or sun; a curved line indicating the eastern horizon; and a thinner curve suggesting a boat traveling across the heavenly ocean.

When the Romans came, they occupied part of Germania but never managed to conquer the greater part, owing to fierce opposition from the Germanic tribes, who won a decisive victory in the year 9 CE, when three Roman legions under the command of Publius Quinctilius Varus were massacred by a force of tribesmen led by Arminius, a native

German who had served in the Roman army. In the areas that they did occupy, the Romans left their legacy, which included customs, beliefs, and religious practices, but they did not forcibly proselytize. Both within the Romanized territories and elsewhere in Germania the native population for the time being continued practicing their ancient religion as they had done since time immemorial. But that would change with the coming of Christianity.

After the Roman Empire adopted Christianity as its official religion in the fourth century CE, it took several hundred years before the conversion of Germany was, at least nominally, complete. A symbolic moment in the conversion was in 723, when an English missionary known as Bonifatius (Boniface) cut down an oak tree sacred to the Germanic thunder god Donar (Thor) at Geismar, now part of the town of Fritzlar in Hessen. In 772 another blow was struck against the old religion when the Frankish King Charles the Great (Charlemagne) ordered the destruction of the Irminsul, a symbolic pillar venerated by the Saxons, which stood on a hilltop near the present-day town of Obermarsberg in North Rhine-Westphalia. A decade later, in 782, a terrible event occurred near Verden, in Lower Saxony, when Charlemagne's Frankish army massacred some 4,500 pagan Saxons. Charlemagne continued his campaign of conquest and Christianization, and in 800 he was crowned Holy Roman emperor by the pope. By the eleventh century, Christianity was dominant in all of Germany.

The old gods were banished but not dead. They lived on in custom, folklore, myth, legend, and in sacred places and certain everyday words and expressions. When one explores the pre-Christian traditions, one finds many hints of a powerful stream running through them—namely, that of shamanism, the shaman being a person who can enter trance states at will and become possessed or travel between the world of the gods and spirits, the everyday world and the world of the dead. Mircea Eliade, in his classic study of shamanism, writes, "In the religion and mythology of the ancient Germans some details are comparable to the conceptions and techniques of North Asian shamanism."[4] This is a theme that we shall encounter again later.

In the centuries following the Christian conversion the church tightened its hold and did its best to stamp out the old pagan values and beliefs, but something deep in the German psyche remained recalcitrant. Despite, or perhaps because of, this tension in the German soul, these centuries produced immortal poets, philosophers, theologians, artists, and mystics. They include figures such as the medieval poet Wolfram von Eschenbach, author of the Arthurian epic *Parzival;* the unorthodox Dominican mystic Meister Eckhart; and the remarkable Hildegard of Bingen, Benedictine abbess, physician, visionary, writer, and composer. Later came Jakob Boehme, the prophetic cobbler of Görlitz; the mystical poet Angelus Silesius; the great sixteenth-century alchemist and physician Theophrastus von Hohenheim, known as Paracelsus; and the half-legendary magician Dr. Johann Faust, immortalized in Goethe's play about him.

Where there is light there is shadow, and the centuries that produced Faust, Paracelsus, and Boehme also produced mass witch hunts and the horrors of the Thirty Years' War. At the same time the century of that war also produced the Rosicrucian tradition, which has spread all over the world and spawned numerous offspring, including, arguably, speculative Freemasonry, which flourished in Germany and produced a crop of exotic high-degree rites such as the Golden and Rosy Cross and later groups like the Fraternitas Saturni.

The Kabbalah, in both Jewish and Christian forms, has left its mark on German culture, as have astrology and alchemy. The latter continued to flourish long after it had declined elsewhere and still has its practitioners in Germany today. It was a German, Frater Albertus, who emigrated to the United States and founded the Paracelsus Research Society. Out of the alchemical tradition came the homeopathic medicine of Samuel Hahnemann, and it was in Germany that the French alchemist Comte de Saint Germain spent his final years as a guest of Prince Karl von Hessen Kassel on the latter's estate near Schleswig. Another powerful body of symbolism that took root in Germany is that connected with the Holy Grail, which repeatedly appears in myth, legend, literature, art, and music.

With the advent of Romanticism in the late eighteenth and early nineteenth centuries, bringing a counterreaction to the rationalism of the Enlightenment, there came a new upsurge of interest in the realm of myth, magic, and the esoteric. The works of the Romantic painters are full of esoteric symbolism. A famous example is one of my favorite paintings, *The Morning* (*Der Morgen*) by the German romantic artist Philipp Otto Runge (1777–1810; see page 8). Painted in 1808, it belongs to an allegorical series depicting different times of day that represent phases of a human life. *The Morning* consists of two images, one framed within the other. The inner one shows a newborn baby lying on a grassy meadow, above which a radiant female figure and several cherubs float against a shimmering dawn sky. The surrounding outer image shows at the bottom a subterranean sun emerging from behind a subterranean moon, which two cherubs are touching with their feet. They appear to pass the underground light upward via other cherubs entangled in a pair of lily plants. At the top, the two images merge in a shining empyrean.

I interpret this work as showing that complementarity between spirit and matter, the solar and the lunar, to which I repeatedly draw attention in this book. In Runge's painting the divine light shines both in heaven and in the depths of the earth. One spiritual path leads directly upward toward the heavenly light. The other goes through the earth and the natural world but leads ultimately to the same divine realm. The latter is the characteristically German path of alchemy and of figures such as Hildegard of Bingen, Paracelsus, Goethe, Hahnemann, and Rudolf Steiner.

The Romantic period was also one in which Germans increasingly looked back to their ancient past and the age of the *Edda*, the Norse sagas, and the Vikings for inspiration. Preeminent in this regard are the operas of Wagner's *Ring* cycle with their evocation of the world of the Norse gods and heroes. The importing of Madame Blavatsky's Theosophical movement to Germany in the late nineteenth century

Fig. I.1. *Der Morgen (The Morning)* by the German romantic artist Friedrich Otto Runge, 1808. (See also color plate 1.)

stimulated a whole new set of esoteric movements, including the Anthroposophy of Rudolf Steiner.

At the same time, Germany held a mystique for people in other countries with a penchant for the esoteric. Germany's reputation as the wellspring of Rosicrucianism had a strange repercussion in England in 1887 when Dr. William Wynn Westcott, coroner for northeast London and a prominent Freemason, came into possession of a manuscript written in one of the ciphers described in a work on cryptography by the Benedictine abbot Johannes Trithemius (1462–1516). When deciphered, the document was found to contain descriptions of initiation rituals similar to those of the Golden and Rosy Cross order and apparently emanating from a German Rosicrucian order called the Goldene Dämmerung (Golden Dawn). Slipped into the manuscript was a piece of paper with a text, also in cipher, that referred to a certain German adept called Fräulein (Miss) Sprengel, who held a high grade in the Goldene Dämmerung. The name she used in the order was Sapiens Dominabitur Astris (the wise person will rule the stars)—the verb is passive but conveys an active meaning. The message also stated that she could be reached via Herr J. Enger at the Hotel Marquardt in Stuttgart.

All of this was a godsend to Westcott, who at the time was intent on founding an esoteric order in collaboration with his friends Samuel Liddell (alias MacGregor) Mathers and fellow Freemason W. R. Woodman. Accordingly he wrote to Sapiens Dominabitur Astris at the stated contact address and received a reply authorizing him and his two friends to found an English subsidiary of the Golden Dawn, which they proceeded to do. The rest, as they say, is history. The Golden Dawn became an immensely influential order that spread to many other countries and spawned numerous offshoots. The only fly in the ointment is that Fräulein Sprengel never existed, and the correspondence was in all probability a forgery concocted by Westcott, as I was able to prove through an examination of the original letters.*

---

*See my article "'Fräulein Sprengel' and the Origins of the Golden Dawn: A Surprising Discovery," *Aries, Journal for the Study of Western Esotericism* 11, no. 2 (2011): 249–57.

The early decades of the twentieth century, despite the devastation of the First World War, were a time of great spiritual and mystical search, which is reflected in the literature of the period, with poets like Stefan George and novelists like Gustav Meyrink and Hermann Hesse. This period was curtailed by the advent of the Nazi regime in 1933. There have been many sensationalized books about how the Nazis worked with occult forces, but the truth is that occultism of the kind that titillates the readers of those books was mostly confined to a limited milieu surrounding Heinrich Himmler, Rudolf Hess, and a few others—and I shall have a few things to say on this topic. But if one adopts a wider definition of the word *occult*—or perhaps *esoteric*—to include the realm of myths and egregores (accumulated thoughtforms in the collective consciousness), then this dimension needs to be taken into account when investigating the Third Reich.

The Germany that emerged after the end of the Second World War in 1945 was dominated by materialism. The country was preoccupied first with rebuilding itself from the ruins of the war and then with the economic miracle and the enormous prosperity that it brought. The prevailing spirit was also marked by rationalism. Esotericism was irrational, and irrationality was associated with Nazism and therefore suspect among the intellectual establishment. For a long time, this attitude has hampered the serious study of the esoteric in Germany, although that situation is gradually changing. Meanwhile, there is a strong interest in things esoteric among people active in various esoteric movements and groups, as well as among a segment of the general public.

Anyone who spends any length of time in Germany today will become aware that the Germans, to a greater extent than most other nations, are engaged in an ongoing attempt to find their national identity and reconcile various contrasting tendencies in the collective mind and soul of the nation. One polarity is expressed in the symbolism of alchemy and astrology. In alchemical texts and illustrations, the symbols of sun and moon, or Sol and Luna, appear prominently. Sometimes these represent the actual celestial bodies, at other times they refer to substances used in the alchemical work. Here is a tentative list of the qualities and principles that I would associate with the two bodies.

Sun	Moon
The male aspect of deity, dawn, daylight, fiery passion, authority, order, discipline, force, militarism, empire, centralization, technology, hierarchy, rationality, practicality, the animus, the phallus.	The Goddess, twilight, night, emotion, feeling, dreams, intuition, secrecy, moodiness, nostalgia, romanticism, intoxication, ecstasy, mysticism, the anima, the female principle, the womb.

This duality overlaps somewhat but not entirely with Friedrich Nietzsche's concept of the Apollonian and Dionysiac forces, which he put forward in his book *The Birth of Tragedy from the Spirit of Music* (*Die Geburt der Tragödie aus dem Geiste der Musik*). The book was written during the tumultuous events of the Franco-Prussian War of 1870–1871, in which Nietzsche served as a volunteer medical orderly, and which led to the founding of Bismarck's new German Reich. The young and sensitive Nietzsche, deeply shaken by the war, felt compelled to address some fundamental questions: Why is suffering inseparable from human life? How can we accept it and still be life affirming? Is there a model that can give us the answers? He believed there was such a model—namely, ancient Greece.

His argument rested on the identification of two conflicting modalities or energies, to which human beings are subject, and which he identified with the gods Apollo and Dionysus. The former was associated with order, measure, balance, proportion, and beauty of form, as well as deeper knowledge—after all, it was the voice of Apollo that was heard by the priestesses at Delphi and the other oracles of the Hellenic world. Dionysus, on the other hand, was associated with ecstasy, intoxication, wild abandon, and the way in which the individual could be swept up in the collective passion of the crowd. At a certain point in history, the Greeks of Apollonian outlook came to acknowledge that their world of beauty and measure rested on a lower stratum of suffering, which Dionysus revealed to them. At the same time, they realized that Apollo could not live without Dionysus and vice versa. How were they to square the circle? The answer was found in the tradition of the Greek tragedy, with its fateful narratives, its choruses, its compelling poetic rhythms, and its powerful music that deepened the audience's engagement with the drama. In this way the Greeks achieved a marvelous coming together of the Apollonian and Dionysiac principles. For a time, Nietzsche appears to have believed that Wagner's operas had achieved something similar, but later he did an about-face and became one of Wagner's fiercest opponents.

Two contrasting modes demand a third mode, a synthesis, in which the dichotomy is resolved. In the case of the ancient Greeks, it was the tradition of tragic drama. In German culture the synthesis is expressed by various images that crop up from time to time. One is that of the hermaphrodite or androgyne, which occurs frequently in alchemical symbolism and also crops up in the work of artists and writers. Another is the Holy Grail. In Christian tradition the Grail is the chalice that was used at the Last Supper and the cup in which Christ's blood was gathered at the Crucifixion, but over time it gathered multiple legends, becoming a lost relic possessing miraculous powers such as that of rejuvenation. For King Arthur's knights it was the object of a sacred quest, but it also appears in alchemical images such as the one shown in figure I.2. from the *Secret Symbols of the Rosicrucians,* published at Altona in northern Germany in 1785. Here, among other symbols, are depicted a sun and moon pouring fluids into a Grail-like vessel. I would suggest that Sol and Luna merging in the Grail, like the rose and the cross combined in the symbol of the Rosicrucians, represent a resolution of opposites that the German collective mind seeks.

One would think that the Grail would be a familiar motif for any

Fig. I.2. Image from *Geheime Figuren der Rosenkreuzer (Secret Symbols of the Rosicrucians),* published in 1785. The solar and lunar principles merging in the Grail make an apt symbol for Germany's quest.

halfway literate German, but unfortunately this is not the case. When I was teaching English at the University of Bremen in 2005, I mentioned the Holy Grail during one lesson and asked the students if any of them knew what it was. Only one young man raised his hand, and all he knew was that it had something to do with rejuvenation. The others had no clue. I found this sad, as it demonstrated the widespread mythical illiteracy in modern Germany. Over centuries the Germans have been subjected to a campaign of indoctrination seeking to teach them to disparage their own mythology. The process dates back at least to the wholesale Christianization campaign of Charlemagne and reached its peak after the Second World War when—in reaction to the Nazi period with its celebration of Germanic tradition, myth, and legend—an ethos of prosaic rationality pervaded the mainstream intellectual establishment. On the other hand, there remains a widespread need for something more vital and more deeply connected with the wellsprings that give life deeper meaning.

One of my preoccupations as a writer has been the interface between myth and history—how history becomes mythologized and how myth can drive history. Myths are the lifeblood of a people—fabled heroes and heroines, the memory of great epoch-making events, national rituals, ancient places of special meaning, folktales, and favorite superstitions. In my native land of England, when I still lived there, the national sense of myth was strong. English history was marked by names, mythical and real, going back to pre-Roman times: Boadicea, Hengist and Horsa, Alfred the Great, King Arthur, William the Conqueror, Good Queen Bess, Robin Hood, Florence Nightingale. And we had our special sites like Stonehenge, Glastonbury, and the Tower of London with its ravens that must never depart lest England fall.

In Germany the situation is rather different. Some Germans have simply no sense of their own historical/mythical heritage. Others are intent on disparaging and belittling it. But there are many who feel a profound need to rediscover that heritage or find substitutes for it. This need manifests itself in a thousand different ways—in the devoted Wagnerites who flock to Bayreuth every year to immerse themselves in his mythical world, in the proliferation of New Age cults and gurus, in the growth of neo-paganism, and in the crowds that gather at various ancient sites to celebrate the solar festivals. In short, the Germans are on a centuries-old quest. In exploring the history of that quest, I came to the realization that the German mind has one particularly outstanding strength—namely, the ability to straddle the realms of the spiritual and the material. In this perspective, the title of this introduction, "Sky-God Land," turns out to be apposite. It suggests the notion of God as a bridge between sky and land, heaven and earth, spirit and matter, soul and body. This theme is a *Leitmotiv* that runs through this book and is found in many of Germany's greatest minds. Now let us begin this journey in a high citadel of German learning and thought—namely, Heidelberg.

1

HEIDELBERG:
AN ENCHANTED GATEWAY

A good way to start a journey into the Germany of mystery, myth, and magic is to take the steep, narrow lane that winds up through Heidelberg to where the remains of its seventeenth-century castle stand. Pausing for breath you can look back and admire a picture-postcard view of the town, strung out along the banks of the river Neckar. Heidelberg is a gateway—and a microcosm of many things that will be explored in this book.

The great castle in its heyday was one of the wonders of the world and still affords an arresting spectacle with the remains of its once magnificent garden laid out on terraces built into the hillside. Here we find ourselves transported into the world of the Rosicrucians, a movement that surfaced in Germany in the early seventeenth century. In a Europe riven by bitter religious conflict that was soon to erupt into the Thirty Years' War, the Rosicrucians proclaimed a holistic vision, bringing together religion, science, and the arts and drawing on ancient esoteric sources. In some mysterious writings, published anonymously, they called for a great spiritual renewal in Europe.

One person who heeded the message was the elector Frederick V,

Fig. 1.1. Heidelberg Castle in 1620, an engraving by Matthias Merian.
WIKIMEDIA COMMONS.

ruler of the Palatinate with his seat at Heidelberg Castle. In keeping with the holistic Rosicrucian spirit, he had the garden of the castle designed by a French Huguenot named Salomon de Caus, a Renaissance man who was not only an architect and garden designer but also an engineer, musician, composer, and scholar well versed in classical philosophy and the esoteric traditions. Fortunately, de Caus left a record of the garden in a beautiful book of engravings.[1] The garden reflected de Caus's belief that the universe, including ourselves and the world of nature, is pervaded by divine musical harmonies based on certain ratios and proportions.[2] Thus, the octave, signifying musical completeness, is incorporated in various features in the garden, such as an octagonal stone basin, which is still there, although the fountain that it contained has vanished. Other surviving remnants include some balustrades, pillars, walls, staircases, and grottoes. Certain features planned by de Caus but never realized include water-driven musical automata such as a Pan figure playing a flageolet (symbolizing the voice of nature) and a device that played the three modes of ancient music.

In its original state the garden must have been a place of great wonder. Its loss is one of the tragedies of history, which came about because Prince Frederick made an unwise move. Early in the Thirty Years' War he made a bid for the crown of Bohemia. A Protestant, he was opposed by the Catholic Habsburgs, who defeated him in 1620 at the Battle of the White Mountain near Prague. Subsequently the Habsburg forces sacked Heidelberg and bombarded the castle, using the garden as an artillery base. In later years further destruction was caused by plundering and vandalism.

The castle suffered a similarly tragic fate. Today only some parts of it are undamaged or restored, but it is still worthwhile to take a tour of the premises, which house a fascinating Museum of Pharmacy. Part of this museum is devoted to alchemy, and this takes us into another esoteric tradition with deep roots in Germany. Alchemy has always been more than an attempt to turn base metals into gold. It is rooted in a worldview that regards the material realm as being in a fallen state; that is to say, fallen from the true divine realm above. However, even in the densest of matter there is a spark of divine light, which can be concentrated through distillation and purification. By this means, substances can be raised to a higher state. In the process of such efforts, many practical discoveries have been made, such as elixirs and medicines, certain metal alloys, and the recipe for Meissen porcelain. Ideally, the alchemist is engaged in an inner process of self-transformation parallel to the work in the laboratory.

In Germany alchemy became particularly vigorous, and it still has its practitioners there today, as we shall see. The great alchemist and physician Paracelsus (1493–1541) was a seminal figure who developed a new approach to alchemy. To the four classical elements of air, fire, earth, and water he added a trinity of salt, sulphur, and mercury. These were not the substances known to chemistry but rather active principles or components corresponding to body, soul, and spirit. Paracelsian

Fig. 1.2. An engraving by Raphael Custos from *Cabala, Spiegel der Kunst und Natur* (Kabbalah, Mirror of Art and Nature) by Stephan Michelsbacher (1616), showing alchemical symbols and a laboratory.

alchemy involves taking a substance—say, the leaves of an herb—separating out the three components, and then bringing them together again, thus greatly increasing the potency of the substance as a remedy.

The rich symbolism of alchemy lent itself to a whole mystical movement, especially in the German lands. The writings of visionaries such as Jakob Boehme (1575–1624) are full of alchemical imagery; later on, various high-degree Masonic and quasi-Masonic orders incorporated alchemical symbolism into their rituals and degree structures. In more recent times the Swiss German psychologist Carl Gustav Jung developed an interpretation of the alchemists' work as being symbolic of what he called the "integration" of the human psyche. Today the legacy of the alchemical tradition can be found in initiatives such as the Soluna Laboratory in Donauwörth, founded in 1921 by the alchemist and poet Alexander von Bernus.

Leaving alchemy and the Museum of Pharmacy behind, we can descend back to the town with its old, cobbled streets opening out into graceful squares, its turreted bridge over the Neckar and its venerable university—echoes of beer-swilling students singing the "Drinking Song" in Sigmund Romberg's operetta *The Student Prince*. Heidelberg is nothing if not romantic, and in Germany romanticism is an old habit. The romantic longs for that which is past or far away or perhaps secret and hidden—like the temples of the Mithras cult, of which the Romans left behind many in Germany.

A beautiful reconstruction of one of these temples can be seen in the Museum of the Palatinate in Heidelberg's main street. It has the form of a narrow, rectangular chamber with deep red walls, white pillars, a blue vaulted ceiling dotted with gold stars, an altar, and on the wall behind the altar, a relief showing the god Mithras slaughtering a bull. Followers of Mithraism were predominantly from the plebian castes—slaves, laborers, soldiers, and the like. The cult had a solar emphasis. The temples were often underground. Lighting was provided by oil lamps or candles, and daylight was shut out except for a small opening in the roof to emphasize the notion of light penetrating darkness. Also in the museum are two original Roman statues of Cautes and Cautopates, the torchbearers who stand on either side of Mithras. Cautes, with torch held aloft, represents life and the rising sun, while Cautopates, with his torch pointing down, symbolizes death and the setting sun. Some writers have seen in these figures a commonality with the theme of symbolic death in Freemasonry. They also point to other common features, such as the star-spangled heaven, which is found both in Mithraic temples and in many Masonic lodges. Be that as it may, Freemasonry is an important current in the context of this book, and one to which we shall return. Further exhibits in the museum relate to the Celts, who occupied the region for several centuries, and to the Romans, who arrived around the first century CE.

Leaving the museum and crossing the river we come to a splendid villa, gleaming white against a wooded slope—the Max Weber House, originally called House Falkenstein but renamed after Professor Max Weber (1864–1920), the great pioneer of sociology who lived there in the early years of the twentieth century. Weber is famous for having proclaimed what he called the "disenchantment of the world" (*Entzauberung der Welt*) in a lecture delivered in 1917. Today he is widely thought of as a rationalist thinker, but on closer examination he turns out to be someone who was not welcoming disenchantment but rather lamenting it as a price we have to pay for rationality and scientific progress. In a doctoral dissertation on Weber and Rudolf Steiner, the founder of Anthroposophy, Aaron French has shown that these two men, who might appear to be polar opposites, in fact had a great deal in common.[3] Both were concerned with the problem of sustaining inner freedom and the life of the spirit in an increasingly technocratic, bureaucratic, and capitalistic world. Both turned to thinkers such as Kant, Goethe, Nietzsche, and the Russian mystical writer Vladimir Solovyov, and both ultimately looked to the wisdom of the East for inspiration. It is also revealing to look at their friends, their activities, and the circles in which they moved.

In Heidelberg, Weber belonged to a private study group called the

Eranos Circle (1904–1908), not to be confused with the famous Eranos seminars at Ascona in Switzerland (1933 onward), which I shall come to later. The Heidelberg Eranos was founded by the Protestant theologian Adolf Deißmann, together with the classical philologist and scholar of religion Albrecht Dieterich, author of an influential book on the worship of Mother Earth titled *Mutter Erde: Ein Versuch über Volksreligion* (Mother Earth: An Essay on Folk Religion), published in 1905. In one lecture, which Weber is recorded as having attended, the audience listened spellbound as Dieterich expounded on the ancient belief that the Earth, as the Mother Goddess, had given birth to human beings. He also spoke of mystery cults such as Eleusis, in which the initiate underwent a ritual of death and rebirth under the aegis of the Great Mother.[4]

In 1910, Weber was among the founders of a philosophical journal called *Logos,* whose contributors included the esoteric writer and teacher Count Hermann Keyserling, the Italian occultist Julius Evola, and the Russian novelist and Anthroposophist Andrey Bely. Someone else who was active in Heidelberg at this time was the esoteric and mystical poet Stefan George, who was not just a poet but also the leader of what amounted to a cult. He treated the members of his inner circles like acolytes whom he was shaping into an elite corps of spiritual aristocrats who would lead Germany into a shining future, but not the future that would later come with the Nazis. Some three decades later one of his followers, Claus von Stauffenberg, inspired by George's teaching, led the unsuccessful plot to assassinate Hitler and paid the price with his own life.[5] George and Weber were, so to speak, sparring friends. They had much in common as well as many points of disagreement.

Another person whom Weber knew in these years was the above-mentioned Alexander von Bernus, poet, Anthroposophist, and later alchemist, who had inherited the former Benedictine abbey of Stift Neuburg just outside Heidelberg, where he hosted meetings of like-minded people, including members of the George circle. Here Weber met people, such as the writer and philosopher of religion Alfred

Schmid Noerr, who was a friend of the occult novelist Gustav Meyrink and had collaborated with the latter in writing the novel *The Angel of the Western Window.*

One significant place visited by Weber was the Monte Verità colony at Ascona on Lake Maggiore, Switzerland, a New Age community ahead of its time, where artists, writers, esotericists, pacifists, anarchists, vegetarians, and others gathered to meditate, commune with nature, dance about naked in the idyllic grounds, and, in many cases, practice free love. It was also conceived as a sanatorium to promote physical and spiritual regeneration. The writer Hermann Hesse went there to cure his alcoholism, and Weber to recover from a nervous breakdown, staying there in 1913 and 1914 for a month each time. At Monte Verità, invigorated by the healthy lifestyle and rejuvenated by some extramarital love affairs, he found a new kind of release and "re-enchantment."

While Monte Verità was located in Switzerland, many of its leading participants were German, and it evinced a mood of optimism, of questing for new spiritual horizons, and of a freer and more vital way of living which was also manifested in Germany itself. Tragically this optimism was blown apart in the First World War. It recovered somewhat after the war, only to be blown apart again in the Third Reich and the Second World War.

Continuing our journey from the Max Weber House, we climb via a path called the Philosophers' Way up a wooded hill called the Heiligenberg, which rises to the north of the town and where the remains of a fortified Celtic settlement are still visible. The name Heiligenberg (Holy Hill) is significant. It must already have been a sacred site in Celtic times, and the Romans built a temple there dedicated to Mercury, as is shown by an amulet in the museum with an inscription to that deity. Also still in place on the hill are the remains of the medieval monastery of Saint Michael, a model of which can be seen in the Museum of the Palatinate. The dedication to the Archangel Michael is in keeping with a tradition found in other parts of Europe. In the Christianization process, hilltop sites dedicated to a solar deity were often reassigned to Michael, who is typically depicted slaying or subduing a dragon. In England, for example, there is a series of such sites forming a ley line that runs from East Anglia down to Saint Michael's Mount in Cornwall, passing through Glastonbury with its ruined hilltop chapel to Saint Michael.

A short way downhill from the monastery ruins is a vast stone amphitheater reminiscent of those built by the ancient Greeks, but this one was built on the initiative of the ill-famed Joseph Goebbels, Nazi propaganda minister, as a place to hold rallies and seasonal ceremonies and was opened in 1935 when Goebbels gave a speech to an audience of thousands. The name given to it was the Thingstätte, from the old Norse word *Thing,* meaning "parliament or assembly," and *Stätte,* which is German for "place." Goebbels planned hundreds more such amphitheaters, but only about sixty were completed before he abandoned the scheme. Despite its murky provenance, the architecture is imposing. There is a stepped amphitheater built to hold twenty thousand people, a circular stage, a massive stone podium, and pedestals for flags, loudspeakers, and floodlighting. In recent years large numbers of revelers have come here to celebrate Walpurgisnacht (Walpurgis Night), the last night of April, but at the time of this writing these gatherings are banned on account of the coronavirus epidemic. One has the feeling that Goebbels's bombastic voice has faded into oblivion and his construction has been taken over by older and more benign powers.

2

PLACES OF POWER

There is no site in Germany more mystique and mystery laden than the Externsteine in North Rhine-Westphalia. Approaching it through gentle, parklike countryside, you suddenly come upon a row of towering sandstone cliffs that were thrust up millions of years ago from a fault in the Earth's crust. Adjoining a lake and surrounded by woods, the site is awe inspiring. Flint implements found there indicate habitation from as early as 10,000 BCE,[1] and we can safely assume that it has been a sacred site for many millennia. Today it draws a constant stream of visitors, including many neo-pagans. For a number of years it was the scene of wild revelries at midsummer, but at the time of this writing these are no longer permitted.

Climbing the highest of the four cliffs via steps cut into the stone and over a humpbacked bridge, you come to a chamber hewn from the solid rock. Measuring about three meters by seven (ten feet by twenty-three feet), it runs from southwest to northeast and has some very puzzling features. At the northeast end there is an arched recess with a sort of pedestal protruding from the wall. In the wall above the pedestal is a mysterious round hole. Equally mysterious is the rectangular niche that is flanked by pillars and cut into the wall at the opposite end. Evidently this was a place of worship of some kind, but was it created as a Christian chapel, as some people maintain, or as a pagan temple in pre-Christian times?

Fig. 2.1. The Externsteine cliffs in North Rhine-Westphalia, a sacred site for many millennia.

PHOTOGRAPH BY THE AUTHOR.

One who took the latter view was a local amateur archaeologist, Wilhelm Teudt (1880–1942), who in the 1920s and '30s made a detailed investigation of the stones and published his findings in a book called *Germanische Heiligtümer* (Germanic Sanctuaries). Teudt argued that several features of the chamber supported his case. For example, the hole in the wall pointed northeast to where the sun rose at the summer solstice, whereas a Christian chapel would have been aligned directly toward the east.[2]

Another much-disputed feature of the Externsteine is a relief carved into the stone at the base of one of the cliffs. It depicts Christ being taken down from the cross, and on the right is a treelike object that appears to be bowing down before a patriarchal, priestlike figure with one hand raised. Teudt identified this object as being the Irminsul, the sacred pillar of the Saxons, which was destroyed by Charlemagne in 772 CE during his Christianization campaign. The shape is curious—a trunk bifurcated at the top with two branches that curl into spirals at the ends. Today this motif is widely accepted among modern pagans as the genuine form of the Irminsul.

Yet another mysterious feature is an open coffin carved out of the rock and lying within an arched niche. Teudt believed this to have been used in the initiation ceremonies of an ancient mystery cult, where the initiate would undergo a symbolic death and rebirth. Visitors often lie in the coffin and sometimes report having experienced remarkable visions or trance journeys.

Teudt's theories are generally rejected by mainstream archaeologists, but he has a certain following among neo-pagans and the New Age public, despite the fact that he blotted his reputation by his membership in the Nazi party and his association with the SS leader Heinrich Himmler, who set up a special foundation to protect and investigate the Externsteine as a sacred site for the ancient Germans.[3]

The Externsteine cliffs are located in the Teutoburg Forest region, which was long thought to have been where the Roman legions were defeated in 9 CE by the Germanic chieftain Arminius (or Hermann, to use his German name). The event is commemorated by the Hermann Monument, which lies about fourteen kilometers (nine miles) northwest of the Externsteine, near Detmold, and was completed in 1875. Standing dramatically atop a wooded hill and approached by a long flight of steps, it features a colossal copper statue of Arminius wearing a winged helmet and raising his sword in a triumphal gesture. In fact, it turns out that his victory took place about eighty kilometers (fifty miles) to the north in the Kalkriese district, near Osnabrück, as archaeological evidence has shown.

Fig. 2.2. The Hermann (Arminius) Monument, commemorating the victory
of the Germanic tribes over a Roman army in 9 CE.

Some thirty kilometers (nineteen miles) to the south of the Externsteine lies a place with a distinctly murky history—namely, the Wewelsburg Castle, a hilltop fortress dating back to medieval times, which was chosen by Heinrich Himmler as a kind of temple for the SS. Nicholas Goodrick-Clarke, in his book *The Occult Roots of Nazism,* relates how Himmler, attracted by the mystique of the Teutoburg Forest, conceived the idea of acquiring a castle in the area for SS purposes. He visited the Wewelsburg Castle in November 1933 and immediately decided to take it over. Among his retinue during the visit was his adviser on occult matters, Karl Maria Wiligut, or Weisthor (Wise Fool), as he called himself. "Weisthor predicted that the castle was destined to become a magical German strongpoint in a future conflict between Europe and Asia. . . . He also had an important influence on the development of SS ritual." The rituals held at the castle included "pagan wedding ceremonies for SS officers and their brides, at which Weisthor officiated with an ivory-handled stick bound with blue ribbon and carved with runes."[4] Today a tour of the castle, which is now a museum, includes the crypt, where the most solemn rituals took place.

It is typical of warlords and monarchs to emphasize their power through the size and magnificence of their castles and palaces. A prime example was the emperor Charlemagne (ca. 747–814), who established his capital at Aachen, now close to the far western border of Germany, but then at the center of his empire. As he had been crowned Holy Roman emperor by the pope, his empire was both a secular and a spiritual institution, as he was determined to emphasize. In the 790s he embarked on the creation of the Palatine Chapel, initially built as part of his palace and now incorporated into Aachen Cathedral.

On the symbolic and geomantic level, the site has multiple significant features. Long before Charlemagne, Aachen had been famous for its numerous thermal springs. The Celts treated it as a sacred site for that reason, and in Roman times it was already a spa town with a nymphaeum, a shrine to the water nymphs. Charlemagne was therefore following a familiar practice of building on an existing sacred site, thus co-opting the subtle energy of the place and emphasizing that it was now under a new creed and a new rulership.

The design of the building was intended to reflect the Holy Jerusalem, as described in chapter 21 of the Revelation of John in the New Testament in which the author describes how an angel carried him away in a vision and showed him the holy city of Jerusalem. The city is described as having twelve gates, three at each of the four compass points, "and on the gates were inscribed the names of the twelve Angels, and names written thereof, which are the names of the twelve tribes of Israel." The chapter goes on to say that the city was in the form of a cube measuring 12,000 furlongs in length, breadth, and height, and the wall measured 144 cubits in height.[5] These figures, converted into Carolingian measures, determined all the essential measurements of the chapel. Furthermore the main part of the building is eight-sided, which again is symbolic, as the octagon in Christian tradition represents rebirth and eternal life. For this reason it is also traditionally the form used for baptismal fonts. In 805 the chapel was consecrated by Pope Leo III.

Supreme symbol of the secular power in the chapel is the Imperial Throne (Kaiserthron), commissioned by Charlemagne himself. On a stone dais with five steps, it is a strikingly plain object made out of marble slabs joined by bronze clamps and devoid of decoration. Its extreme austerity stands in contrast to the lavish ornamentation of the rest of the chapel and suggests that it was intended to convey the message that the emperor, while supreme secular ruler, was ultimately the humble servant of God. Up to the early sixteenth century a succession of monarchs were crowned on this throne, which was therefore the symbolic center of power of the entire Holy Roman Empire of the German nation.

Four centuries later another figure occupied the imperial throne—namely, Frederick I (1122–1190), known as Barbarossa on account of his red beard. Barbarossa's grandson Frederick II (1194–1250) ruled for most of his reign from the Kingdom of Sicily and was renowned for his powerful personality, wide learning, and the splendor of his court. After the death of Frederick II, a prophecy arose that he would one day return to bring peace and unity to the strife-ridden German lands. Later this legend somehow became transferred to his grandfather Barbarossa. By the sixteenth century, rumors were circulating that the latter was asleep in a cave in a small mountain range called the Kyffhäuser, located almost exactly in the center of present-day Germany. Here he sat at a stone table, his beard growing ever longer, while he waited for a new age to begin. Every hundred years he would wake up and ask a dwarf whether the ravens were still circling around the mountain. If the answer was yes, then he would go back to sleep for another century. For anyone familiar with the old Germanic mythology, this is strongly reminiscent of the figure of Odin with his two ravens, Hugin and Munin.[6]

In a striking example of how myth can impinge on history, when King Wilhelm of Prussia was proclaimed emperor of Germany in 1871, some hailed him as the fulfillment of the Barbarossa prophecy. This symbolic connection was further emphasized in the gigantic sandstone monument erected in 1896 on a peak in the Kyffhäuser Mountains in honor of Kaiser Wilhelm I. Below a bronze equestrian statue of the kaiser is a stone statue of Barbarossa, sitting in a very Odin-like pose under an arch with a raven carved in relief.[7] In the Second World War the same legend was invoked when the Nazi invasion of Russia was code-named Operation Barbarossa.

Another monarch who has taken on a mythical dimension is Ludwig II of Bavaria (1845–1886), who tried to live out an epic fantasy of kingship and created wondrous castles but overreached himself and died a tragic and lonely death after being deposed. Everyone knows his fairy-tale castle, Neuschwanstein, perched on a dizzying peak at the edge of the Bavarian Alps—Ludwig's dream of a Grail castle, built partly as homage to his hero and the recipient of his munificent patronage, Richard Wagner. Thousands of visitors flock through it every year, gazing entranced at the sumptuous detail of the interior, the acres of mural painting, the rich tapestries, the elaborate carvings in stone and wood.

What few of the tourists know is that geomancers have discovered powerful energies present in the site itself. As David Luczyn writes in his book on enchanted sites in Germany:

> A group of para-scientists visited Ludwig's fairy-tale castle in 1988 and investigated the premises with pendulums, dowsing rods and electronic sensors. In the Throne Room of the castle, exactly at the spot where King Ludwig's throne had stood, they found intensive radiation and a positive energy field. Some of them said they had never before experienced such strong emanations.[8]

Luczyn reports that, even as a child, Ludwig was drawn to this place because of the energies present there. In earlier times others had evidently been attracted there for the same reason. Neuschwanstein is built over the ruins of a medieval castle that had belonged to the Knights of Schwangau and that in turn was built on a Roman or possibly a Celtic settlement. Luczyn adds that some geomancers believe that where there is a concentration of positive energy there may also be a negative pole. In the case of Neuschwanstein this appears to be located in the waterfall opposite the castle, where the river Pöllat plunges into a deep gorge. This is evidently a favorite spot for suicides.[9]

In Neuschwanstein we encounter again the ubiquitous theme of the Holy Grail. As I say in my biography of Ludwig, *The Swan King,*[10] the building itself was an attempt to re-create the castle of Monsalvat, home of the Grail King Parsifal, whose son Lohengrin is the hero of Wagner's opera of that name. In the opera, which was Ludwig's favorite, Lohengrin sings of a sacred castle far away and within it a temple where the Grail is kept. At Neuschwanstein the equivalent of this temple is the throne room at the heart of the building, a breathtaking vision of Byzantium with acres of gold leaf, mosaic, and rich murals. The focal point of the room is an empty alcove. Why empty? Perhaps not for a throne after all but for the absent Grail—absent because to place a real vessel there would seem banal. That is only speculation, but it is striking how the motif of the Grail was something of profound fascination, even obsession, for Ludwig. He read avidly about it in medieval epics such as Wolfram von Eschenbach's *Parzival* and Albrecht von Scharfenberg's *Young Titurel,* and on August 21, 1865, he wrote to Richard Wagner: "Today I read a description of the Grail Temple! Away to new ecstasies!"[11]

Perhaps appropriately, it was at Neuschwanstein that the penultimate scene in the final drama of Ludwig's life took place. In the middle of the night of June 11–12, 1886, a party of doctors, asylum orderlies, and policeman arrived at the castle and took Ludwig into medical custody before bringing him in a carriage to Berg Castle on Lake Starnberg. There, on the evening of June 13, he drowned in the lake along with his doctor under mysterious circumstances, leaving behind an undying legend.

3

FOLLOWING ANCIENT
FOOTPRINTS

There is a kind of archaeology that is not about digging for bones and pottery shards but rather about probing into myths, legends, customs, symbols, and words. These things, too, have their layers, their buried messages, and their footprints of the ancestors. In Germany this kind of excavation reveals a substratum of paganism, magic, and shamanism, which many would rather not uncover but which is an essential part of the German heritage. That heritage suffered a hiatus as a result of the Christianization process, which had profoundly traumatic consequences. Although to a degree the same applies to other countries, in Germany the trauma was particularly acute. Consider, for example, the religious edict issued by Charlemagne (Charles "the Great") in the 780s, which contained the following clauses:

> Henceforth whoever among the Saxons hides himself and disdains to be baptized and wishes to remain Heathen, he shall be put to death. . . . Whoever reveres springs or trees, or worships in groves or performs sacrifices according to Heathen customs, he shall be punished with a fine.[1]

Repeatedly the Christian clergy found that the old beliefs were deeply rooted, and their efforts to stamp them out were commensurately ruthless. For example, in the wave of witch-hunting in the fifteenth to seventeenth centuries, more so-called witches were tortured and burned at the stake in Germany than in any other country.

Significantly, most of the victims of this persecution were women, and this tells us something about the role of women in pre-Christian Germanic culture in contrast to Christian culture and why women in particular aroused the ire of the inquisitors. I have already drawn attention to the strain of shamanism in the Germanic world. It is important to note that the Nordic/Germanic form of shamanism, *seidh* (alternatively *seidhr* or *sejd*), was traditionally the preserve of women, although later on men also took up the practice. Odin's ordeal on the world tree to gain the secrets of the runes was certainly shamanic, but it is worth noting that, according to the *Edda,* it was the goddess Freya who instructed him in the art of seidh.[2] Apart from those who were shamans and seeresses, women as a whole played a key role in Germanic society as midwives, herbalists, and healers. As mothers they passed on to their children the traditions and collective memory of the tribe through songs and stories. And the sagas and Eddic poems are full of stories of strong, determined women.

A woman who practiced seidh was called a *seidhkona.* An alternative term was *heid* (seeress), and this word is perpetuated today in a number of first names for women, such as Heide, Adelheid (noble seeress), Heidelinde (seeress of the linden), and Heidrun (seeress of the runes). These names are echoes of the old pagan/shamanic religion, which has surfaced repeatedly over the centuries in various different disguises, even within Christianity. One of its essential features is what we would now call a holistic worldview that sees life as emerging from the interaction of nature and spirit. This is what lies behind, among other things, alchemy, the Rosicrucian tradition, and the eighteenth-century movement called *Naturphilosophie* (nature philosophy). There are many echoes of this worldview, as the following selected examples from lore, legend, and custom illustrate. Many of these still have lessons for the present age.

THE TREE

Veneration of trees is an age-old tradition among all the Indo-European peoples,[3] but perhaps especially among the Germans. It was from Germany that there came the tradition of the Christmas tree, and the song "O Tannenbaum" (Oh, Fir Tree) is now sung all over the world in different versions. The *Edda,* the collection of old Norse poems, even tells us that human beings originated from two primal trees, Ask and Embla (ash and elm), which were animated by the gods and given human qualities. In the Germanic mythology the world itself is a tree, the Yggdrasil, as the *Edda* describes—a tree divided into nine sub-worlds. One is reserved for the gods and one for human beings. Then there are worlds for the elements fire and water; for the Black Elves, the White Elves, and the giants; and for the netherworlds of Hel and Niflheim. It was on the world tree that Odin, the Nordic god of wisdom and poetry, hung for nine days and nights to obtain the secrets of the runes in what was clearly a shamanic ordeal. In shamanism the world tree is also the central axis of the world, which the shaman re-creates symbolically in his or her own space—for example, in the form of a tent pole. The Christmas tree is a relic of the same practice. For the duration of the Christmas holiday the tree becomes the center of the household and symbolically the center of the world.

For the German tribes of pre-Christian times the groves were their places of worship, as Tacitus confirms:

> The Germans, however, do not consider it consistent with the grandeur of celestial beings to confine the gods within walls, or to liken them to the form of any human countenance. They consecrate woods and groves, and they apply the names of deities to the abstraction which they see only in spiritual worship.[4]

For the Christian missionaries the worship of trees presented a threat, and they were quick to act against it, as the English emissary Winfried, known as Boniface, did when, in 723, he felled the Donar oak at Geismar, now part of Fritzlar in Hessen. With the wood from the tree Boniface had a church built, which led to the founding of the town of Fritzlar in 724. In 1999, to commemorate the 1,275th anniversary of the foundation, the municipality erected a bronze statue by the sculptor Ubbo Enninga, depicting Boniface holding an ax and standing on the stump of the felled oak. Set into the paving beside the statue is a plaque with an explanatory text. All of this rankled with the pagan community, and in 2012 a group of pagans led by Thomas Vömel (alias Phoenix), a practicing shaman, held a peaceful demonstration at the statue. They proposed, in a spirit of interreligious understanding, to plant a new oak tree and install another plaque, marking the anniversary from the pagan point of view. Further demonstrations were held in 2014 and 2016, but neither the Catholic diocese nor the town authorities took the proposal seriously.

The reverberations created by Boniface's action have continued until today, as witness the musical about him, which premiered in Fulda in 2004 and enjoyed an enormous success. Boniface is portrayed sympathetically as a man of genuine piety and an essential goodness, who comes to see the felling of the Donar oak as an act of hubris, which he regrets. Boniface's enemy, the pagan chieftain Radbod, is presented as a man with his own sense of honor, even though he murders Boniface.

Despite the efforts of the missionaries, the Germans' age-old sense of kinship with trees could not be eradicated. It used to be—and perhaps in places still is—the custom for a forester, before felling a tree, to ask it for forgiveness. Trees are still personified among the Germans. One speaks of "Father Oak," "Mother Linden," and "Lady Hazel." The linden or lime tree is especially loved, and its name, *Linde* in German, is cognate with the verb *lindern,* meaning "to soothe"—think of linden tea. The village linden (*Dorflinde*) is a feature of many a town square, and in some cases its place is occupied instead by a village oak (*Dorfeiche*).

Fig. 3.1. The Dorflinde (village linden) in the Borgfeld district of Bremen. Such trees feature in many town and village centers in Germany.

Photograph by the author.

There is another tradition that illustrates the importance of the tree in the German psyche. Passing a house under construction and nearing completion, you will often see what looks like a kind of maypole attached to the roof ridge. This is the topping-out wreath (*Richtkranz*), which is erected when the timbers are in place but the roof tiles have not yet been laid. The basic form is a wreath of pine branches surrounding a pole and with colored ribbons tied to it. I believe there is some profound symbolism involved here. It suggests the world tree, male and female, and possibly the axis of the world stretching out to the polestar and surrounded by the circle of the zodiac. A slightly different form is where the branches are bent into the shape of a crown. In whichever form, the object is surely a variant of the shaman's tent pole, a way of marking the center of the house and symbolically the center of the world for those who are going to live in it. The topping-out ceremony typically involves one of the building team standing on the roof and drinking a glass of schnapps, then throwing the glass to the ground. It is taken as a good omen if the glass smashes and a bad one if it remains unbroken. By such customs is the German sense of kinship with trees kept alive.

In recent years a German forester from the Eiffel district, Peter Wohlleben, has scored a huge public success with his books, films, and courses revealing how trees are intelligent, social, and sentient beings. Since reading his book *The Hidden Life of Trees,* I have found that a walk in the woods has taken on a whole new perspective, making me aware how each tree is constantly at work, combating harmful parasites, monitoring climatic conditions, making strategic decisions for its growth, and passing messages on to the other trees in the wood. A tree is a wondrous creation whose mysterious properties are still not fully understood—for example, the way in which trees pump water up through their trunks in defiance of all the known laws of mechanics. Wohlleben's book is not overtly spiritual, but it awakens the kind of awe about which the nature mystics talk. For that reason it has been criticized by some members of the scientific establishment as being fanciful and unsound. But the trees themselves bear witness to a truth deeper than the purely scientific mind can understand.

PSYCHEDELIC PLANTS

In early Germanic culture one of the ways in which the shamans attained altered states of consciousness was through narcotic plants, of which they had a variety at their disposal. One of the most common was the psychedelic mushroom *Amanita muscaria,* or fly agaric. Early evidence for this is found in Scandinavia in the Bronze Age rock carvings, typically depicting a ship bearing a mushroom-shaped object. Archaeologists and ethnologists were long puzzled by this object. Was it a sail or perhaps a tree? But it now seems clear the object not only looks like a mushroom but *is* a mushroom and relates to the use of psychedelic mushrooms by the shamans of that region.[5] Scott Olsen, author of authoritative works on shamanism, has made a special study of entheogens, a term coined in the 1970s and meaning something like substances "causing one to become god-inspired." He finds many symbolic references to them in the Nordic mythology. For example, he believes the shape of Thor's hammer also represents a mushroom.[6]

The ethnobotanist Christian Rätsch has indicated how the *Amanita muscaria* mushroom, or fly agaric, to use its common name, features in German folklore. The German word for it is *Fliegenpilz* (fly mushroom). The reason for the name is possibly because of the visionary flight that can be caused by consuming the mushroom. German tradition links it with Wotan (Odin), and Rätsch quotes a south German folktale that Wotan was riding one on Christmas eve and was suddenly pursued by devils. The horse went into a gallop and began to foam at the mouth. Where the foam fell the fly agaric sprang up the following year.[7] The fly agaric, which is toxic unless taken in small doses, is not only a narcotic but also an aphrodisiac and a medicine.

Rätsch has also written about the use of cannabis or hemp as an entheogen and as an aphrodisiac, which was already happening in Germanic society by the fifth century BCE. The plant was cultivated by women and was sacred to the love goddess Freya. The sowing and harvesting of the plant were accompanied by a ritual involving intense sexual arousal—one became erotically "high." Rätsch connects this ritual with the German word for a wedding, *Hochzeit* (meaning "high time"). For the people of that time, aphrodisiacs were not something indecent but rather sacred substances that furthered procreation.

Another plant that was much valued by the Germans and Celts for its aphrodisiac and intoxicating qualities was the black henbane (*Hyoscyamus niger*), for which the popular German word is *Bilsenkraut*. In a slight variation the *B* in *Bilsen* becomes a *P*—hence the town of Pilsen in the Czech Republic, home of the famous Pilsner beer. For the ancient Germans, beer made with the addition of henbane was sacred to the thunder god Thor.[8] Thus Germany's high reputation in beer-making has a long and venerable history behind it.

WATER

Germany is rich in traditions connected with the veneration of water, as witness the number of place-names ending in variations of the word *Brunnen,* meaning "spring or fountain." Hence names like Heilbrunn, Heilbronn, and Heilborn, all meaning "healing" and/or possibly "holy spring," and hence the names of towns like Paderborn and Bad Schönborn. Many of these places were spa towns that grew up around a sacred spring. Such springs were revered by the ancient Germanic and Celtic tribes, and the tradition was continued by the Romans. Wherever they settled, the Romans would seek out a spring and build a temple around it dedicated to one of their deities such as Venus, Diana, Hercules, Mercury, or Mithras. Hot springs were especially valued by them. Thus these shrines were places of worship as well as places for bathing and drinking the health-giving waters.

An age-old practice going back to pagan times is to collect water from a spring at or close to the vernal equinox in honor of the spring goddess Ostara, whose name was Christianized in German to Ostern (Easter). In certain Catholic parts of Germany, on Easter morning young women collect water from a spring or river. The practice of *Wasserschöpfen* (collecting water) at Easter has now been revived among neo-pagan groups. It is supposed to take place at sunrise, and the water must be gathered in silence if its special properties are to be preserved.

These traditions and customs are based on the realization that water has extraordinary properties that cannot be detected by laboratory methods. "The 'water corpse' that is subjected to such procedures will . . . never be able to reveal its laws. Only from the messages of moving water can a few conclusions be drawn."[9] These words were written by Viktor Schauberger (1885–1958), Austrian philosopher, scientist, inventor, and seer. Schauberger came to his remarkable insights about water while working as a forester in the Austrian Alps and observing the mountain streams. Schauberger saw water as the primal substance, the interface that enabled spirit and matter to interact and thus become the very first material manifestation and the source of all the rest of creation. He was therefore very much in the tradition of German nature philosophy. He came to the conclusion that water is an active organism with a sort of consciousness and the ability to record and store information. As such, it can give off positive energies, but to do so it must be treated in accordance with its own natural laws derived from nature. Tap water that has been processed and chemically treated is in effect dead, but Schauberger invented various devices—filters, energizers, and vortices—that can reanimate the water.

Schauberger's findings have subsequently been followed by other researchers, such as the German Anthroposophist Theodor Schwenk (1910–1986), who was a pioneer in the development of flow forms, constructions in which water cascades down through a series of basins designed so that the water constantly twists and turns. I knew some people in London who had such a form in their garden and were using it to treat the wastewater from their bathroom, which they then used to irrigate the garden, resulting in abundant growth.

In the early 1960s Schwenk cofounded the Institute of Flow Sciences at Herrischried in the Black Forest, which he led until 1971. Recognizing the essential role of water for the health of human beings and nature, the Institute is devoted to researching the miraculous properties of water and finding and promoting policies for better water use and management. Schwenk and his colleagues developed a method of photographing the manifold shapes and patterns of water as it drops, flows, spirals, and interacts with the air element. They were convinced that these patterns contain lessons from a higher level of the cosmos as to how we can use water more responsibly. Today the institute, which is linked to the Anthroposophical movement, continues its work in the spirit of the founders.

There are some simple tests that anyone can do to test the quality of water. If you pour water down a plug hole it will rotate in either a clockwise or counterclockwise direction, and 80 percent of water is of the latter variety The geomancer Eike Hensch explains in his book *Geomantische Reisen* (Geomantic Journeys) that the clockwise variety has electromagnetic properties that combat decay and can heal a variety of illnesses. Sometimes such water can switch to the counterclockwise mode, but there is a kind that always returns to its clockwise nature as the default option. Springs containing the latter kind have always been specially valued for their health-giving properties.[10]

FIRE

In addition to the drawing of water at the vernal equinox, another ancient pagan practice connected with Ostara is that of the Easter fire. This was and still is part of a celebration to bid farewell to winter and hail the coming spring. The tradition has also been adopted by the Christian churches but in a slightly different form. In Catholic churches on the night of Easter Sunday, a small fire is lit outside the church. The priest lights a candle from the fire and carries it back into the darkened church to symbolize the light of Christ illuminating the world. The secular or pagan version of the custom is a very different affair, as I can remember, having attended Easter fire celebrations in Lower Saxony. In an open field a huge fire is lit, and a big crowd gathers for much singing, dancing, drinking, and, in some cases, leaping over the fire. The poet and naturalist Hermann Löns (1866–1914), bard of the Lüneburg Heath, wrote a beautiful poem about this custom. He describes wandering over the heath, reflecting gloomily on the passing of the old ways and the old gods, when he comes upon an Easter fire:

> I walked on further across the twilit land,
> Behind which the sun sank down, round and red.
> On the other side across the brownish marsh,
> A glowing red flame rose toward a starless sky.
>
> The white smoke billowed up before a pitch black forest,
> Until it slowly disappeared in the evening clouds.
> And I stood and stayed, gazing at the fire's glow,
> And I listened to the girls' cheering and the young boys'
>   shrill shouts,
> And I laughed and thought:
> Despite it all, the joyful ways of our ancestors
> Have been kept alive by my people.[11]

While the Easter fire is in origin a celebration of the vernal equinox, the St. John's fire, which takes place in June, celebrates midsummer. This again is a festival that is celebrated by both pagans and Christians.

On the subject of fire, the practice of pyromancy (fire divination) should be mentioned. Some years ago I had a house in the state of Brandenburg, and I remember an elderly woman, who was my neighbor, telling me about a method of fortune-telling, practiced in the region, called "speaking to the Red Man," which involved sitting by the fire and reading messages in the flickering patterns made by the flames and smoke.

AIR

Jacob Grimm attributes the element air to the god Odin, or Wuotan in old Germanic. The word *wuot* conveys impetuosity and wildness as well as also spirit or mind and is possibly cognate with *od,* the breath of life or the life force. In his *Germanic Mythology,* Grimm tells us that "Wuotan was the all-pervading essence, equivalent to Vishnu, the fine ether that fills all of space."[12] Possibly, therefore, what we see in the figure of Odin/Wotan is a personification of the notion of a subtle, all-pervading fluid that links everything in the universe—something that was recognized by Franz Anton Mesmer, Karl von Reichenbach, and others, as we shall see later on.

Odin has many of the characteristics of a shaman, and one of the typical traits of shamanism is the great importance attached to birds. The Buryat and Yakut shamans of Siberia have a legend that an eagle was the father of the first shaman.[13] Birds often feature as totem creatures, and the ability to transform oneself into a bird is found in many forms of shamanism.[14] Odin, a distinctly shamanic figure in the Germanic mythology, is accompanied by two ravens, Hugin and Munin (Thought and Memory). Birds also function as psychopomps, guides who bring souls into the world and accompany them to the afterworld. A well-known example is the stork, which in many European countries is said to bring children into the world. In old German the word for "stork" is *adebar,* and in old Norse *odabaro.*[15] The name means "carrier of the od" and the word *od* refers to the breath of life or the life force, the Nordic equivalent to the Chinese concept of *chi,* or *prana* in the Indian tradition. The legend has it that the stork goes to a pool where new souls, cradled in water lilies, wait to be incarnated. The stork takes a soul from the pool and places it in the womb of its future mother. Storks are much loved creatures in Germany, and their arrival around April is greeted in many places with a *Storchenfest* (stork party).

EARTH

As Jacob Grimm writes, "In nearly all languages the earth is feminine and, in contrast to the paternally embracing sky, is conceived as a supporting, birth-giving, fruit-bringing mother."[16] The worship of the earth goddess Nerthus among the tribes along the west coast of the Baltic Sea is described by the Roman historian Tacitus in his *Germania:*

> They believe that she interests herself in human affairs and rides through their peoples. In an island . . . stands a sacred grove, and in the grove stands a car [i.e., a wagon] draped with a cloth which none but the priest may touch. The priest can feel the presence of the goddess in this holy of holies, and attends her, in deepest reverence, as her car is drawn by kine. Then follow days of rejoicing and merry-making in every place that she honours with her advent and stay.[17]

In a different Germanic tradition the earth goddess is Jörd, wife of Odin. Reverence for the earth among the Germanic tribes is also shown by the custom of swearing an oath on the soil.

In Germany there is a rich mythology concerning the little people of the earth, the elves and the dwarfs. These are especially connected with mountainous areas where precious metals are mined, such as the Harz Mountains. The dwarfs are thought to be the guardians of these metals, and, as such, according to mining tradition, they have to be treated with respect. Often they are portrayed as miners wearing leather aprons and carrying lanterns, picks, and hammers. This is the image that was immortalized in Walt Disney's cartoon film *Snow White and the Seven Dwarfs,* based on the Grimms' fairy tale. Statues of dwarfs adorn many a garden in Germany, as in other countries. The ethnobotanist Wolf-Dieter Storl writes in his book on plant devas, "The red-capped plaster dwarfs, scorned by cock-sure intellectuals as the epitome of bourgeois kitsch, are in fact visual representations of the etheric forces present in a garden." These figures, he says, attract invisible helpers who find shelter in the statues and cause them to be animated.[18]

4

FALL AND RISE OF
THE OLD GODS

By tradition, every five years the town of Oberstdorf in Bavaria puts on a strange and deeply pagan ceremony called the Dance of the Wild Men, involving a group of thirteen dancers, dressed in costumes made out of a fiber obtained from fir tree bark, which make them look like the fabled Big Foot of the California mountains. In July 2010, I went by car from my home in Bremen down to Oberstdorf with my old friend Jörg Rohfeld to see the performance. We checked into a hotel in the hills above the town and in the evening walked down to the Oybele Hall, where the event was to take place. We found it already packed, with several hundred or so people in the audience. Traditional clothes were much in evidence—*Loden* jackets, leather shorts or knee breeches, and *Dirndl* dresses. A few nuns in their black robes were also present. A stage at one end of the room was decked out with fir tree branches. Waitresses were serving enormous mugs of beer.

A brass band played, and a few couples danced on the stage. Then, after a pause, the Wild Men entered for the main performance. Over their shaggy costumes they wore crowns of holly and girdles made from fir branches. The band struck up again, and the men began to dance, making strenuous-looking hopping, leaping movements. The dance proceeded in eighteen stages of three or four minutes each with pauses in between. In the final scene they assembled an image of a huge, bearded face, apparently depicting the Nordic god Thor, then they danced around it, each bowing in turn to the figure. We wondered what the nuns thought of it all. Such a pagan performance seemed distinctly out place in Catholic Bavaria.

Evidently this extraordinary ritual represents a dim memory of a mysterious race—the wild folk—that once lived in various parts of Europe. Accounts vary as to what they looked like. According to some they were small in stature, but more often they were described as giants. In the early centuries of the Christian era, as waves of new settlers arrived, the wild folk sought refuge in the mountains and in the depths of the forests. On the whole they kept to themselves, but occasionally they came into contact with the newcomers. Sometimes there were fights, but there were also occasions when the wild folk used their knowledge of herbal medicine to help the settlers. Sightings of wild folk were recorded in many different areas of Europe.

The town of Wildemann (Wild Man) in the Harz Mountains took its name from an incident that is said to have happened in the early sixteenth century when miners were beginning to probe into the hills in search of the precious metal ore. In one secluded valley they encountered a wild man and woman living together. The miners were commanded by their ruler, the Duke of Braunschweig, to capture the wild man. After several failed attempts they wounded him with arrows and tied him up to take him to the duke, but on the way he died.[1] While this may be part legend, there are enough comparable reports to suggest that the wild folk really existed.

Over time the wild folk increasingly took on a mythical character. They figured in plays, courtly pageants, and the performances of mummers. They became a favorite motif in heraldry, where they sometimes appear on the shield of a coat of arms or more often as supporters standing on either side of the shield. Sculptures of the wild man as well as of his near relative, the green man, are often found in medieval churches, as though in an attempt to tame and Christianize them. The wild folk also appear frequently in works of literature. In the medieval epics there are stories of knights encountering wild men in forest clearings or themselves living for a time in the wild state. Goethe refers to them in his drama *Faust,* where he writes:

> *The Wild Men, as they are named,*
> *In the Harz Mountains greatly famed,*
> *In nature's nakedness and might,*
> *They come, each one of giant height.*[2]

These figures inspired a mixture of fear, awe, and fascination. They represented the unbridled forces of nature, the carnal drives, and a more primitive state of humanity.

While the Oberstdorf Dance of the Wild Men is highly unusual in its form, it overlaps with other folk traditions in which, for a short space of time, things that are dark and uncanny are let out within the confines of a procession or festival. One such comparable tradition celebrated in the German-speaking world involves the figure of Percht, usually portrayed as a witchlike woman with a hideous, demonic face. Legend has it that she goes from house to house at the end of the year, making sure that everything is clean and tidy, and woe betide any housewife whose house does not pass muster. In certain places in Austria, Switzerland, and southern Germany it is customary, during the twelve days of Christmas, to hold processions in which locals, dressed as Percht and wearing appropriately frightening masks, parade through the streets to the delighted shrieks of the children.

Similar figures appear in festivals at the beginning of Advent, held, for example, in the region of Berchtesgaden (named after Bercht or Percht). Here the various processions look similar but have different names, depending on the locality. In some places the participants are called Perchts, in others Buttmandeln or Krampus.

Plate 1. *Der Morgen* (*The Morning*) by the German romantic
artist Friedrich Otto Runge, 1808.

Plate 2. The Kabbalistic Instruction Tableau of Princess Antonia, dating from the 1660s, in the Church of the Trinity at Bad Teinach in the Black Forest.

WIKIMEDIA COMMONS.

Plate 3. Distillation work in progress at the Soluna Laboratories at Donauwörth, Bavaria.

PHOTOGRAPH COURTESY OF SOLUNA.

Plate 4. The park at Wörlitz in Saxony-Anhalt,
showing the area known as the Labyrinth.

Plate 5. Icehouse in the form of a pyramid
in the Rosicrucian park at Potsdam,
created by King Frederick William II of Prusssia
(1744–1797).

PHOTOGRAPH BY THE AUTHOR.

Plate 6. *Wandervögel,*
a painting by Max Frey, circa 1931.

Plate 7. *Shambhalah,* a visionary work
by Melchior Lechter, painted in 1925.
IN THE COLLECTION OF THE MEININGEN CITY MUSEUMS, THURINGIA.

Plate 8. Entrance to the Octagon, the esoteric library
created by Thomas Hakl in Graz, Austria.

PHOTOGRAPH BY THE AUTHOR.

The Buttmandeln, in addition to wearing demonic masks, are encased in costumes made of sheaves of straw. They have heavy cowbells attached to them and make a great din as they move along. These processions are held on December 5, the eve of Saint Nicholas Day, and they are led by a Saint Nicholas figure carrying a crozier and dressed in a robe and bishop's miter. His role is to impart the good news of Advent. Thus what was originally a pagan ceremony has been given a Christian character. To take part in these processions wearing a heavy costume is a strenuous experience and is regarded as a rite of passage for young men. To be a Krampus one has to be at least fifteen years old and unmarried. Possibly in pagan days the experience was a kind of shamanic initiation.

When Europe was converted to Christianity the old festivals were either given a Christian wrapping or they were categorized as something atavistic and demonic. Thus Halloween (an English abbreviation of "All Hallows Eve"), which was originally an occasion when one remembered and paid homage to dead forebears, became, thanks to British and American influence, a time to get out the ghost and witch costumes and make lanterns from hollowed out pumpkins carved into faces that glowed eerily in the candlelight.

Something similar happened to the traditional festival held in the Harz Mountains on Walpurgis Night; that is, the night from April 30 to May 1 (named after Saint Walpurga or Walburga). In pagan times it was a joyful festival to thank Wotan for the advent of spring and probably involved a good deal of drinking, dancing, and lovemaking. With the coming of Christianity it acquired a lurid reputation as an orgiastic gathering of witches and demons presided over by the devil. The focal point of the revels was the Brocken, the highest mountain in northern Germany, which not long ago straddled the border between the two Germanies. Today some revelers still make their way to the top of the Brocken, often via a steam train called the Mephisto Express. But most of the revelry takes place at various other venues in the Harz, notably the Hexentanzplatz (Witches' Dance Arena), a plateau in the hills high above the town of Thale, which lies in the deep valley of the Bode River.

Effigies of witches are still burned in bonfires, a practice that deeply offends present-day witches.

In the old days, so it was said, the witches used to fly there on broomsticks or pitchforks. My wife, Donate, and I did the nearest thing to flying, which was to take the cable car from Thale. The glass walls and floor of the cabin afforded dizzying views of the river far below and the steep gorge with its breathtaking cliffs on either side, the rock in places resembling craggy faces or the remains of ruined castles. Even in the most precipitous places there were trees growing—sycamore, beech, chestnut, oak—some of them appearing to rise directly out of an almost vertical surface.

Arriving at the Hexentanzplatz one wonders how the old gods would react to what the tourist industry has created here: the bronze devilish figures disporting themselves on a circle of boulders; the half-timbered Witch House, which is upside-down along with its furniture and contents; and above all the Walpurgis Night celebration, when some ten thousand people gather here, displaying a variety of witch costumes and demonic masks. There is a laser show, a firework display, and much wild dancing to live music.

Walking back toward the cable car station for the downward journey, we were looking forward to visiting the Mythical Way, which takes you along the riverside and through the town past a series of statues of the old Germanic gods and mythical creatures: the Midgard Serpent, Odin and his eight-legged horse, the messenger squirrel Ratatosk, the three Norns, and others. How curious that in Thale, contrary to tradition, the demons are up above and the gods down below.

But wait! What is this imposing building close to Hexentanzplatz? A sign bears the name Walpurgishalle (Walpurgis Hall). The entrance is flanked by rugged stone pillars and surmounted by a wooden gable bearing a great bearded face with a winged helmet. The blind eye and the silhouettes of two wolves flanking the gable remove any doubt. We are looking at Wotan, chief of the Nordic pantheon. However, when one enters the building it is clear that this is not just a pagan

Fig. 4.1. Statue of the three Norns forming part of the Mythical Way at Thale in the Harz Mountains.

PHOTOGRAPH BY THE AUTHOR.

Fig. 4.2. The Walpurgishalle at Thale. The portico features the god Wotan (Odin), while the interior evokes the world of Goethe's *Faust*.
PHOTOGRAPH BY AXEL SEILER.

temple but also an homage to the Faust legend, as the interior murals show. The one on the far wall as you enter depicts the Walpurgis Night scene on the Brocken from Goethe's *Faust*. In the sky is a flock of naked witches on their broomsticks. In the foreground various figures dance while others huddle over a cauldron, doubtless containing some noxious potion. Presiding over it all is a winged and horned devil perched on a high rock.

The building and the murals were the creation of the artist Hermann Hendrich (1854–1931), a leading activist in the pagan revival of the late nineteenth and early twentieth centuries. In addition to the Walpurgishalle (erected in 1901), he also designed the Nibelungenhalle in Königswinter (opened in 1913), a monument to Richard Wagner, of whom Hendrich was a fervent admirer. Hendrich was cofounder in 1901 of an organization called the Verdandi-Bund, one of a number of neo-pagan groups, such as the Wodan Society and the Germanic Faith Community, founded in Germany and Austria in the early twentieth century. The Verdandi-Bund was named after one of the three Norns, the goddesses of fate and time in the Nordic tradition—Urd, Verdandi, and Skuld. Urd governs the past, Verdandi the present, and Skuld the future. Another person associated with Thale was Hendrich's friend and fellow pagan Ernst Wachler, an artist and cofounder of the Wodan Society. Wachler was the creator of the Harz Mountain Theater, an amphitheater cut into the slope of the mountain not far from the Hexentanzplatz. Opened in 1903, it put on dramas celebrating Germany's pagan past. Today it offers a varied program of plays, operas, and musicals.

At this point let us take a look back and trace the story of the gradual resurgence of the old gods. This was not exclusive to Germany. Something similar took place in Italy and other countries. However, when the scholars, poets, and artists of the Italian Renaissance began to celebrate the gods of classical mythology, they had the advantage of access to an abundance of ancient literature on the subject. Similarly, in Iceland there were the texts of the *Edda,* containing a wealth of information about the gods and myths of the North.

By contrast, in Germany there was very little written evidence to go on apart from Tacitus's *Germania* and two tiny fragments of verse dating from about 900 CE known as the Merseburg Spells after the town of Merseburg, where they were discovered in the cathedral library. One of these is a spell for freeing someone from chains. The other describes how Odin, or Wotan, and two goddesses heal the horse belonging to the god Baldur, which has dislocated a leg joint. The latter text, scanty though it is, gives us an important insight as to the shamanic nature of the culture that produced it. The horse is one of the traditional shamanic totem animals. It was considered particularly sacred among the Germanic peoples, and it would have been quite normal for a shaman

Fig. 4.3. Crossed horses' heads on the gable of a farmhouse in Lower Saxony. The horse is a sacred animal in Germanic tradition.

PHOTOGRAPH BY THE AUTHOR.

to treat an injured horse by pronouncing a spell over it. The importance attached to the horse as a sacred animal is shown today in the custom of having a wooden gable decoration in the form of crossed horse heads, a tradition especially common in my home state of Lower Saxony. If you drive through Lower Saxony today, you will see countless farmhouses and barns decorated with this motif.

You will also see, not only in Lower Saxony but elsewhere in Germany as well, offerings of fruit, flowers, and such, left at ancient sacred places in honor of the local deities and bearing witness to some deep-seated need to reconnect with the ancestral past. Such places are particularly plentiful in certain areas. For example, any comprehensive sightseeing tour of the hilly Eifel district on the left side of the Rhine west of Bonn and Cologne would include the remains of a series of temples dating back to the second and third centuries CE, when the

Romans occupied the area, and dedicated to a trio of female figures known as the Matronae (plural of *matrona,* a Latin word meaning, roughly, "dame" or "gracious lady" or "respected mother"). Typically the three are depicted in relief on a stone stele, seated in a row and holding baskets of fruit. The one in the center is a young woman with long hair, uncovered and unbound. The other two are older women, usually with a curious hair style—or possibly a hat of some sort—in the form of a large, balloon-like shape protruding from the head.

What we are dealing with here is evidently a Celto-Germanic cult that was adopted by the Romans and possibly merged with some existing Roman elements. The motif of the Triple Goddess is found in many pre-Christian traditions and is thought to symbolize the three phases of the female life cycle—namely, maiden, mother, and crone—also corresponding to the three phases of the moon: waxing, full, and waning. These were household deities to whom obeisance was paid so that they would bring abundance and well-being to the family and the homestead and protect them from harm. These shrines are found mainly in the Celtic and Germanic areas formerly occupied by the Romans, with the largest concentration in the vicinity of the Eifel, where there are some eight hundred such sites. In some cases the remains of the Roman structure are remarkably well preserved, as in the Temple of the Matronae at Pesch in the Eifel, where, on the basis of the remaining walls, it has been possible to create a model of the building, which consisted of a perimeter structure in the form of a pillared loggia and an inner sanctum with a Matronae stele on either side of the entrance.[3]

Such ancient sites were not always valued as they are today and over the centuries were often plundered for building material. But by the eighteenth century, attitudes toward the relics of the past were changing, including the literary relics. In 1777 the first German version of the *Edda,* translated by Jacob Schimmelmann, was published at Stettin in Prussia, just in time for the advent of the Romantic era, which seized upon the stuff of Germanic mythology and nourished a new enthusiasm for the culture of the German folk, which scholars and folklorists began to study eagerly. In the early decades of the nineteenth century the prolific brothers Jacob and Wilhelm Grimm produced not only their famous collection of fairy tales but also a new translation of part of the *Edda,* a study of the runes and a monumental work on German mythology. Another key work of the early nineteenth century was a collection of folk songs by Achim von Arnim and Clemens Brentano titled *Des Knaben Wunderhorn* (The Boy's Magic Horn), which appeared in three volumes from 1805 to 1808.

All of this went together with a romantic nationalism that was burgeoning at the same time in many countries of Europe and grew in strength throughout the nineteenth century. One of the ways in which it manifested itself was in a passion for building heroic monuments such as the colossal Arminius Monument at Detmold in North Rhine-Westphalia, completed in 1875, and the Parthenon-like Valhalla Monument overlooking the Danube at Regensburg, built in honor of heroic men and women of the German-speaking lands and opened in 1842. The name of the monument is significant, Valhalla being the abode of slain warriors in the Nordic tradition. The stage was now ready for a call to the old gods, and onto the stage stepped the composer Richard Wagner.

My own introduction to Wagner was his opera *Lohengrin,* which had the same intoxicating effect on me as it had on King Ludwig II of Bavaria when he first heard it at the age of fifteen. Years later I was delighted to discover that my American grandmother, as a young woman on the grand tour of Europe, had attended a performance of *Lohengrin* in Berlin at the end of the nineteenth century, with the great Wagnerian tenor Ernst Kraus in the title role. In her diary she described the performance as the loveliest thing she had heard on the tour.

Wagner's achievement was all the more remarkable in view of his lack of a formal musical education. Born in Leipzig in 1813, probably the illegitimate son of the actor Ludwig Geyer, Wagner was a child prodigy. At an early age he became stagestruck and had hardly learned to read before he was planning to write dramas of Shakespearean scale. Soon he turned his ambitions toward the opera. Enthused by Beethoven's music, he taught himself composition and embarked on a career that would involve years of penury and flight from creditors before he was rescued by King Ludwig, who supported him financially and gave him the security to write the music and text of his greatest work, the *Ring* cycle, based partly on the German medieval epic *Nibelungenlied* and partly on old Norse works such as *Völsunga Saga*. A central theme in these epics is the theft of a treasure, which sets off a whole chain of disasters. In Wagner's narrative the treasure is a hoard of gold that lies at the bottom of the Rhine and is guarded by three Rhine maidens. The dwarf Alberich steals the treasure and makes himself king of the Nibelungs, who are a race of dwarfs. Wotan then steals the treasure from Alberich with the help of Loge (Loki), leading to a series of tragic events culminating in *Götterdämmerung* (Twilight of the Gods). With help from King Ludwig, Wagner built an auditorium specifically for the performance of his works, the Bayreuth Festival Theatre, which became the mecca of the Wagner cult.

Wagner's works created a greatly increased awareness of the Nordic gods by presenting them in a highly dramatic way in combination with powerful music, and thus he helped to nourish the emerging neopagan movement in Germany and Austria. One particularly fervent admirer of Wagner was the above-mentioned Hermann Hendrich, whose Nibelungenhalle (Hall of the Nibelungs), close to Königswinter on the Rhine, is a kind of temple to the composer and was completed in 1913 to commemorate the hundredth anniversary of Wagner's birth. Conceived by Hendrich, it was designed by the architects Hans Meier and Werner Behrendt. The building is suitably imposing. There is a massive stone portico that might be the entrance to Valhalla, with the name Nibelungenhalle in gold, quasi-runic letters on the architrave. The circular, domed interior has a kind of altar piece with Wagner's head in relief, and the walls are hung with Hendrich's powerfully eerie paintings of scenes from the story of the Nibelungs. The floor of the main hall is inlaid with a pentagram and a mosaic of the Midgard Serpent. Close to the building is a feature added in 1933, the Dragon's Cave, containing a stone sculpture of Fafnir, the dragon who guards the Rhinegold. Appropriately the building stands on the hill called the Drachenfels (Dragon Cliff), part of the Siebengebirge (Seven Hills) range.

During the early years of the twentieth century, the nascent Germanic pagan movement encompassed several different groups and factions, which were constantly quarreling, splitting, merging, and competing. Probably the most significant was the German Faith Community (Germanische Glaubens-Gemeinschaft), led by the prominent painter and writer Ludwig Fahrenkrog (1867–1952). Many of its assemblies were held in the dramatic environs of the amphitheater above Thale. Another member of the German Faith Community was Fahrenkrog's close friend and fellow artist Fidus (pseudonym of Hugo Höppener), noted for his evocations of an idealized nature-oriented way of life. Typical of his work are radiant images of naked figures saluting the rising sun or dancing in idyllic landscapes. Fidus was among the visitors to the Bohemian colony at Monte Verità in Switzerland, along with Hermann Hesse, Max Weber, and others. During the Third Reich, although a member of the Nazi party, he was cold-shouldered by the Nazi establishment, and Hitler himself condemned his paintings. Fahrenkrog fared little better and was after a time forbidden to exhibit his works in Germany. On the whole, Germanic pagans were not well treated by the Nazi regime, which tended to see them as cranks and crackpots.

Typical was the Nazi attitude toward the millionaire entrepreneur Ludwig Roselius, inventor of HAG decaffeinated coffee and a proponent of the Nordic pagan worldview. In the Böttcherstrasse, a street off the town square in his hometown of Bremen, Roselius commissioned the architects Eduard Scotland and Alfred Runge and the sculptor and architect Bernhard Hoetger to design a series of buildings full of motifs from Germanic mythology and built of red brick in a striking, expressionist style.

Today the street is considered a landmark of expressionist architecture and attracts a constant stream of tourists and shoppers, but it has a troubled history, especially its most prominent building, the House Atlantis, which now houses a Hilton hotel. Hoetger's design for this building was inspired partly by the ideas of the folklorist and ethnologist Herman Wirth, author of works of a Nordic/folkish tenor in which he connected Plato's Atlantis with the early history of the Nordic race. Hence the choice of the name House Atlantis. The facade had three metal-clad columns decorated with images of the three Norns, the goddesses of fate. Above them was a huge wooden sculpture depicting Odin hanging on the world tree, Yggdrasil, to receive the secrets of the runes. In his speech at the opening of the building in 1931, Roselius said the following:

> House Atlantis leads back to the prehistory of humankind. Bearing witness to the past, shaping the present, holding out a promise for the future, it rises up in the street of the Tree of Life. Three Norns bear the mighty roots, drawing our attention to the age-old meaning of spiritual sacrifice, surrounded by the circle of eternal life, raising to heaven the cross of the savior that, freed from any human image, bears only the solar shield of truth.[4]

This facade was severely damaged in the Second World War and subsequently removed, but the interior has been preserved and can be visited by checking at the hotel reception. A spiral staircase leads up to the astonishing art deco Atlantis Hall with its parabola roof of glass tiles arranged in patterns suggesting runes.

Roselius and Hoetger hoped that their creation would meet with the approval of the Nazi regime, but they were severely disappointed. The street and its contents were dismissed as decadent art, and Hitler himself disparagingly referred to "Böttcherstrasse culture." In an effort to win over Hitler, Roselius had a striking relief mounted over the entrance to the street. Titled *Der Lichtbringer* (*The Lightbringer*), it is covered in gold leaf and shows a sword-wielding angel fighting a dragon,

Fig. 4.4. *Der Lichtbringer (The Lightbringer)*, a gilt relief in the Böttcherstrasse, Bremen. The angel fighting the dragon was intended to symbolize Hitler's victory over the powers of darkness.
PHOTOGRAPH BY THE AUTHOR.

intended to symbolize the victory of the führer over the powers of darkness. After much petitioning on Roselius's part, Hitler finally agreed with a shrug to let the Böttcherstrasse stay.

While Roselius was supervising the construction of the Böttcherstrasse, his contemporary, the sculptor and painter Michael Bossard, was busy with his own celebration of the old gods at his property in Lüneburg Heath about an hour's drive northeast of Bremen. The Swiss-born Bossard had, in 1911, acquired a piece of land surrounded by woods near the town of Jesteburg and built a house cum studio. In 1926 he married the much younger Jutta Krull, his former pupil at the Hamburg Art College and a sculptor in her own right, and the couple set about creating a total work of art (*Gesamtkunstwerk*) in the Wagnerian spirit with an emphasis on mythical and pagan motifs. The main feature is a Temple of the Arts, built in red brick in a style reminiscent of the Böttcherstrasse. There is also a Hall of Odin (Odinhalle), full of images of the one-eyed god with whom Bossard identified, having lost an eye as a child as the result of scarlet fever. Today the place is a museum, the Bossard Site of Arts (Kunststätte Bossard). The museum has been the subject of some controversy due to Bossard's attitude to Nazism. Like Roselius, he appears to have initially placed great hope in the regime, only to become disenchanted with it. At the time of writing there is talk of expanding the site to encompass the work of a wider range of artists.

While on the subject of neo-pagan movements of the interwar period, it is worth mentioning the Independent Free Church (Unabhängige Freikirche, UFK), founded by Friedrich Hielscher (1902–1990) in 1933. As a young man Hielscher was involved in the national conservative movement and was a close friend of the writer Ernst Jünger, one of the leading figures of that movement. He was, however, vehemently against the Nazis, whom he regarded as rabble. Already at the age of twenty-seven he was writing to Jünger, speaking of the need for an "invisible church" celebrating the Germanic forebears and their gods. In 1930 he began publishing a periodical titled *Das Reich,* which he followed up in 1931 with a book of the same title. In due course he attracted a circle of about fifty people, who formed both a religious group and a political resistance movement.

The essence of Hielscher's belief system was a form of panentheism (the belief that the world is contained in one God) combined with a polytheistic theology involving twelve messengers of that God with names taken or adapted from Nordic mythology, such as Wode, Frigga, and Loki. To each of these were assigned festivals, colors, musical notes, plants, and zodiacal signs. The festivals were marked by rituals incorporating complex symbolic correspondences. Hielscher also conducted baptisms, weddings, and funerals. As part of their resistance effort, members of the movement infiltrated various branches of the Nazi apparatus. Hielscher was arrested by the Gestapo in 1944, narrowly escaped execution, and was sent to the front. After the war the UFK resumed its activities, but by the time of Hielscher's death in 1990 the active membership had virtually shrunk to himself and his wife, Gertrud.[5]

By then others had taken up the cause of the old gods, and the stage was set for their return on a larger scale, which I shall speak about in a later chapter.

5

MYSTICS, MAGICIANS, AND WITCHES

The river Rhine flows romantically past the town of Bingen, framed by vineyard-covered banks and hilltop castles. Bingen is associated in my memory with a visit to the German headquarters of the Japanese Sokka Gakkai movement, a form of Buddhism and one of the most active of the oriental religious groups that have gained a foothold in Germany, but the town is also famous for another reason. Up in the hills above Rüdesheim on the opposite bank, the twin towers of a monastery rise over the vineyards, imposingly medieval in appearance but in fact built in the early twentieth century. This is the Benedictine Abbey of Saint Hildegard, named after Hildegard of Bingen (1098–1179), one of the most extraordinary women of the Middle Ages—abbess, poet, composer, theologian, visionary, physician, herbalist, and author of a series of remarkable writings including works on medicine that remain influential to this day.

Although living strictly within the rules of her order and the teachings of the church, Hildegard was in effect a sort of traditional wise woman and seeress. Born into a noble family, already as a teenager she became a nun in the Benedictine order, rose to become prioress, and subsequently founded two monasteries herself. From early childhood she experienced mystical visions, which she began to write down in her forties, having received papal authorization to do so. The first was an apocalyptic and prophetic work titled *Scivias,* meaning "May you know the ways." Later writings included the *Liber Divinorum Operum* (Book of Divine Works), the *Liber Vitae Meritorum* (Book of Life's Merits), the *Liber Simplicis Medicinae* (A Simple Medicine Book), and the *Liber Compositae Medicinae* (Book of Composite Medicine).

What is particularly fascinating about Hildegard's worldview is her conviction that the divine light is present within the world of matter, in contrast to the tendency in medieval Christianity to separate spirit and matter. In the *Liber Simplicis Medicinae* she wrote, "In all creation, trees, plants, animals and gem stones, there are hidden secret powers which no person can know of unless they are revealed by God."[1] This notion of the sacred in material creation is something that is found repeatedly in German thought. We find it in the writings of other German mystics, in the nature philosophy movement of the eighteenth century, and in alchemy, as we shall see later on.

How Hildegard arrived at her medical expertise is an intriguing question. She had no formal medical training and maintained that it was from her visions that she derived her remarkably accurate descriptions of physiological processes. As for her knowledge of herbal and other remedies she must have absorbed much from traditional and folk medicine as well as from her own observations. At any rate, her recipes have stood the test of time remarkably well, although some of them appear extremely bizarre. Wighard Strehlow and the late Gottfried Hertzka, two German doctors who have applied Hildegard's methods, describe her recipe for a cancer treatment as consisting of "a complicated honeywine-vinegar extract out of eel gall, ginger, long pepper (*Ocimum basilicum*), ivory powder, and the powder from vulture beak," a preparation that involved great difficulties. Vultures being a protected species, the two doctors had to wait five years to obtain one that had been killed in an accident. The use of medicines derived from vultures is evidently very ancient and was already being applied in Germany at that time. Strehlow and Hertzka write positively about the use of the remedy in homeopathic doses.[2]

Hildegard is rightly admired as one of the bright figures in the history of Christianity, but commensurately dark was a figure born a year or so after her death—namely, Konrad of Marburg (ca. 1180–1233), who entered the priesthood at a time when the church was using the newly formed Inquisition to combat what it saw as heretical movements, such as the Albigensians and the Waldensians. Konrad took an active part in these efforts and participated in the brutal Albigensian Crusade in southern France. Returning to Marburg he became confessor to Elisabeth, wife of Landgrave Ludwig IV of Thuringia. After Ludwig's death he obtained total control over Elisabeth, placed her two children in adoption, and subjected her to a regime of savage whippings and extreme physical austerities from which she died at the age of twenty-four. Having virtually murdered her in this way, he successfully pleaded for her canonization, then went on a rampage of heresy hunting that resulted in many innocent victims dying at the stake. Much hated, he was murdered while returning to Marburg after a visit to Mainz.

It is part of the strange *chiaroscuro* of medieval life in Germany that the age that produced the crazed, woman-hating Konrad also produced a school of poetry, influenced by the French troubadours, that idealized women and celebrated the tradition of courtly love. Preeminent among the German poets of this school was Walter von der Vogelweide (1170–1230), the epitome of the wandering bard of noble birth, going from castle to castle, singing his exquisite verses and occasionally having a love affair with some highborn lady.

A close contemporary of Walter was Wolfram von Eschenbach (ca. 1170–1220), most celebrated for his great epic *Parzival,* which deals with the Arthurian legend and the quest for the Holy Grail. Here we encounter a theme that crops up repeatedly in German culture. What is the Grail? In the Arthurian epics of Britain and France it is either the Crucifixion cup or the chalice used at the Last Supper. In Wolfram's epic, although he is careful to emphasize his Christian credentials, the Grail is not a Christian relic but apparently a kind of precious stone possessing miraculous powers. In Wolfram's words, "Flegetanis the heathen saw with his own eyes in the constellations things he was shy to talk about, hidden mysteries. He said there was a thing called the Grail whose name he had read clearly in the constellations." Flegetanis goes on say that a host of angels "left it on the earth and then flew away up over the stars."[3] Later on in the narrative a hermit reveals more to Parzival about the Grail:

> It is called *lapsit exillis*. By the power of that stone the phoenix burns to ashes, but the ashes give him life again. . . . There never was a human so ill but that, if he one day sees that stone, he cannot die within the week that follows. And in looks he will not fade. His appearance will stay the same, be it maid or man, as on the day he saw the stone. . . . Such power does the stone give a man that flesh and bones are at once made young again.[4]

When I read this passage it immediately struck me that what is being described here is alchemy. The phoenix that burns to ashes and is then reborn in full splendor is a common alchemical symbol for transmutation, and the stone that rejuvenates corresponds closely to the philosopher's stone of the alchemists. In alchemy we see the same notion of the sacred in matter that is present in the work of Hildegard of Bingen and that runs counter to the Christian tendency to privilege spirit over matter. Another heterodox aspect of alchemy was the way it dealt with sexuality and the role of women. In the alchemical treatises the erotic and the spiritual, separated in the Christian mind, come together. There are beautiful images of kings and queens in a sexual embrace and of female and male alchemists working side by side in the laboratory.

I am not the only one to have spotted the alchemical message in Wolfram's epic. Emma Jung and Marie-Louise von Franz, in their book *The Grail Legend*, write:

Wolfram connects the Grail with the psychologically important *realm of alchemical symbolism*. As Jung has pointed out, this latter formed something like an undercurrent to the Christianity which ruled the surface layers and it endeavored to fill in those lacunae which the tension of opposites in Christianity had left wide open.[5]

An undercurrent of heterodoxy was also present within the church. One who gave expression to it was Meister (Johann) Eckhart (1260–ca. 1328), a Dominican who rose to high office within the order. In his writings and sermons he taught a mystical philosophy that was in many ways at odds with official church doctrine. One of his most striking assertions was that the human soul is at one with God. "God," he wrote, "enters the soul in his entirety, not with only part of himself. . . . No one touches the depths of the soul but God alone."[6] And again, "How are we one with God? In that we are one being with him."[7]

This is reminiscent of the Vedanta tradition of India, which teaches that the soul is identical with Brahma, the supreme deity. Often he interprets scripture in surprising ways. For example, when the Bible says that God sent his only begotten son into the world, Eckhart takes that as referring not to the outer world but to the inner world of the human soul.[8] He also professes his own kind of pantheism, in which he sees both the world and God as being dissolved in a soul-like realm beyond time and space.[9]

No wonder Eckhart fell afoul of the Inquisition, for if God is entirely present in each human soul, what need do we have of priests, liturgies, and dogmas? Having been arraigned for heresy in Cologne, he brought his case before the pope in Avignon but died before a verdict was reached. After his death the pope issued a bull in which some twenty-six of Eckhart's statements were condemned as heretical.[10] Nevertheless, Eckhart's works went on to be read by an ever-widening audience, both Catholic and Protestant. On the Catholic side some attacked his works vehemently while others welcomed them as a fresh wind in the church. To this day he continues to have his admirers and opponents.

In the fifteenth century, the esoteric and mystical undercurrents to mainstream Christianity in Germany were joined by Hermetic and Kabbalistic influences from Renaissance Italy. The philosopher Pico della Mirandola (1463–1494) had pioneered a Christian application of the Jewish Kabbalah. His work in turn influenced the German Hebraist Johannes Reuchlin (1455–1522), author of a seminal text of Christian Kabbalah, *De arte cabalistica* (1517). Reuchlin was also influenced by Jewish exponents of the classical Hebrew Kabbalah. It was a dangerous time to be an admirer of Jewish traditions. In Spain the Jews had been expelled from the country in 1492, and in many European countries they were subjected to persecution, which was particularly intense in Germany. Reuchlin, conspicuous for his respectful attitude toward Jews, came under attack, especially from a fanatical Jewish convert to Christianity named Johannes Pfefferkorn, who advocated a campaign of forced conversion and the confiscation of Jewish holy books. Reuchlin fiercely opposed this policy. The Dominican inquisitor in Cologne, Jacob Hochstraten, joined in the fray and attempted to have Reuchlin condemned for heresy. The affair turned into a storm of controversy that spread through Germany and even involved the pope and the emperor.[11]

Reuchlin was beleaguered, but he had loyal friends, one of whom was the great artist Albrecht Dürer (1471–1528). Like Reuchlin, Dürer was a Christian Kabbalist and had studied Hebrew; he went into battle for Reuchlin with the weapons of his art. The artist and art historian Zhenya Gershman has made a searching study of Dürer's work and has shown how his famous engraving *Melencolia I* can only be understood in the light of Christian Kabbalah, the Reuchlin controversy, and the Renaissance humanism that both Reuchlin and Dürer embraced. The title was in fact given to the picture after Dürer's death because of the fact that the word *Melencolia* appears in the top left-hand corner, grasped in the claws of a strange, bat-like creature. Zhenya has shown that the word is in fact an anagram of "cameleon," with certain letters added, and that the creature depicted is indeed a chameleon, ripping

Fig. 5.1. *Melencolia I,* an engraving by Albrecht Dürer, dated 1514. The picture is packed with esoteric symbolism.

WIKIMEDIA COMMONS.

open its skin to reveal the anagram—hinting that the picture has an inner meaning that can only be revealed by following certain clues.

The rest of the picture is densely packed with symbols, most of which have to do with Jewish mystical and prophetic themes and Christian Kabbalistic notions. As Zhenya has convincingly argued, the main figure in the foreground is not a woman symbolizing melancholy, as many art experts have thought, but rather the angel Metatron, divine messenger, keeper of secrets (symbolized by a set of keys on his belt), measurer of time (symbolized by an hourglass), weigher of human deeds (symbolized by scales), and herald of a new dispensation in which it will be shown that the Jewish and Christian holy scriptures point to one truth (the angel's wing pointing to the figure one on a magic square carved in stone).[12] Thus Dürer emerges not just as one of the greatest artists of all time but also as a profound esoteric thinker and a champion of interreligious understanding.

In the age of Dürer one is again struck by the juxtaposition of light and darkness. While Dürer was a teenager there appeared one of the most evil books ever written, the *Malleus Maleficarum,* meaning "Hammer of the Malefactors" (i.e., witches), by two Dominicans, Heinrich Krämer und Jacob Sprenger (although the extent of the latter's involvement is uncertain). First published at Speyer in 1486 in Latin, it subsequently went through numerous editions and appeared in many languages including German. The book was a witch hunter's manual and included detailed instructions for the extraction of confessions through torture. It helped to foment a wave of persecution of so-called witches in which countless innocent people, mainly women, were burned at the stake and which lasted for more than two and half centuries.

One who bravely stood up against the witch persecution was Heinrich Cornelius Agrippa (1486–1535), a remarkable man of many facets—physician, legal expert, soldier, theologian, and occultist. Agrippa led a commensurately roving life, studying in Cologne and Paris, soldiering in Spain and Italy, lecturing at various universities, at times working as a court physician and at other times as a legal adviser.

It was in his legal capacity as adviser to the magistrate of Metz that he became involved in a famous case of alleged witchcraft in 1519. A woman had been accused by the Inquisition on the grounds that she had inherited a pact with the devil made by her mother. Agrippa, entrusted with the defense, cleverly argued that the sacrament of baptism was stronger than any pact with the devil. His argument convinced the court, and the woman was acquitted, much to the fury of the Dominican inquisitors, who made life so uncomfortable for Agrippa that he was forced to leave the city.[13]

It is astonishing that, in addition to all his travels and various assignments, Agrippa was able to produce an impressive volume of writing. His books include a defense of Reuchlin's work on the Hebrew scriptures and a treatise titled *On the Nobility and Preeminence of the Female Sex* (1529). The latter was most unusual in an age of widespread misogyny. Drawing on Kabbalistic and other esoteric sources, Agrippa argued that women were the superior sex, being the mediators between the human and the divine realms.[14] Chiefly Agrippa is known for his three-volume work *De Occulta Philosophia* (Of Occult Philosophy), published in 1533. The first volume deals with the elemental world—that is, phenomena categorized according to the four classical elements of fire, earth, air, and water—and with scientific and technological matters. The second is concerned with what Agrippa calls celestial magic, which covers areas such as astrology, numerology, and music. The third is about ceremonial magic, using a system of practical Kabbalah. *De Occulta Philosophia* for centuries remained the classic reference work on Western magic and is still widely read today.

Roughly contemporary with Agrippa was another magus whose legend soon vastly outgrew the person behind it—namely, Johann Faust, immortalized in the plays by Johann Wolfgang von Goethe and Christopher Marlowe in an opera by Charles Gounod and in the adjective *Faustian,* which has passed into the English language. A Faustian bargain is one in which a person sacrifices their soul or moral integrity in return for the granting of a wish, as Faust is said to have done in making a pact with the devil. The real Faust is a somewhat shadowy figure, and the legend possibly conflates more than one person of that name, but the original is thought to have been one Johann Georg Faust, born at Knittlingen in Württemberg circa 1480. Little is known about his childhood and education, but by the early sixteenth century, styling himself Doctor Faust, he had become a familiar figure in the marketplaces of Germany, a combination of sorcerer, spirit conjurer, astrologer, and the equivalent of the American snake oil merchant, selling miracle cures for all ailments. After his death, circa 1541, his legend grew to immense proportions, resulting in sensationalized accounts of his life and a number of spurious Faustian books of magic. One Faustian work that appears to be genuine is *Magia naturalis et innaturalis* (Natural and Unnatural Magic), of which there are several printed editions, based on a manuscript dated 1505. It includes a hierarchy of demons corresponding to the hierarchy of the Holy Roman Empire, from the emperor himself, in descending order through kings, princes, electors, counts, and so on down to the peasants. Evidently even in hell everyone knows their place.[15]

It is striking how many remarkable minds were produced by this period straddling the fifteenth and sixteenth centuries—polymaths like Reuchlin, Dürer, Agrippa, and another figure of the time who stands out as a universal genius—namely, Theophrastus Bombastus von Hohenheim (better known under the name of Paracelsus (1493–1541)), alchemist, astrologer, theologian, scientist, and physician. He was born at Einsiedeln in Switzerland, the son of a physician, and followed his father's profession. Like Agrippa, he led a wandering life that included a short period as town physician and university lecturer in Basel, where he caused astonishment by lecturing in German as well as in Latin and ruffled feathers in the faculty and the town council by questioning the ancient medical authorities such as Galen. After further wanderings through various parts of the German Empire, he died at Salzburg in 1541, leaving behind a massive body of writing ranging over medicine, alchemy, astronomy, theology, and magic. His approach to medicine is what we would now call holistic and rested on four "pillars"—namely,

Fig. 5.2. The great alchemist and physician Theophrastus Bombastus von Hohenheim, known as Paracelsus.

philosophy, astronomy,* alchemy, and morality. As mentioned earlier, one of his innovations in the field of alchemy was his theory of a "primal trio" in the material realm, three principles that he termed salt,

---

*Astronomy at that time would have included what we now call astrology.

sulphur, and mercury (see page 18). Salt was the principle of solidity, sulphur of combustibility, and mercury of volatility. In Paracelsus's view these principles did not replace the traditional four elements of earth, water, air, and fire. Rather, the elements were building blocks that were subject to the active influence of the three principles. This theory had a strong influence on the development of chemistry and is still applied by modern alchemists and practitioners of Paracelsian medicine—a theme to which I shall return later. In the field of theology Paracelsus put forward the notion of their being two "lights," the light of nature and the light of religion.[16] This and other aspects of his thought were to have a profound influence in the following century on the Rosicrucian movement, to which we shall turn in the next chapter.

6

ROSICRUCIANS, FREEMASONS, AND ALCHEMISTS

In 1614 a curious figure arrived in the town of Kassel in Hessen and made his way to the premises of the court printer, Wilhelm Wessel, bearing a mysterious manuscript. The visitor was Benedictus Figulus, an itinerant pastor and alchemist with a reputation for promiscuity. The manuscript he was carrying was the *Fama Fraternitatis des löblichen Ordens des Rosenkreuzes* (Fame or Proclamation of the Praiseworthy Order of the Rosy Cross), which came to be known as the first Rosicrucian manifesto. This work, written in German by an unnamed author, had been circulating in manuscript form since about 1610 and had already stirred up a good deal of controversy. It told a story about a man called Christian Rosenkreuz, a German born of noble parentage who had entered a religious order and then embarked on a journey to the Middle East, where he gathered knowledge and wisdom from the sages of that region. Returning to Germany, he gathered a group of like-minded followers and formed a fraternity, the Brotherhood of the Rosy Cross. The house they built for themselves was called the House of the Holy Spirit. Apparently Christian Rosenkreuz died at the age of 106 and was buried in a vault, which remained hidden for 120 years, until it was discovered by one of the brethren while carrying out repairs to the House of the Holy Spirit. Here, in a chamber lit by an artificial sun, they found the perfectly preserved body of Christian Rosenkreuz.

Wessell successfully applied to Landgrave Moritz, ("the Learned," as he was known) to publish the manuscript, which duly appeared in print in 1614. It was followed in 1615 by a second manifesto, this time in Latin, the *Confessio Fraternitatis* (Confession of the Fraternity), and in 1616 appeared the third and final manifesto, the *Chymische Hochzeit Christiani Rosenkreutz* (*Chymical Wedding of Christian Rosenkreuz*), which, in fact, was not so much a manifesto as an allegorical tale full of alchemical and other symbolism. The key figure in this movement and the main author of the first manifesto was the Protestant theologian Johann Valentin Andreae, who was at the center of a circle in Tübingen composed of like-minded scholars, physicians, and theologians.

It remains something of a mystery what precisely the strategy was behind these writings, but the essential vision they conveyed was of a great spiritual renewal in Europe based on a holistic worldview, bringing together religion with all branches of learning to create what the *Fama* called "a perfect development of all the arts"[1] and at the same time healing the great religious divide caused by the Protestant Reformation a century earlier.

This vision was strongly influenced by the teachings of the great alchemist and physician Paracelsus, who had a holistic view of medicine in which the human being is a microcosm of the universe, and spirit and matter are intertwined. In this respect he was following the well-established alchemical tradition that in the depths of matter there are divine forces present that can bring about true healing. This can be contrasted with the stereotypical image of the alchemist striving to make lead into gold, which is explicitly condemned in the *Fama* as irrelevant to the true philosophy (i.e., alchemy). Just as Paracelsus spoke of there being two lights, of nature and of religion, so the *Fama* speaks of God's name "written in the book of life."[2]

The *Fama* ended with an appeal to all learned people in Europe to come forward and contact the Brotherhood, but unfortunately no mailing address was given. Nevertheless, many people tried to contact them. Some people wrote open letters, some wrote books defending or attacking the Brotherhood, and some claimed to be members of it. Among the people who have been linked with the early Rosicrucian movement was the elector Frederick V of the Palatinate, as mentioned in chapter 1, and for a time his court at Heidelberg was a place marked by the Rosicrucian spirit.

Then in 1618 came the outbreak of the Thirty Years' War between the Catholic and Protestant states, and everything collapsed into chaos, the elector Frederick had to flee, and the whole Rosicrucian vision appeared to have gone up in smoke—but not quite . . . because the Rosicrucian spirit lived on in less conspicuous ways. One of the people who kept it alive was Princess Antonia of Württemberg, daughter of the Duke of Württemberg—a profoundly spiritual and highly educated woman who had been in close contact with Johann Valentin Andreae and was deeply interested in the Kabbalistic tradition in its Christian application. She left behind a remarkable treasure in the form of an altarpiece in the church at Bad Teinach near Stuttgart. It is known as the *Lehrtafel* (instruction tableau) of Princess Antonia, dating from the 1660s (see page 80).

The side panels show various biblical scenes, but the main feature is the central panel, which shows a woman, symbolizing the soul, entering a labyrinthine garden surrounded by a hedge of roses, in the center of which is the figure of Christ. In the background is a temple with various female figures representing the sephiroth of the Kabbalistic Tree of Life. Christ is shown in the position of the tenth sephira, Malkuth, the Kingdom.

Apart from such exceptions as Princess Antonia's altarpiece, the Rosicrucian current went more or less underground in Germany for most of the seventeenth century, although it spread to other countries,

Fig. 6.1. The Kabbalistic Instruction Tableau of Princess Antonia, dating from the 1660s, in the Church of the Trinity at Bad Teinach in the Black Forest. (See also color plate 2.)

including Britain, where it found strong apologists such as the physician and alchemist Robert Fludd (1574–1637). In Germany it revived in
the eighteenth century with the emergence of a new Rosicrucian order,
called the Golden and Rosy Cross. This order was part of high-degree
Freemasonry. To be admitted one had to have passed through a regular
Masonic lodge. And from then on, we find various Masonic systems of
one kind or another invoking the Rosicrucian symbolism.

The Golden and Rosy Cross order was grouped into circles of
nine members each and had nine grades of initiation, each involving
elaborate initiation rituals. This grade structure, slightly modified, was
adopted by the English occult order, the Golden Dawn, and later by
other Rosicrucian orders. The initiation ceremony for each grade was
accompanied by a symbolic tableau. For example, the tableau used at
the initiation of members into the fifth grade, that of Minor, showed a
form of the Kabbalistic Tree of Life with the Sefiroth arranged in two
pentagonal figures. At the top was the eye of God in a triangle, and in
the center of the tableau, a sort of Adam Kadmon figure. The crosses
on his clothing and in the sphere underneath emphasized the basically
Christian nature of the order.

Members of the order had to go through a study curriculum covering Christian theosophy, mysticism, Kabbalah, and alchemy. In particular, alchemy played a major part in the order's activities. Alchemical
symbolism featured in the initiation ceremonies, and members were
supposed to have their own laboratories and work diligently at their
furnaces, retorts, and crucibles. There survive today many alchemical
manuscripts that circulated among the fraternity, and, as one progressed
up through the order, one received more and more alchemical secrets.

If you look at the alchemical books and manuscripts that circulated among the brethren, you will see that they are very much practical recipe books containing very detailed and precise instructions about
alchemical processes, often with drawings of alchemical equipment. So
we are not here in the realm of those who would see alchemy merely as
a set of symbols for a spiritual process. This was very much physical,

nitty-gritty work in the laboratory but combined with a spiritual process in which the work of refining substances went hand in hand with a process of inner refinement.

This approach to alchemy was closely bound with a gnostic worldview. Gnosticism is the belief that the material world was not created by God but by a mischievous creator called the demiurge, whose aim is to keep human beings trapped in dense matter. At the same time, gnosticism teaches that a heavenly spark exists in us and in nature, and, through the correct knowledge or gnosis, we can reconnect with the true divine world above. In the Golden and Rosy Cross this comes out very clearly in the stated aim of the order, which was "to make effective the hidden forces of nature, to release nature's light which has been deeply buried beneath the dross resulting from the curse, and thereby to light within every brother a torch by whose light he will be able better to recognize the hidden God."[3] This may sound dualistic, but in fact what it is saying is that spirit is present in the depths of matter if you know how to find it. And here we encounter again that notion of the interpenetration of spirit and matter that we have already seen in Hildegard of Bingen, Meister Eckhart, and Paracelsus, a notion that we can follow like a vein of gold through the centuries up to the present day and that accounts for the fact that alchemy has survived in Germany to this day and has enabled a revival to take place in many other countries.

If you had traveled to one of the numerous German kingdoms, dukedoms, or earldoms at any time up to about the early nineteenth century and called at the residence of the local ruler you would not have been surprised to find a cellar or outbuilding containing a well-equipped alchemical laboratory. A famous example of a royal alchemist was Frederick William II (1744–1797), who became king of Prussia in 1786 upon the death of his uncle Frederick the Great. He already, as crown prince, had been initiated into the Golden and Rosy Cross through the influence of his military aide de camp Johann von Bischoffswerder, and he appears to have been a keen member. When he came to the throne, he built a palace at Potsdam and laid out a park with many Rosicrucian features and a special building for his laboratory. A striking feature of the park is an icehouse in the form of a pyramid, a common motif in Masonic and Rosicrucian symbology (see the next chapter).

A contemporary of King Frederick William and a fellow Rosicrucian was Prince Karl von Hessen-Kassel (1744–1836), one of the most fascinating and influential figures at the time in the world of Freemasonry, Rosicrucianism, and Hermetic studies. He belonged to innumerable orders and rites and was a practicing alchemist. His house at Louisenlund in Schleswig-Holstein contained a room for Masonic meetings, and in the park was an alchemist's tower with a laboratory and another Masonic lodge room. We shall return to the design of the park in the next chapter.

In 1778 a mysterious and legendary character of great personal charisma arrived at Louisenlund and presented himself to Prince Karl as a French aristocrat and alchemical adept with the title Count of Saint-Germain. Most likely he was not a real count, and the Hungarian American Hebrew scholar Raphael Patai makes a convincing case that he was Jewish. Patai cites the Austrian statesman Count Philipp Cobenzl, a close friend of Saint-Germain, as saying:

> In brief, he is a man of universal culture, as is but rarely found in one person; he speaks all the languages, Hindustani as Italian, Yiddish as French.

Patai goes on to say:

> In the eighteenth century only a Jew would know Yiddish. . . . Although Hebrew was by that time studied by some gentile scholars . . . a knowledge of Yiddish seems to be prima facie evidence of a Jewish background.[4]

Many rumors to this effect were circulating at the time, but they did not prevent Saint-Germain from pursuing a remarkable and many-faceted career. Apart from being an alchemist, he was a physician, composer, painter, diplomat, and much more.

After many travels over the length and breadth of Europe, involving some shadowy diplomatic missions, he came to Louisenlund and offered his services to Prince Karl. The prince, initially cautious, was won over by Saint-Germain, and they were soon conducting alchemical experiments together in the alchemist's tower. They worked on a number of projects, including developing various remedies and a metal alloy, similar to gold in appearance, that came to be called the Karl metal. In addition, in the nearby town of Eckernförde, Prince Karl set up a factory for the count, where he worked on techniques for dyeing silk. Prince Karl came to have great admiration for his guest, who remained at Louisenlund for the last four and half years of his life.

By the early nineteenth century, alchemy had become marginalized in favor of what we now call modern chemistry. But in the German-speaking lands the alchemical worldview never died out. There it remained an important side current that continued to exert an influence in various ways. An example can be seen in the homeopathic medicine developed by Samuel Hahnemann (1755–1843). One of the basic principles of homeopathy is that "like cures like," as opposed to the traditional allopathic approach in which the remedy opposes the symptoms of the ailment. This principle was not an invention of Hahnemann but had already been formulated by Paracelsus, who wrote, "Never a hot illness has been cured by something cold, nor a cold one by something hot. But it has happened that like has cured like."[5]

The other distinguishing feature of homeopathy is the practice of diluting remedies—the higher the dilution, the stronger the remedy. This may appear paradoxical, but it becomes comprehensible if one takes the view that, say, a plant is the dense physical manifestation of the plant's matrix on a higher and more subtle plane of existence. As one increases the dilution of a plant extract, one goes higher up toward the primal formative forces, which act upon the lower ones. The homeopathic approach, in an adapted and expanded form, later became the basis of the Anthroposophical medicine developed by Rudolf Steiner and still produced today under the Weleda trade name, among others.

A near contemporary of Hahnemann was the poet and universal genius Johann Wolfgang von Goethe (1749–1832), whose worldview in many ways partook of the esoteric stream that we have been following. At the age of nineteen, Goethe became seriously ill with a swelling on his neck and was confined to bed for several months. One of the doctors who treated him was Dr. Johann Friedrich Metz, a man touched by an aura of mystery and who was a member of the Pietist movement of radical Protestantism as well as an alchemist and Rosicrucian. Metz produced a vial containing a crystalline salt with an alkaline taste, which reduced the tumor and set Goethe on the road to recovery. The grateful patient set about reading some books that the doctor had recommended and was soon immersed in the esoteric realm of alchemy, Kabbalah, and Hermetism as well as in investigations of the nature of life and the properties of the natural world. Encouraged by his mystically minded friend Susanna von Klettenberg and with the help of Dr. Metz, Goethe set up a small laboratory where he carried out experiments in alchemy.[6]

Goethe's interest in matters esoteric passed through various phases but remained with him throughout his life. Its influence can be seen in much of his work, including his great drama *Faust,* and it profoundly informed his studies of nature and comes across in his work on botany. Dissatisfied with the classifying approach of the Swedish botanist Linnaeus, Goethe set out to answer the question: What is the ultimate essence that all plants have in common and that makes them what they are? He looked for the answer using not only the eye of the scientist but also the vision of the artist and poet, and he came to the conclusion that all the thousands of plant species are variations of a single template that he called the "primal plant" (*Urpflanze*). This primal plant, he believed, exists in some realm of ideal forms and is invisible except when it takes on the characteristics of the various species—size, color, shape, and so on. While he spoke about this primarily in relation to botany, he believed that the same principle applied to all organisms in nature.[7]

Goethe was for most of his life a Freemason, as was his near contemporary Wolfgang Amadeus Mozart. While Goethe's *Faust* is his most occult work, the most esoteric of Mozart's operas is *The Magic Flute* (*Die Zauberflöte*) with a libretto by his friend and fellow Mason Immanuel Schikaneder. This opera has been much misunderstood. While the sublime music speaks for itself, the profound symbolic content of the story has often been ignored or dismissed as a kind of pantomime. For example, in Peter Schaffer's famous play *Amadeus* the work is presented as spectacle for popular entertainment, and there is no hint that it is in fact something much deeper—namely, a story about initiation, self-perfection, and the reconciliation of opposites, drawing on the symbolism of Freemasonry and alchemy. As the French musicologist Jacques Chailley has written, "Far from being that 'fable pieced together like Harelquin's cloak' which, with complaisant scorn, it is still accused of being, the action of *Die Zauberflöte* is a remarkably constructed symbolic story rigorously developed."[8]

The story of *The Magic Flute* features two couples: a young prince, Tamino, and the woman he loves, Pamina; and the birdcatcher Papageno and the object of his love, Papagena. Their struggle to be united is played out against a background of struggle between two forces represented by the solar figure Sarastro, high priest of the Temple of Wisdom, and the lunar figure of the Queen of the Night, mother of Pamina. So here we have again the polarity of Sol and Luna that is so central to alchemy. Both couples are subjected to a series of initiatory tests for admission to the Temple of Wisdom. Tamino and Pamina are proved worthy, while Papageno and Papagena fail and must be content with a less exalted destiny. These tests involve passing through the four elements, as in the higher-degree Masonic rites with which Mozart and Schikaneder would have been familiar. Furthermore, the magic flute itself, whose tones are heard at critical moments, combines all four elements. It was made of wood (earth) on a night of rain and lightning (water and fire) and is brought to life by the breath of the flautist (air). There is a masterly interplay of story and music, with changes of key, tempo, and instruments to mark different characters and themes. Altogether *The Magic Flute* stands out as one of the most glorious creations to be born out of the combination of superb music and deep symbolic meaning. Goethe was so enthused by *The Magic Flute* that in 1795 he began writing a sequel to the story, but this was never finished except for a fragment that appeared under the title *Fairy Tale*.

To read Goethe's works and to come into contact with his colossal mind has been a transformative experience for many people. One of them was Rudolf Steiner (1861–1925), founder of the Anthroposophical movement, which he started after breaking with the Theosophical Society, whose German branch he had belonged to for some years. In his introduction to *The Metamorphosis of Plants,* Steiner explains his intense admiration for Goethe: "With him it is not a question of discovering new facts, but rather of opening up a new point of view, a certain way of looking at nature." The scientist who merely observes and collects facts fails to perceive the essential being or animating soul of the organism he is studying; in other words, he cannot see the forest for the trees.[9] So great was Steiner's regard for Goethe that when he built a headquarters for the Anthroposophical Society at Dornach in Switzerland he called it the Goetheanum.

In 1910, Steiner met a young poet and man of letters named Alexander von Bernus, who had inherited the former Benedictine abbey of Neuburg, near Heidelberg. Bernus, a man in search of spiritual orientation, was greatly inspired by Steiner and in 1911 entered the Theosophical Society, about a year before Steiner left it to found the Anthroposophical Society. Around this time Bernus began to study alchemy, which was to be his main vocation for the rest of his life. In 1921 he founded the Soluna Laboratory at Neuburg to develop alchemical remedies. After selling Neuburg Abbey to its original owners, the Benedictine order, in 1926 he moved the laboratory to Stuttgart, where it was destroyed by bombing in 1943. Bernus then carried on the work at his mansion, Schloss Donaumünster at Donauwörth in Bavaria.

Fig. 6.2. Distillation work in progress at the Soluna Laboratories at Donauwörth, Bavaria. (See also color plate 3.)
PHOTOGRAPH COURTESY OF SOLUNA.

Following the death of Bernus in 1965, Soluna was continued by his widow, Isa, but in 1988 was taken over by the Italian Marino Lazzeroni, who revitalized the firm and created a subsidiary at Averara in northern Italy. Soluna continues to operate after some changes of management and the building of a new laboratory at Donauwörth in 2014. At the time of this writing, the firm is run by Karin Proeller and Christoph Proeller.

At Soluna the work of preparing medicines begins with the cultivation of their constituent plants. Water from a mountain spring flows into a fountain via a spiral tube with seven rings made from seven different metals corresponding to the seven planets. The water, thus energized, then flows into the plantations where the medicinal plants are grown. Each plant is harvested at the time of day when its vital force is at its highest. For example, camilla is picked between 6:00 and 10:00 a.m. and calendula around midday. The harvesting is done by hand so that the vital energy is not conducted away by metal. The plants are then laid out on silk and dried. Later they are left to mature in an octagonal pavilion at a temperature of 37 degrees Centigrade, the body temperature of a healthy person. At certain times their position is changed in accordance with the rising and setting of the sun and moon so that they harmonize with the solar and lunar forces. Metals and minerals used for medicaments are also treated in this way.

The final stage is the spagyric process (the word *spagyric* meaning "separating and putting together"). This is according to the system of the sixteenth-century alchemist Paracelsus, who conceived of three fundamental principles in matter, which he called salt, sulphur, and mercury. Salt is the body of a substance, sulphur is its soul or individual properties, and mercury is its spirit or vitalizing principle. If you are working with plants, for example, you macerate (chop up and ferment) the substance of the plant (the salt, or body), distilling it to make an extract that contains both alcohol (the sulphur, or soul) and etheric oil (the mercury, or spirit), then burn the remains of the plant to a powder and combine the powder with the extract to make the finished medicine.[10]

Another firm manufacturing spagyric products is Phylak, founded in 1996 and operating from a state-of-the-art laboratory at Spreetal in Saxony. Phylak has its own way of making spagyric preparations, based on the methods developed by Carl-Friedrich Zimpel (1801–1879), a remarkable man whose biography reads like the most extravagant adventure novel. Born in Lower Silesia, now part of Poland, he lost his parents to tuberculosis while still a teenager and joined a Prussian infantry regiment, where he served as an officer for ten years until he was dismissed as a result of a scandal over an attempted elopement. He then emigrated to the United States, acquired American citizenship, qualified as an architect and engineer, and worked on important railway and construction projects, much of the time having to endure the alligator-infested swamps of Louisiana. To this day there is a street in New Orleans named after him.

He returned to Europe in 1837 and continued to work as a railway engineer on important intercity routes in Germany and Hungary before turning his attention to medicine. Being himself prone to illness, he experimented with various treatments and became convinced of the value of homeopathy. While training as a homeopathic practitioner he found time to study at the University of Jena, where he was awarded a doctorate in philosophy and a somewhat pro forma doctorate in medicine on the basis of a short treatise about his experiences with yellow fever.

Then began a decade of wandering that took him to London,

Fig. 6.3. Equipment at the Phylak Laboratory, Spreetal, Saxony: vials containing plant substances that have been dried (left) and calcinated (right). The calx will be united with the extract made in the copper distilling apparatus.

Photograph by courtesy of Phylak.

Italy, and Palestine, among other places. By this time, he had become a devotee of the Swedish visionary and scientist Emanuel Swedenborg (1688–1772). He took to writing endless esoteric exegeses of the Bible and looked forward to a new millennium and the return of the Messiah. At the same time, he continued to pursue his medical interests and practice. In Italy he met the colorful politician, writer, and healer Count Cesare Mattei, one of the people credited with having rediscovered alchemical medicine in the nineteenth century. Mattei introduced Zimpel to the spagyric art, and the latter was immediately enthused. This was apparently the system he had long been looking for—one that surpassed any other treatments. Because Mattei was not willing to reveal the full secrets of his preparations, Zimpel set about creating his own series of spagyric medicines. These are what became known as Dr. Zimpel's remedies. Zimpel handed over their production to the apothecary Friedrich Mauch in Göppingen, and thence they passed into wider use.[11]

Thus the alchemical tradition branched out into many different streams. One of them fed into Anthroposophical medicine, developed by Rudolf Steiner together with the physician Ita Wegman, drawing partly on Paracelsian alchemy but largely based on Steiner's own conception of human beings and their connection with the cosmos. They also founded the firm of Weleda, which continues to produce medicaments according to Anthroposophical principles. In Anthroposophical medicine the patient is treated as an entity with three levels: body, soul, and spirit. The physical body is divided into three regions corresponding to three basic functions: the head (control center and focus of the nervous system), the limbs (motor system), and the middle region, which has a rhythmic function (breathing, heartbeat, digestion). At the same time there are cosmic formative forces that act on these different levels, and the Anthroposophical approach to treatment involves taking all of these factors into account.

I was given a good insight into Anthroposophical medicine by Elisabeth Pahnke, a practitioner in Bremen. She told me that Steiner arrived at his insights through clairvoyance, a faculty that he believed was in former times possessed by all human beings as a divine gift and is still often present in children. Today, because of the plunge of modern society into materialism, we have largely lost this gift and can only reattain it by a conscious effort of will. An interesting fact pointed out by Elisabeth Pahnke is that southern Germany, Austria, and Switzerland are far more open to alternative healing methods than northern Germany.

The same holistic approach to science, evinced by Steiner, Hahnemann, Goethe, and Bernus, is also found in the work of Rudolf Hauschka (1891–1969), an Austrian-born chemist who became a follower of Steiner. Alongside Steiner's Weleda, Hauschka founded the WALA enterprise, which produces medicaments and cosmetic products. When I read his book *The Nature of Substance* (*Die Substanzlehere*, 1950) it transformed my view of chemistry and opened up amazing vistas. Essentially Hauschka argues that what we see as chemical elements and reactions are only the material manifestation of cosmic laws and processes, which we can come to understand if we look at the world with our souls and feelings and not just with our analytical faculties. So when we speak, say, of carbon, we should really be speaking of a carbon principle, a kind of ray that becomes progressively more material and solid as it descends from the immaterial macrocosm.

These principles are constantly inter-reacting in a dynamic way according to great cosmic rhythms. For example, Hauschka points out that carbon, hydrogen, and oxygen are basic to all organic matter. Carbon is the principle of form, hydrogen of force, and oxygen of life. He writes:

> Life oscillates between form and fire, rigidity and dissolution. When life moves to the etherealizing pole, then water, the "solvent of life" (H_2O), is its expression. When it becomes tied at the opposite pole to carbon, "earth substance," the carbonic acid (CO_2) thereby produced may be termed "paralysed life."

He adds that "it would be appropriate to call carbo-hydrates 'formed and fire-quickened cosmic life.'"[12]

To illustrate the rhythmic relation between life and the cosmos, Hauschka writes about the composition of air, which consists of approximately 78 percent nitrogen, 20 percent oxygen, and 2 percent carbon-dioxide. The balance of nitrogen to oxygen determines how quickly or slowly we breathe. The number of breaths that we take on average in a day is 25,920, which is the number of years that the vernal equinox (or any other point in the solar year) takes to move through the entire zodiac.[13] By such observations, Hauschka illustrates the interaction between macrocosm and microcosm. Hauschka, being a trained chemist, was able to back up his insights with solid chemical evidence.

Another German who helped to keep the alchemical worldview alive was Albert Riedel (1911–1984), who wrote under the pseudonym Frater Albertus. Born in Dresden, Riedel emigrated to the United States in the early 1930s and joined the Ancient and Mystical Order Rosae Crucis (AMORC), founded by H. Spencer Lewis and based in San Jose, California. Riedel, having attended a series of seminars on alchemy at AMORC, went on to play a key role in promoting alchemy in the United States. In 1960 he published a manual titled *The Alchemist's Handbook,* and in the same year he founded the Paracelsus Research Society in Salt Lake City, which had an immense influence through its courses on alchemy until Riedel's death in 1984.

With Riedel's entry into AMORC and his creation of the Paracelsus Research Society, it seems that some kind of cycle was completed that had begun long ago in Germany. A young German seeker arrives in balmy California, joins an American version of a German tradition—namely, Rosicrucianism—and founds a society named after another German, Paracelsus. Thus did occult Germany leave a significant stamp on American culture.

SYMBOL-STREWN SPACES

Gardens have often been imagined by poets as settings for courtly love, or by mystics as offering a memory of a lost paradise or a foretaste of a future one, or by alchemists as places of alchemical transmutation. Literature and art are full of such imaginary gardens. But what about real gardens as places of inner transmutation or initiation? The notion of a garden with an initiatic or esoteric message is one that many people find hard to understand. The plot behind the suburban house, with a patch of lawn, herbaceous borders, a place for barbecues, and perhaps a swing and a sandpit for the children hardly conjures up the idea of initiation. But some of the most beautiful gardens in Europe were created precisely with this idea in mind, and Germany is particularly rich in gardens of this kind. Why? Perhaps because the German combination of nature mysticism, alchemy, and esoteric thought was particularly conducive to the creation of such "symbol-strewn spaces or landscapes," as I call them.

I have already mentioned the garden at Heidelberg, designed for the Elector Frederick V of the Palatinate by the French garden architect Salomon de Caus, a Renaissance man who was also a composer, an engineer, and a philosopher—in a word, a polymath. In the garden he strove to express the holistic Rosicrucian vision of a world pervaded by divine harmonies and structured according to heavenly mathematical ratios and proportions. For example, eight, the number of the musical octave and signifying completion, is repeated in many of the features, such as an eight-sided fountain basin and eight parterres. De Caus's intention was that visitors to the garden would come away uplifted and awe inspired by a vision of an earthly Eden.

By the mid-eighteenth century, many landowners and garden builders were Freemasons, and the influence of Freemasonry can be seen in a number of gardens of the period. The symbolic journey of initiation is a feature often found in such gardens. Another theme in Freemasonry is the idea of architecture and building as a metaphor for the inner work of moral and spiritual development undertaken by the Freemason. This goes together with the idea of a search for the lost ancient wisdom that was reflected in the architecture of classical antiquity, of ancient Egypt, and of the vanished Temple of Solomon. The imaginary landscapes of Masonic art, with their classical temples, pyramids, obelisks, sphinxes, broken columns, and so on, possibly served as the models for a number of Masonic gardens, although one did not necessarily have to be a Mason to want to place a pyramid or a classical temple in one's garden or to create a symbol-filled itinerary that conveys a message of a philosophical, moral, or esoteric nature.

One of the most striking of such itineraries is found in the Wilhelmshöhe Park in Kassel, essentially mainly created by two of the rulers of Hessen-Kassel, Landgrave Karl (reigned 1677–1730) and his grandson Landgrave Frederick II (reigned 1760–1785). During the reign of the former, a prestigious technical college, the Collegium Carolinum, was founded in Kassel. It was also Karl who essentially shaped the basic design of what is the largest hillside park in Europe, laid out along a seemingly endless axis that extends arrow-straight from the heart of the town into the park and up a long water cascade to the summit of the hill, on which stands a somewhat forbidding fortresslike building surmounted by a steep pyramid topped with a gigantic copper statue of Hercules, symbolizing strength, courage, and virtue. On the facade of the pyramid,

Fig. 7.1. Statue of Hercules in the park of Wilhelmshöhe, Kassel.
PHOTOGRAPH BY THE AUTHOR.

just below the statue, are two angels blowing trumpets and representing fame or glory. Originally there were additional statues on the pyramid, incorporating various qualities and virtues including victory, knowledge, freedom, prudence, justice, faith, and concord. The whole structure is therefore a kind of symbolic sermon, acting as a reminder of the ideals and virtues that the ruler should strive to embody.

Some of the landgraves, like many German princes, practiced alchemy, and one of them, Moritz "the Learned," had a purpose-built laboratory erected on the estate. Landgrave Frederick II was also an alchemist and had Moritz's laboratory restored. Furthermore, it seems likely that he was a Freemason in view of the fact that all the leading faculty of the Collegium Carolinum were Masons, including the naturalist Johann Georg Forster, who was also a member of the Golden and Rosy Cross. Landgrave Frederick added to the park many features with mythological and symbolic associations. One of them is a pyramid, a familiar motif in Masonic iconography. Others include a Temple to Mercury, a Tomb of Virgil (based on the supposed original in Naples), a Grotto of the Sybils, and a Hermitage of Socrates.[1] Thus, as you go through the park you commune with the spirit of classical antiquity and receive inspiration.

Another of my favorite symbol-strewn landscapes is the park at Wörlitz in Sachsen-Anhalt, built in the latter part of the eighteenth century by Prince Friedrich Franz von Anhalt-Dessau around a watery area formed by a salient of the river Elbe so that as you go through the park you are never far from water. The prince had spent a great deal of time in England and may very well have been initiated there as a Mason, although we do not know for sure. But certainly the whole park is unmistakably initiatic in a way similar to the Kassel park. A key role in planning it was played by the prince's privy counsellor August von Rode, who had a profound knowledge of classical literature and mythology and employed it to great effect in the design and scenic features of the estate. He wrote a remarkable and delightful description of the house and park, which visitors can still use as a guidebook.

In one part of the park you are led through a labyrinth of rocky passages, past inscriptions in stone that warn the visitor "Choose your way with reason" or "Here the choice becomes difficult but decisive." Going deeper into the park, the initiatic theme becomes more dramatic. You cross a rather precarious chain bridge over a chasm, and on the other side you come to a small open space surrounded by rocky walls intended for a few moments of meditation. From there a tunnel leads to a sort of rocky alcove, which Rode calls the "Cell of the Initiator into Sacred Mysteries." Here you have a choice between two paths. The one to the right, Rode says, "is comparable to the thoughtless, wearisome path of the person without knowledge or culture. On rough-hewn, intermittent steps he clambers up the slope between gloomy trees, now hither, now thither, zig-zagging, but without any joyful variety nor pleasant view." By contrast, the left-hand way

is the path of the mystic, the apprentice in pursuit of lofty wisdom. . . . He soon strays into a cave, now quite dark, now sparsely lit from above, now more brightly lit from a high opening at one side. By virtue of this wandering one has the sense of understanding the language of the mysteries, of crossing Proserpina's threshold and of standing on the border between life and death.[2]

One of the most striking buildings in the park is the Temple of Venus, which is built on a small hill over two grottoes, one dedicated to earth and fire, the other to water and air. You enter the grottoes through an entrance at the base of the hill, then you progress symbolically through the elements. In the second grotto you find yourself standing directly beneath the Temple of Venus, and you can look up into the round, hollow pedestal on which a statue of the goddess stands. The pedestal resembles a lantern with panes of yellow glass, and "a soft light falls into the grotto, like sunshine during an eclipse."[3] This is a strikingly alchemical image, evoking the notion of a divine spark lying deep in the earth in the form of gold. You exit from the grotto of water

Fig. 7.2. The park at Wörlitz in Saxony-Anhalt, showing the
area known as the Labyrinth. (See also color plate 4.)

PHOTOGRAPH BY THE AUTHOR.

and air through an opening close to the Venus Temple to behold the expanse of the river Elbe—for the water element. The original idea was that at this point you would hear the sound of an aeolian harp, evoking Aeolos, god of the winds. Unfortunately there is no aeolian harp today, but if there ever was one it would have been a marvelous experience to hear it as one came out of the grotto.

Prince Franz was in friendly contact with the poet Goethe, who lived not far away at Weimar. Goethe was privy counsellor to Duke Carl August of Weimar, and he helped the duke to create a beautiful park along the river Ilm. The name *Weimar* means "sacred moor," and there is indeed a sacred quality about the park. Goethe is well known to have been a Freemason, and this may account for some of the features that are found in the park, such as a sphinx, a familiar symbol in Masonic iconography, reclining in a grotto. There is also an object called the Snake Stone in the form of a serpent curled around a stone pillar. When I first saw this, it reminded me of the ouroboros of Masonic and alchemical iconography, but I subsequently discovered that the stone is based on an altar at Herculaneaum and was carved by Martin Gottlieb Klauer at the request of Duke Carl August, evidently in honor of Goethe. Carved into the stone is the Latin inscription GENIO HUIUS LOCI (to the spirit or genius of this place). The stone that one sees in the park today is in fact a copy of Klauer's original, which had become weathered and is now in the Roman House, a small museum on the edge of the park. Interesting also is a monument in the grounds of Goethe's Garden House in the park. It's called the Stone of Good Fortune and is in the form of a simple cuboid surmounted by a sphere. There is very little documentation about this monument, but possibly it is a symbol of heaven and earth or of the fixed and movable principles in nature.

Another fascinating garden of about the same era is the New Garden at Potsdam, built by the Rosicrucian King Frederick William II of Prussia, nephew of Frederick the Great. He became king of Prussia in 1786 when his uncle died. Already as crown prince, he had been initiated into the Golden and Rosy Cross, which I spoke about in the previous chapter. Historians have not been very kind to Frederick William. He has generally been portrayed as a weak and rather ineffectual successor to Frederick the Great. But I feel he must have been a rather likeable and engaging figure. He was a curious combination of mystic, libertine, and artistic patron. He had several mistresses and a couple of bigamous marriages. At the same time, he kept an orchestra with a European reputation, he patronized composers such as Mozart and Beethoven, and he built the beautiful Marble Palace by the Holy Lake at Potsdam and created a park to go with it, the New Garden, filled with Rosicrucian motifs. As crown prince he had acquired the land. Then, after he became king, he set about laying out the garden and building the Marble Palace. When the building work on the Palace was about to start, there were some acacia trees in the way, which the king himself had planted and refused to cut down, so the palace had to be built out into the lake on special foundations.

The most striking object in the New Garden is an icehouse in the form of an Egyptian pyramid. This reflects the mystique of ancient Egypt, which goes right back to the Hermetic writings, but it became particularly fashionable in the eighteenth century, partly through the novel *Sethos,* by the French priest Jean Terrasson, published in 1731, which tells the story of the young prince Sethos, who is taken through an initiatory process by the sage Amedes to prepare him to become king. This book also influenced the Egyptian setting of Mozart's *Magic Flute.* King Frederick William's pyramid has some Egyptian hieroglyphs and a set of seven alchemical symbols in gilded wrought-iron work over the doorway, underlining the key role that alchemy played in the Golden and Rosy Cross. The Egyptian theme also appears in the design of the orangery, which is made to look like an Egyptian temple with a sphinx over the portico and two figures of gods in black marble flanking the doorway. This orangery was designed by the architect Carl Langhans, who also designed the Brandenburg Gate in Berlin. There were a number of other interesting features in the park, including a figure of Isis,

Fig. 7.3. Icehouse in the form of a pyramid in the Rosicrucian park at Potsdam, created by King Frederick William II of Prusssia (1744–1797). (See also color plate 5.)

PHOTOGRAPH BY THE AUTHOR.

a grotto, and a hermitage with a ceiling painted with images of the planets—possibly this was where Frederick William had his alchemical laboratory. Unfortunately all of these features have disappeared.

Another interesting example of a symbol-strewn landscape is the park at Louisenlund in Schleswig-Holstein, built in the late eighteenth century by Landgrave Carl von Hessen-Kassel and now the property of a private school. As mentioned in the previous chapter, the landgrave was a prominent Freemason, active in numerous exotic rites and head of an order called the Asiatic Brethren, which incorporated Rosicrucian and alchemical elements. He is also famous for having harbored the mysterious alchemist, the Comte de Saint-Germain. The park that he laid out was a striking example of a landscape crammed with symbolic features. There was an alchemist's tower, where alchemical work and

Masonic rituals were conducted, and there was an initiatic itinerary that involved the candidate passing through a dense wood, finding his way through a labyrinth, and encountering various allegorical images such as a figure of a hermit. There was also a pond with a secret grotto concealed behind a waterfall where the most solemn rituals were held. Sadly, over the years most of the symbolic features have disappeared. All that remains of the alchemist's tower, for example, is an Egyptian stone doorway, which was moved to a different position and cemented into the wall of a stable, where it stands completely out of context. The Louisenlund School and other parties are, at the time of this writing, engaged in a project to restore the alchemist's tower and various other features in the park.

Moving to the twentieth century, one of my favorite symbol-strewn landscapes, Thieles Garden, is tucked away in a suburb of the workaday town and port of Bremerhaven on the Weser estuary. It was created not by a rich aristocrat but by three people of modest means but remarkable vision: the brothers Gustav and Georg Thiele and Georg's wife, Grete. When you go there it may take awhile to find it among the sprawl of residential streets, but when you do . . . what a wonderland opens up! A path leads past a small house, which the Thieles built in a Middle Eastern style, and into the garden, where, passing a sculpture of a pair of wrestlers, you are soon greeted by a jovial, goat-legged faun sitting on a rock and wearing a slightly devilish smile. Not far away is a young woman embracing a sort of wild man, half human, half ape—or is she perhaps whispering a secret into his ear? More sculptures follow: footballers; children playing leapfrog or splashing about in fountains; Pan sitting cross-legged, playing his pipe; a Venus figure emerging from a shell and surrounded by nymphs and other mythical beings; a naked woman with arms raised as though greeting the sun, standing in front of a circular, colonnaded temple like something out of a painting by Claude Lorrain. Wherever a woman is depicted in these sculptures the model is Grete Thiele, a woman of great beauty and grace who worked as an assistant in the

Thieles's photographic shop and studio in Bremen and then married Georg in 1929. Both of the brothers had frustrated artistic ambitions, Gustav as a sculptor and Georg as a painter.

In 1923 the brothers bought a plot of land on the northern edge of Bremerhaven, where they tried unsuccessfully to set up a small construction business, but the piece of land came into its own two years later when they were inspired to create their own sculpture garden after reading an article in the gardening magazine *Gartenschönheit* (Garden Beauty). Georg, with his artist's vision, set about landscaping the area, creating ponds, groves, and meandering paths, while Gustav began creating a series of sculptures, using cement over a wire framework. Some

Fig. 7.4. The author (on the right) with a faun in
Thieles's Garden, Bremerhaven.
PHOTOGRAPH BY DR. DONATE McINTOSH.

of the sculptures depict everyday images, like the footballers, but the majority have some mythological association.

When their house and studio in Bremerhaven were destroyed by a bomb in 1944, they moved fully into the Moorish House. After the war they opened the garden to the public and in the 1950s offered to sell it to the City of Bremerhaven, which turned down the offer, as the local Art Association had described the garden as kitsch. Instead a wealthy local builder bought and extended the property and allowed the Thieles to go on living there and further developing the garden. Finally the city changed its mind and acquired the property after all. The Thiele brothers and Grete must have had a considerable library containing works on mythology, art, architecture, and other things. Unfortunately we can never know what their sources were, as the library was never catalogued and was sold off after Grete's death in 1990—Georg having died in 1968 and Gustav the following year. Today the garden draws many visitors. It is a venue for concerts and other events and has rooms that can be hired for wedding parties and other receptions. Sadly, some of the sculptures have been damaged by vandalism.

The question arises: Does the garden have a message? In my book *Gardens of the Gods,* I speculate that it might have been intended as an interface between the everyday world of human beings and the world of the gods and nature spirits. I suggest that the wrestlers, the footballers, and the woman bathing belong to the former, while the Pan figure, the sun priestess, and the goat-legged elf belong to the latter, and perhaps the young woman embracing the wild man represents the two worlds coming together.[4]

8

SEERS AND SOMNAMBULISTS

In the summer of 1901 a young man named Gustav Meyer was admitted to a hospital in Dresden, dangerously ill with tuberculosis of the bone marrow.[1] Meyer was later to become famous under the name of Gustav Meyrink, author of a series of remarkable occult novels, most notably *The Golem,* a haunting tale of myth-laden Prague. Born in Vienna in 1868, the illegitimate son of an actress and a German nobleman, he had lived since the age of fourteen in Prague, where he had founded a banking business, cut a dandyish figure, and embarked on a mystical quest, joining various occult groups and immersing himself in the study of parapsychology, alchemy, Kabbalah, and the like. He had also pursued a certain mind-body practice developed in the previous century by the Freemason and opera singer Johann Baptist Kerning (1774–1851) that involved the vibrating of certain letters and sounds, mantra-wise. Meyer found the system powerful, but in quite the wrong way. It was this activity to which he attributed his bone marrow disease, which was successfully treated in the Dresden hospital.

We shall return to Meyrink later on, but first a flashback to the period of the late eighteenth and early nineteenth centuries and to Kerning and his Masonic milieu. Johann Baptist Kerning, whose real name was Johann Baptist Krebs, was born into a poorish family in a village in the Black Forest. He was earmarked for the priesthood but instead embarked on an operatic career and worked for most of his life at the Stuttgart Opera, first as a singer and then as director and teacher. His main importance, however, lies in his Masonic career. The founder and long-standing member of a Stuttgart lodge, he exemplified the mystical and esoteric strain in Freemasonry that we have seen in the Golden and Rosy Cross and in Mozart's *Magic Flute*.[2]

What is fascinating about Kerning is that he was far ahead of his time. Transcendental meditation, the Hare Krishna movement, and Baghwan Rajneesh and his ilk were all in the future, but here was Kerning teaching a yoga-like mind-body practice that would not have been out of place in a twenty-first-century New Age center. His system involved vibrating the sounds of letters while visualizing them in different parts of the body, starting with the feet, the idea being that they would act as lenses opening up higher states of consciousness. An account of the system was published by his student and successor Karl Kolb in 1908.[3] The intended results of the system are described in Kerning's book *Wege zur Unsterblichkeit* (Roads to Immortality). The book is a fictional work in the tradition of the German novel of education and involves an interchange between Silbert, a young seeker after wisdom, and his guru figure Fielding. After years of struggle to master Fielding's teaching he finally acquires "the ability of forming a lens in all the parts of his body, from the toes to the top of the head, and to see in its true shape whatever object he chose."[4]

The exercises formed the basis of a Masonic degree called the Sabbith Grade, founded by Kerning/Krebs; subsequently their influence flowed in many directions.[5] Gustav Meyrink came into contact with the system through Alois Mailänder (1843–1905), a South Tyrolean who had settled near Frankfurt and founded a society of Christian-mystical orientation. Notwithstanding Meyrink's negative experience with the Kerning system, it continued to gain practitioners such as the Czech occultist Karl Weinfurter (1867–1942), who wrote about it in his book *The Burning Bush* (originally published in Czech as *Ohnivý keř*, in three parts, 1923–1930), and the Viennese Maecenas Friedrich Eckstein (1861–1939), who in 1887 founded the first Austrian lodge of the Theosophical Society. By further roundabout routes the Kerning system, in modified forms, percolated through Germany's esoteric milieux, including Rudolf Steiner's Anthroposophical movement where it is applied in the dance method called eurythmy. This is based on the idea that the letters of the alphabet correspond to primal forces active in the body and through movement we can come into harmony with these forces. In Anthroposophy there is also a related system called speech formation, based on the theory that the meaning of a word is contained in the actual sound and can be conveyed to a person by speaking the word in a very clear and deliberate way, even if the listener does not know the language being spoken. Thus Kerning's legacy has had wide reverberations.

Kerning lived during a golden age of German philosophy, when the German language had come into its own as a medium of philosophical discourse, and philosophers like Kant, Fichte, Schelling, Hegel, and Schopenhauer were grappling with vast and profound questions about life, the universe, and meaning of human existence. Within philosophy as a whole, there was a movement that came to be called nature philosophy (*Naturphilosophie*). It can be seen as a continuation of the alchemical-Rosicrucian stream that we have encountered, which sought to close the gap between spirit and matter, soul and body, the divine realm and the natural realm. One of its predecessors was Jakob Boehme (1575–1624), the visionary cobbler of Görlitz. At the age of twenty-four, Boehme had a transformative experience. While he was sitting in his workshop in a melancholy mood, perplexed at the thought of a world remote from God in which evil was ever present and good went unrewarded, his eye caught a beam of light reflected on a pewter vessel, putting him into visionary state in which he had the sense that he was looking into the very center of nature. The vision was subsequently reinforced during a walk in the countryside. Suddenly he was overwhelmed with a feeling of being embraced by divine love and the realization that God was present in all of nature.[6]

Boehme's heritage was influential among nature philosophers such as F. J. W. von Schelling (1775–1854), who spoke of there being a "World Soul" in his youthful work of that title (1797), and the Catholic mystical philosopher Franz von Baader (1765–1841), whose writings embraced both religion and science; the list of his works includes titles such as *On the Substance of Warmth* (*Vom Wärmestoff*) and *On Lightning as the Father of Light* (*Über den Blitz als Vater des Lichts*).

Another key figure of the same period was the Romantic poet and nature philosopher Novalis, whose real name was Friedrich von Hardenberg (1772–1801) and who was also an outstanding example of a mind that straddled the realms of spirit and matter. Having grown up in a noble family of deep Christian piety, he studied at the universities of Jena, Leipzig, and Wittenberg, taking courses in philosophy, history, and mathematics, and already showing sublime gifts as a poet. Much of his best work was inspired by grief at the death of his idealized fiancée, Sophie von Kühn, whom he had met when she was only twelve and who died just over two years later. He might have devoted himself fully to a literary career, but instead he enrolled at a mining academy and on graduating took up a position in the royal salt mines of Saxony while continuing to write. At that time a certain mystique was attached to mining and metallurgy, which often went hand in hand with alchemy. Novalis's nature mysticism was enriched by his work as a mining engineer and comes across clearly in much of his writing. His unfinished novel *Die Lehrlinge zu Saïs* (*The Apprentices of Saïs*), for example, opens with the following passage:

> Many are the paths that human beings pursue. Whoever follows and compares them will see astonishing figures emerge—figures that seem to belong to that great cipher script which can everywhere be

discerned—on wings, on eggshells, in clouds, in snow, in crystals and in rock formations, in frozen water, in the surfaces and depths of mountains, in plants, in animals, in humans, in the lights of heaven, . . . in iron filings around a magnet, and in strange coincidences. In these things, one suspects, lies the key to the miraculous script and its language.[7]

This was a time when scientific advances, such as Benjamin Franklin's experiments with electricity and Lavoisier's discoveries in chemistry, were capturing the imagination of the age. But the question was, How does God fit in? Do electricity, magnetism, and the chemical elements explain God away? Or are they in themselves evidence of a divine order? For those who took the latter view, science could easily be seen as another kind of magic, which opened up breathtakingly exciting vistas. Increasingly the boundary between science and the occult became blurred. *Animal magnetism* was the term used by Franz Anton Mesmer (1734–1815) to describe the workings of a subtle, invisible, and all-pervading fluid, which he was able to manipulate for healing purposes. The figure of the scientist often merged with that of the magus, as in the case of Mary Shelley's Frankenstein in her novel of that name, published in 1818 and subtitled *The Modern Prometheus*. As the subtitle suggests, the story is partly a warning against the consequences of scientific hubris.

One of Mesmer's admirers was Justinus Kerner (1786–1862), a physician, writer, and indefatigable investigator of the visions of somnambulists and other paranormal phenomena, which he called the "Nightside of Nature." While carefully seeking a scientific explanation for such things, at the same time he remained convinced that nature was ensouled by higher spiritual powers. One of his most famous cases was that of a young woman called Friederike Hauffe, who was tormented by strange voices and visions. She lived for only three years after Kerner began treating her, but during that time she became famous for her visionary trances, which Kerner believed were made possible by her nearness to death. Her reputation spread far and wide, and she was visited by some of the most prominent philosophers of the time, such as the above-mentioned Franz von Baader and F. J. W. von Schelling. Shortly after her death, Kerner published a book about her titled *Die Seherin von Prevorst* (*The Seeress of Prevorst*). As Wouter Hanegraaff has written, "*Die Seherin von Prevorst* is one of the earliest attempts at an empirical study of paranormal phenomena, but is also interesting for its philosophy of illness and bodily disintegration as a condition necessary for experiencing spiritual realities."[8]

An equally bizarre case investigated by Kerner involved a young woman named Magdalena Grombach in the Swabian town of Orlach. She spoke of being visited by the spirit of a medieval monk who could not find rest because he had seduced and murdered several women. He indicated that their remains lay under the foundations of Grombach's house, and he wanted them to be dug up and given a Christian burial. The excavation was eventually carried out, and indeed human bones were discovered. After they were buried there were no more visits from the monk.[9]

Kerner's methods for accessing the "nightside" of the mind included what he called *Kleksographien* (roughly translatable as "blotographs"), obtained by making an ink blot on a piece of paper and then folding the paper over the blot—a method that foreshadowed and possibly influenced the famous ink-blot tests of the Swiss psychiatrist Hermann Rorschach (1884–1922). As Hanegraaff writes, "To Kerner's imagination they [the blots] suggested the shapes of spirits . . . and by adding extra pencil strokes he indeed turned them into weird demonic or semi-demonic figures."[10]

To an esoterically minded observer at that time, it must have seemed that something uncanny was breaking through in the zeitgeist. Over in America it broke through in 1848 when two sisters, Margaretta and Kate Fox, living on a farm in upper New York State, began to communicate with the spirit world by means of knocks, thus launching the Spiritualist movement, which rapidly spread to Europe, including

Germany. Knocks began to be heard in darkened drawing rooms in Berlin, Munich, and Frankfurt. Books and journals on Spiritualism appeared, as publishers cashed in on the craze.

The year of the Fox sisters' breakthrough, 1848 was also the so-called Year of Revolutions, when masses of people took to the streets all over Europe. In France and elsewhere the monarchies fell. In most of the German lands they didn't, and soon the old order seemed more secure than ever, but things were changing. Technology, industry, and commerce were flourishing, and the German states were growing closer together economically. Prussia was increasingly setting the tone, and in 1871, in the wake of the Franco-Prussian War, came the formation of Bismarck's new German Reich.

In the same year the French occultist Éliphas Lévi (alias Alphonse-Louis Constant) made his way to Elberfeld, now part of Wuppertal in the Ruhr district, to visit his pupil Marie Gebhard. The daughter of an Irish couple named L'Estrange, she had grown up in France and become one of Lévi's most devoted followers. She then married the German industrialist Gustav Gebhard, a fellow spiritual seeker (who joined his surname to hers to become Gebhard L'Estrange), but she stayed in contact with Lévi and visited him every year. She and her husband had six children, and their house at Elberfeld became a venue for like-minded people.* One room of the house was called the Occult Room, and it was there, on July 22, 1884, that the German section of the Theosophical Society was founded.[11]

The main Theosophical Society had been founded in New York in 1875 by Helena Petrovna Blavatsky, a Russian seeress of undoubted charisma, and her associate, Henry Steel Olcott, with three chief objectives: (1) to form a nucleus of Universal Brotherhood without distinction of race, creed, sex, caste, or color; (2) to encourage the study of comparative religion, philosophy, and science; and (3) to investigate the unexplained

---

*I had the pleasure of knowing her grandson Vidar L'Estrange in the 1970s when he was living in London.

laws of nature and the powers latent in man. It subsequently established a world headquarters at Adyar, India, and branches were founded in many countries. In Germany, Theosophy fell on particularly ripe soil and would serve as a gateway for many a seeker of new spiritual vistas. The stage was set for a flowering of esoteric movements in the German lands in the period straddling the threshold of the twentieth century.

9

SEEKERS OF THE LIGHT

As the nineteenth century drew to a close, Germany was on the ascendant. The army had spiked helmets, "jingling johnnies," and state-of-the-art weaponry. The universities had dueling fraternities and world-famous professors. Rudolf Diesel had recently produced the first diesel motor. Otto Lilienthal had successfully tested an aircraft several years before the Wright brothers. The railway network was expanding. The Krupp factories were turning out steel of incomparable quality. Wagnerites were flocking every year to the Bayreuth Festival.

The maestro himself, Richard Wagner, had died in 1883 some six months after the first Bayreuth performance of *Parsifal*, which he considered the apex and culmination of his life's work. *Parsifal* was not just an opera but what Wagner called a *Bühnenweihefestspiel*—a virtually untranslatable word meaning something like "staged sacred festival drama." Wagner considered it so sacred that he wished it only to be performed at the Bayreuth festival theater. Based on the epic *Parzival* by the medieval poet Wolfram von Eschenbach, it tells the story of the "pure fool," Parsifal, and his journey to the court of the Grail King, Amfortas, who lives with his knights and his father, Titurel, in the castle of Monsalvat, where they guard the Holy Grail, the chalice used by Jesus and his disciples at the Last Supper. Another sacred relic, the

Fig. 9.1. The German tenor Heinrich Hensel as Parsifal in
a Bayreuth performance of Wagner's opera, ca. 1920s.
INTERNET ARCHIVE BOOK IMAGES VIA WIKIMEDIA COMMONS.

spear that pierced the side of Jesus at the crucifixion, is in the possession
of the evil magician Klingsor, who lives in a castle near to Monsalvat.
Here he has a retinue of seductive women who are a continual tempta-
tion to the Grail knights. Amfortas is suffering from a festering wound
that only the touch of the sacred spear can heal. Parsifal overcomes
Klingsor, regains the spear, and heals Amfortas, whom he then succeeds
as Grail King.

Wagner's mature works, especially *Parsifal,* are more like religious
rites than operas, and they had, and still have, a corresponding effect
on his devotees. The sublime music and the powerful symbolic and

mythical motifs create an experience of great intensity. Especially after Wagner's death, he became the focus of a cult. The journey to Bayreuth became for many a kind of pilgrimage to a shrine, and they came from far and wide. The French Wagnerite Albert Lavignac began his book *Voyage artistique à Bayreuth* (Artistic Journey to Bayreuth) with these words, "One can travel to Bayreuth as one wishes, on foot, on horse-back, in a coach, on a bicycle, by train, but the true pilgrim must go there on their knees."[1]

The motif of the Grail, which is the central symbol in *Parsifal*, resonated with the turn-of-the-century mood of romantic longing for something more than Krupp steel and railways. The mythos of the Grail and Monsalvat was ubiquitous. Wagner's patron, King Ludwig II, even built his own version of Monsalvat in the form of Neuschwanstein Castle, as we have seen. In 1899 the romantic artist Hans Thoma painted a typically evocative picture titled *The Grail Castle*. In the twi-light some knights on horseback make their way along a path leading through dark pinewoods and up to where the castle stands on a lofty peak, gleaming in the rays of the setting sun. Another artist, Melchior Lechter (1865–1937), picked up the Grail motif in his painting *Panis Angelorum* (*Bread of the Angels*). The Grail theme was also exploited commercially. In 1913 the household supplier Carl Boller in Bayreuth published an advertisement in German, French, and English offering some items including "Gral [*sic*] of purple glass with metal foot, *the only correct original shape*. Gral cans, breadbaskets, goblets, knight's cloak, staff and several novelties."[2]

LIGHT FROM THE EAST

The notion of the Grail quest answered the German romantic long-ing for that which is unattainable or far away in space or time, and at the same time it was rooted in European and Christian tradition. But there were those who wanted to go further afield in their search for the light. One of them was Franz Hartmann (1838–1912), physician, occultist, prolific author, Theosophist, and prominent member of the esoteric milieu of that time. He had wide contacts and fingers in many esoteric pies. For some reason he is often described as a disreputable character, but there is no denying that he had a remarkably versatile and adventurous life.[3]

Born in Donauwörth, Bavaria, he served for a brief spell in the army then studied pharmacy and medicine at Munich University but interrupted his studies to emigrate to the United States, where he remained for eighteen years, completing his medical training and leading a wandering existence. Between spells of practicing as a doctor, he worked at various jobs, including farming and mining for precious metals. He also found time to attend Spiritualist séances and to read literature about Theosophy and the paranormal. In 1882 he joined the Theosophical Society in the United States and the following year left for the society's headquarters at Adyar in India, where he became a close associate of Madame Blavatsky and an important figure in the Adyar establishment.

Returning to central Europe in 1885, he displayed a remarkable talent for pursuing several different careers at the same time, establishing a sanatorium at Hallein near Salzburg, becoming head of a new German Theosophical Society in Berlin (the original one having been dissolved), and cofounding with Alfredo Piota and Countess Constance Waldmeister a kind of Theosophical lay monastery at Ascona in Switzerland, which later became the Monte Verità colony (of which more later). He also founded a monthly Theosophical journal called *Lotusblüten* (Lotus Blossoms), engaged in various publishing activities, and produced many books and articles of his own on magic, mysticism, Rosicrucianism, and the like. In addition to all of the above, Hartmann was involved in various occult orders such as the Ordo Templi Orientis and the Rite of Memphis and Misraim.

Many threads connect Hartmann with the occult world of his age, and to follow them is to enter a veritable cat's cradle of interconnected orders, societies, movements, and splinter movements. One thread leads into the embryonic German astrological movement through a trickster figure called Hugo Vollrath (1877–1943).[4] In about 1899, Vollrath abandoned his studies at university to become Hartmann's disciple, assistant, and companion on the older man's lecture tours. Vollrath soon developed ambitions of his own and managed to be appointed librarian of the Leipzig Theosophical group. From this vantage point he conjured up a "Literary Department" of the main German section of the TS, compiling a list of honorary members and patrons without their knowledge or permission. He then went on to found the Theosophical Publishing House, based at Leipzig with himself as proprietor. By this time he had a tarnished reputation in the local TS, and his enemies complained to Rudolf Steiner, general secretary of the German section who expelled Vollrath from the section. Vollrath then went over Steiner's head and appealed to Annie Besant, who had succeeded Madame Blavatsky and was running the TS from London. Mrs. Besant accepted Steiner's expulsion of Vollrath from the German section, but at the same time confirmed the latter's continued membership of the International TS. She then made him the German representative of her Order of the Star in the East, which she had founded to proclaim the new world messiah in the person of a young Indian called Jiddu Krishnamurti (1895–1986), something that Steiner could not accept. For Steiner, the Vollrath affair, coming on top of the Krishnamurti affair and other disagreements, was all too much, and he resigned from the TS, subsequently going his own way and creating the Anthroposophical Society.

Meanwhile Vollrath was thriving as an esoteric publisher in Leipzig. So was a rival in the same field—Max Altmann, publisher of the monthly journal *Zentralblatt für Okkultismus* (Central Bulletin for Occultism), which had been launched in 1908. The following year Vollrath followed suit with a rival periodical called *Prana,* a "Journal for Experimental Secret Sciences," adding insult to injury by employing as editor Karl Brandler-Pracht, who had previously been editor of Altmann's journal. Brandler-Pracht, an enthusiast of astrology, added a supplement titled the *Astrologische Rundschau* (Astrological Panorama) and around the same time founded the German Astrological Society.

Vollrath, Brandler-Pracht, and a handful of others now formed the core of a fledgling astrological movement in Germany, which looked to England as the fount of astrological wisdom. The main works of the English astrologer Alan Leo were published by Vollrath in German translation and were much admired by German astrologers. However, at this time only a small minority of Germans were interested in astrology. There were no horoscopes in the mainstream press, and very few people knew their astrological sign. That would all change after the First World War, and by the 1920s there would be a large volume of popular astrological literature in circulation. In the Nazi period astrology suffered a setback following Deputy Führer Rudolf Hess's flight to Britain in the hope of negotiating a peace settlement. Because Hess was believed to have taken astrological advice for his mission, there was a mass arrest of astrologers, and many died in concentration camps—but after the war, astrology flourished again in Germany and continues to do so today.

EROS AND OTHER MYSTERIES

The seekers who found their way to Theosophy soon discovered that it opened doors to other paths to illumination. France had given birth to the current loosely known as Martinism, in which a leading role was played by Gérard Encausse, who wrote under the pseudonym Papus. He had joined a French lodge of the Theosophical Society in 1887 but resigned five years later to pursue his own highly eclectic path. A tireless organizer, he was soon at the center of a network of initiatic orders encompassing a conglomeration of esoteric currents including fringe Masonry, Rosicrucianism, Kabbalah, ritual magic, and the teachings of Louis Claude de Saint Martin and Martines de Pasqually—a heady mixture that soon attracted seekers in the German-speaking world.

One of these was a colorful and many-faceted man called Theodor Reuss (1855–1923), a singer, journalist, Freemason, early feminist, radical political activist, and precursor of the New Age movement. Reuss was born in Augsburg, the son of an innkeeper. Initially trained as an apothecary, he became an operatic and music hall singer and then a journalist and foreign correspondent and, some have suspected, a spy for Prussia. While working from London he joined a regular Masonic lodge.[5]

As a young man he became an enthusiastic Wagnerite and, according to his own account, came into contact with the maestro himself at Bayreuth and attended the rehearsals and premiere of *Parsifal* in 1882. Soon he was attracted to the world of fringe Masonry and exotic initiatic orders. He was in contact with Papus, who introduced him to Martinism, and with Franz Hartmann and Karl Kellner (1850–1905). The latter was a businessman and fellow Freemason with some knowledge of Indian mysticism and possibly of sexual tantric techniques. Whether thanks to Kellner or to his own research, Reuss had a flash of insight into what he saw as the essential mystery celebrated in Wagner's operas—namely, the mystery of sexuality. It was there in the love potion in *Tristan and Isolde;* in Siegfried's sword, Nothung; in the holy lance and the Grail in *Parsifal*. This mystery was to become the core of a new order, the Ordo Templi Orientis (Order of the Oriental Temple, usually abbreviated OTO), but Reuss still had some way to go in his fringe Masonic career before he was ready to launch the OTO.

Meanwhile he began collecting charters to operate a variety of fringe Masonic rites. In England he came into contact with William Wynn Westcott, head of the Societas Rosicruciana in Anglia (Rosicrucian Society in England, or Soc. Ros. as it was often called), who gave him a charter to form a Berlin college of the Soc. Ros. He also met the Masonic researcher John Yarker, an inveterate collector of rites, from whom he obtained charters to found German sections of various high-degree rites including versions of the Rite of Swedenborg, the Ancient and Accepted Rite, and the Rite of Memphis and Misraim. The early years of the twentieth century found Reuss publishing a periodical called the *Oriflamme* and presiding over a network of fringe Masonic orders. During this period he was contacted by Rudolf Steiner, then still head of the German section of the Theosophical Society, who was looking for an order that he could use as a vehicle for the work of an inner group called the Esoteric School, which he had founded. Reuss obliged by giving him a charter to found a section of something called the Antient and Primitive Rite, one of Yarker's collection of orders. Steiner accordingly did so and called his section the Mystica Aeterna.[6]

In 1905, Karl Kellner died, and Reuss's career in Germany began to founder. Dogged by negative gossip and with his fringe Masonic network coming apart at the seams, he returned to London. By now the theme of sexuality was central to his thinking. While Sigmund Freud, ensconced in his somber apartment in Vienna and surrounded by his collection of idols and fetishes, was probing the unconscious mind for suppressed sexual neuroses, Reuss was exploring sexuality as a means of transcendence. In 1906 he produced a work titled *Lingam-Yoni,* based largely on Hargrave Jennings's book *Phallicism,* published in 1884.

Reuss was now poised to found the OTO. It is not clear when precisely the founding took place, but it must have been sometime between 1906 and 1912 and entailed the incorporation of the Gnostic Catholic Church, or Ecclesiastica Gnostica Catholica (EGC), as the ecclesiastical arm of the OTO. The EGC had been founded in France by Joanny Bricaud. Unlike many of the rites in which Reuss had been involved, the OTO was and remains open to both sexes. Sometime in the embryonic phase of the OTO, Reuss met Aleister Crowley, who then played an essential role in shaping the organization and its rituals. It was Crowley who wrote the Gnostic Mass, the central ritual of the EGC and a key ceremony for the OTO. However, unlike the initiatic rituals of the OTO, the Gnostic Mass is open to nonmembers of the order. The mass is marked by strong sexual symbology and involves a form of eucharist. Today most people who have heard of the OTO associate it with Crowley, although Reuss was the main progenitor.

When the First World War broke out, Reuss moved to neutral Switzerland, where he became involved in the proto–New Age colony of Monte Verità at Ascona on Lake Maggiore and founded an OTO lodge there. A predecessor of the colony was the short-lived

Theosophical lay monastery project of Franz Hartmann and Countess Wachtmeister, and the same idyllic spot on a hill overlooking the lake became the location of the new colony, which took the name Monte Verità (Mountain of Truth). Although located in Switzerland it had strong links with the German-speaking world, where its reverberations were felt in various ways. The main moving spirits behind it included the Austrian artist and poet Gustav ("Gusto") Gräser, the pianist and author Ida Hoffmann, and Ida's lover Henri Oedenkoven, son of a rich Belgian industrialist. Gräser, gaunt faced, with long hair and beard, and dressed in a flowing robe, was a hippie ahead of his time. A fervent pacifist, during the First World War he served a term of imprisonment in Germany for refusing to serve in the military.

The heyday of the colony lasted essentially from its inception in 1900 until about 1927, when the property was taken over and made into a wellness center. Outside the protected enclave of Switzerland, the world was changing rapidly. The new century opened with a surge of optimism, which soon gave way to the maelstrom of the First World War and the austerity of the postwar years. Through it all, the participants of the Monte Verità colony went on living their alternative lifestyle in the conviction that they were creating a blueprint for a better world. They were artists, writers, dancers, musicians, nudists, mystics, Theosophists, political revolutionaries, dietary reformers, nature worshippers, and advocates of sexual liberation. Photographs of the time show groups of them disporting themselves naked throughout the grounds or dancing, white-robed, in circles. Famous visitors included the artists Paul Klee and Hans Arp (cofounder of the Dada movement), the writers Hermann Hesse and Gerhard Hauptmann, and some strange political bedfellows such as the anarchist writer Erich Mühsam and the folkish artist Fidus (Hugo Höppner), who later threw in his lot with the Nazis.

Theodor Reuss evidently felt at home in this motley community. As a pacifist and feminist he was among kindred spirits, and he found the atmosphere of sexual freedom congenial. The colony was also a good place to find recruits for the OTO. One of them was Rudolf Laban

(1879–1958), the choreographer and modern dance pioneer, one of the most influential figures among the Monte Verità habitués. Laban, of Hungarian extraction, was born in Bratislava, then part of the Austro-Hungarian empire, attended a military academy in Vienna, then for many years pursued a wandering and Bohemian life, which included a spell at the École des Beaux Arts in Paris. There he became interested in dance as an art form and began to develop the system of dance for which he became famous. This was more than just body movement and was intended to develop the three essential human faculties of understanding, feeling, and will. The underlying philosophy was that the whole cosmos is performing a dance and that the dancer could connect with the cosmic dance by moving according to certain patterns based on the five Platonic solids, the geometrical forms considered by Plato to be the essential building blocks of the universe. One of the forms most frequently used in Laban's movements was the dodecahedron (with twelve sides). Dancers would practice inside a dodecahedron made of a framework of assembled rods. In developing his system Laban was to some extent influenced by Rudolf Steiner's eurythmy dance method, although the two differed markedly in many ways. He is also famous for the dance notation that he devised, a sort of shorthand using signs for forward, backward, and sideways movements. This is now used by dancers, choreographers, and dance teachers all over the world.

Monte Verità provided the perfect milieu for Laban's dance activities, and his summer courses there became legendary. One high point was in the summer of 1917 when he orchestrated a nocturnal ritual called "Song to the Sun," a kind of Wagnerian total work of art with music, dancing around a fire, and a culminating ceremony in which everyone paid homage to the rising sun.

Laban left Switzerland in 1919 and went to live in Germany, where he founded a dance school in Hamburg, whose graduates went on to found similar schools in various countries. After the Nazi seizure of power in 1933, Laban, although never a party member, at first went along with the regime and was employed by Josef Goebbels's Propaganda

Ministry to administer all matters connected with dance, including festivals and dance academies. To what extent Laban was really in sympathy with the regime is a controversial matter. At any rate, in 1936 he fell out with the Nazis over the banning of one of his works, and in 1937 he emigrated to Britain, where he remained for the rest of his life, founding a dance school and continuing to promote his method.

CHILDREN OF NATURE

The Monte Verità colony was part of the wider *Lebensreform* (life reform) movement that emerged in the late nineteenth century as a reaction against the stiff, materialistic ethos of Germany under Kaiser Wilhelm II, but whose roots lay deep in the German past. In an article on the influence of this movement, Gordon Kennedy writes of the natural religiosity of the Germanic peoples:

> Wherever their nature can unfold itself freely, their faith emerges in that form which religious scholarship has described as "nature religion" or "earth religion." To remove the German soul from the landscape is to kill it. The Romans knew this, and once Christianity had become the state religion of the Roman Empire, Christian missionaries were then eager to chop down the Germanic forests and set their temples on fire.[7]

But from time to time the old nature religion reasserted itself.

By the second half of the nineteenth century, the time was ripe for a concerted revival of the old religiosity. One of its avatars was a former Protestant minister named Eduard Baltzer, who between 1867 and 1872 published a four-volume work titled *Die natürliche Lebensweise* (The Natural Way of Life), setting out wide-ranging policies for social reform and the promotion of physical health. He advocated vegetarianism and the provision of small gardens where families could grow their own food.[8]

The essential aim of the Lebensreform was to open shutters that had too long been closed and let in the light, whether it shone from the human body, erotic love, the world of nature, or folk culture and traditions. One important initiative in this context was the nudist movement, pioneered around the turn of the nineteenth to twentieth century in the German-speaking lands, where it is called *Freikörperkultur* (free body culture), or FKK for short. One of its pioneers was Richard Ungewitter, author of a book published in 1913 titled simply *Die Nacktheit* (Nakedness), a passionate paean to the liberating and health-giving effects of nudism. It is full of images of lithe naked bodies, including some drawings by the artist Fidus. One of Fidus's striking images (not included in Ungewitter's book) is his *Lichtgebet* (*Prayer to the Light*), which became an iconic work in Lebensreform circles. It shows a naked youth bathed in sunlight and standing on a rocky promontory, arms raised in the age-old gesture of pagan ecstasy. It is significant that the word *prayer* appears in the title, as it underlines the ethos of nature mysticism and sun worship in the image and in nudism as a whole.

Soon there were journals and associations devoted to the FKK movement, and the number of adherents grew steadily, especially in Germany and Austria. With the Nazi seizure of power in 1933, nudism was forbidden, although the ban was eased somewhat during the war. After the war the movement flourished anew in both East and West Germany, and today it is a well-established part of German life with many FKK areas. One of them is by a lake near where I live. It is not fenced off, and on sunny days it is crowded with naked people swimming, picnicking, or just sitting around chatting in a very un-self-conscious way.

Out of the same spirit as the Lebensreform came a youth movement called the Wandervögel (Birds of Passage). It was started in Berlin in 1895 by a group of students motivated by youthful wanderlust, a desire to escape the confines of the city, and a romantic desire to roam through the countryside singing lustily. The Californian writer Gordon Kennedy, who has made a special study of such movements, writes of the Wandervögel:

Fig. 9.2. *Wandervögel*, a painting by Max Frey, circa
1931. (See also color plate 6.)
WIKIMEDIA COMMONS.

They spread to all parts of Germany and eventually numbered fifty thousand. Part-hobo and part-medieval, they pooled their money, wore woolen capes, shorts and Tyrolean hats, and took long hikes in the country where they sang their own versions of Goliardic songs and camped under primitive conditions. Both sexes swam nude together in the lakes and rivers.[9]

The symbol of the Wandervögel was a crane in flight, as shown in the painting by Max Frey, circa 1931, which captures the romantic ethos of the movement.

CHANNELED WISDOM

Many are the channels through which the voices of the gods or sages have been heard by those disposed to listen. In the early part of the twentieth century, one of them was a young man named Oskar Schlag, who was to become a key figure in the esoteric domain in the German-speaking world. Born in Landshut, Bavaria, in 1907, he began even as a teenager to show paranormal abilities and came to the attention of Albert Schrenk-Notzing, one of the pioneers of parapsychological research. For a time he acted as a test subject for Schrenk-Notzing before moving to Switzerland, where he lived for the rest of his life. He studied graphology, applied psychology, and psychoanalysis, and, equipped with these skills, he became a highly successful psychological consultant in Zürich. A man of wide learning, especially in the area of esotericism, he amassed over the years a remarkable library containing some 26,000 books, one of the largest collections of esoterica in the world.

In addition, Schlag himself was actively involved in various esoteric groups, notably one called the Hermetic Society, founded in Zürich in the 1920s by a group including the psychiatrist and parapsychologist Eugen Bleuler, the businessman Fritz Alleman, the graphologist Max Pulver, the psychologist and art historian Rudolf Bernoulli, and the latter's wife, Katharina. Among other things the society produced a set of tarot trumps designed by the Swiss artist Max Hunziker under Schlag's instructions. A major activity of the society consisted of weekly séances at which Schlag acted as a medium for an entity calling himself Atma. These were recorded but published only after Schlag's death as *Die Lehren des A.* (The Teachings or Instructions of A.). Carl Gustav Jung is said to have been a member of the society and at one séance to have engaged in a long conversation with Atma. Unfortunately, as Oskar Schlag told Thomas Hakl, "The psychologist's expulsion was made necessary by the rivalry between 'Atma,' the guiding spirit of the Hermetic Society, and 'Philemon,' Jung's spiritual guide, whom he claimed had accompanied him since the age of three."[10]

Antoine Faivre describes the pronouncements of Atma as follows:

> His Instructions constitute a kind of never-ending story or dream.
> As his inspiration goes, he dwells and comments on a great variety
> of symbols, themes and myths for a while, then suddenly leaves them
> for others, only to take them up again later. He extensively deals
> with alchemy, kabbalah, the Tarot, Egyptian and Greek mythology,
> Buddhism, Hinduism, and last but not least a great variety of Yoga
> theories and practices.[11]

There is a possible connection between the Hermetic Society and
the Eranos series of seminars, held from 1933 at a property in Ascona,
the Casa Gabriella, not far from the site of what had been the Monte
Verità colony. Thomas Hakl, the historian of Eranos, writes, "Allegedly
. . . the building of the Eranos lecture hall and possibly even the founding of the Eranos meetings themselves can be traced back to an initiative that came from this society."[12]

Whatever the original impulse behind Eranos, its creator and moving spirit was an Anglo-Dutch woman, Olga Fröbe-Kapteyn, who saw
its main purpose as being a meeting ground between the spiritual traditions of East and West. The meetings began in the fateful year 1933,
when the Nazis came to power in Germany, and continued under Olga
Fröbe's leadership until her death in 1962. The sessions at the Casa
Gabriella continued until 1987, when a dispute arose over the future
of the institution and a splinter group was formed, which met at other
venues including the Monte Verità property. The meetings of these two
Eranos associations are still continuing at the time of this writing. A
third initiative, the Eranos Conference Group, now appears to concen-
trate on publications. Although based in Italian-speaking Switzerland,
Eranos in its heyday always had strong connections to Germany and
German scholarship.

One Eranos meeting is particularly relevant here—namely, that of
1946, which focused on the theme of "Spirit and Nature." The par-

ticipants included, for the first time since Eranos began, a number of distinguished scientists including the Nobel Prize–winning Austrian physicist Erwin Schrödinger and the Swiss biologist Adolf Portmann. The latter was exceptionally well suited to speak on the chosen topic, as he opposed the kind of science that attempted to reduce all biological phenomena to chemistry and physics. He was also against a purely mechanistic view of evolution based entirely on chance mutation and natural selection. He believed that evolution was much too complex to be explained in such simplistic terms. He saw all living things as sharing a quality that he called *Innerlichkeit* (meaning, roughly, "indwelling spirit"). He even spoke of "alchemical thinking," a type of thinking that he described as "para-scientific, not pre-scientific, for what is aimed at here is a human goal which science does not strive towards and which today appears more urgent than ever—namely the goal to come back into contact with ourselves and into harmony with the world in its totality."[13] In other words, Portmann belonged to the tradition of spirit-and-matter thinking that forms a Leitmotiv of this book.

Eranos also connects with the theme of the Grail, as is shown by a letter that Olga Fröbe wrote to her mentor C. G. Jung on March 11, 1960, in which she wrote:

> You once talked about the Eranos Round Table, as you came down the path to my house, and you spoke of a Grail, suspended between heaven and earth. The festive table resembled a picture that one might see in some old manuscript. That was right at the beginning of Eranos, and I have not forgotten your words.[14]

10

JOURNEY TO THE SELF

*The life of every man is a way to himself. . . . No man has
ever been utterly himself, yet every man strives to be so.*

HERMANN HESSE, *DEMIAN*

In my mind I am on a train on my way to London sometime in the
1970s, oblivious to the suburbs rolling past the window as I am deeply
immersed in a book—namely, the novel *Der Golem* (*The Golem*) by
the Austro-German writer Gustav Meyrink (1868–1932), already mentioned in connection with the Kerning exercises. The book was published in 1915 and is set in Prague around the same era, a Prague of
mystery, magic, dark alleys, and shadows thick with legend. Even the
appearance of the book holds an allure for me—the Gothic type, the
curious esoteric symbols on the binding, and the name of the publisher
on the copyright page: Kurt Wolff of Leipzig. Information on the same
page tells me that the print run of this edition was 150,000. This was
the book that brought fame and fortune to Meyrink. It was followed
by a series of other novels in the same genre, written during the First
World War and in the period that followed it. That period was a grim
and troubled one for Germany in the wake of military defeat, yet it was
an enormously rich one for the arts—literature, drama, music, painting,

and film—including those that dealt with occult and esoteric themes. On the literary scene there were various writers in the occult genre, whom I shall come to shortly, but Meyrink remains my favorite. The occult was not just the subject matter of his stories but also something in which he was deeply involved. He was connected with a network of prominent occultists in different parts of Europe. In view of his importance, it is worth going into his life and career in some detail.

Gustav Meyrink, whose original name was Gustav Meyer, was born in Vienna in 1868, the illegitimate son of Baron von Varnbüler, a minister of the Württemberg court, and the actress Marie Meyer. Contrary to what has sometimes been claimed, Meyrink was not Jewish and was brought up in the Lutheran faith, though Jewish traditions and the milieu of the Prague ghetto came to fascinate him. He was educated in Munich, Hamburg, and Prague, and he spent some twenty years of his life in the Czech capital. There he cut a colorful figure as a man-about-town, champion oarsman, and bon viveur, fond of keeping strange pets such as dancing mice and Chinese bullfrogs. For a time he ran a banking concern that he ironically named the First Christian Banking House in Prague.

His inclination to épater les bourgeois and his flamboyant way of life made him disliked in respectable society, and one of his bitterest enemies was the brother of the woman, Philomena Bernt, who became his second wife. This man, an Austrian army officer, caused Meyrink to be prosecuted on a false charge of fraud, which led to the collapse of his banking business and a spell of several weeks in prison before he was cleared. Such experiences led him to nurture a hatred toward the bourgeois establishment, officialdom, and the officer class for the rest of his life.

Already known as a raconteur among the artists and writers whose company he kept in the cafés of Prague, Meyrink began in 1901 to contribute articles to the journal *Simplicissimus* and other periodicals. Meanwhile he was developing a profound interest in occultism and mysticism. On the point of suicide because of the emptiness of his life, he had come across an article on Spiritualism. Forgetting his intention of suicide, he began a serious investigation of Spiritualism, which he later rejected but which led him to explore the whole realm of occult and mystical belief. In 1904 he moved to Vienna, where he frequented the circle of Friedrich Eckstein, founder of the Vienna lodge of the Theosophical Society. In 1906 he moved to a house on Lake Starnberg in Bavaria, where he remained until his death by suicide in 1932.

The range of Meyrink's activities and contacts in the esoteric world was extraordinary. The people he knew or corresponded with included Annie Besant, successor to Madame Blavatsky as head of the Theosophical Society; Rudolf Steiner, founder of Anthroposophy; the rustic guru Bô Yin Ra; and the English occultist William Wynn Westcott, supreme magus of the Societas Rosicruciana in Anglia and cofounder of the Hermetic Order of the Golden Dawn. As regards the groups in which he was involved, these included orders with exotic names such as the Royal Order of Ape and of the Sat Bahai, the Fraternity of the Ancient Rites of the Holy Grail in the Grand Orient of Patmos, the Ancient Gnostic Church of Eleusis, and the Aquarian Foundation.[1]

The success of *The Golem* brought Meyrink recognition and financial security, and he went on to write a series of other novels as well as short stories. All of his mature writings deal with the borderland between the mysterious and the everyday and with an individual's quest for self-realization. All are fascinating and highly readable, although none achieved the same degree of success as *The Golem*.

The action of *The Golem* takes the form of a kind of vision experienced by an unnamed narrator who himself appears only at the beginning and end of the story. The novel opens with the narrator in bed, trying to sleep but tormented by the memory of a passage he has read in a book about the life of Buddha, comparing those who forsake the Buddha to a crow that sees a stone that looks like a piece of fat then, realizing it is only a stone, flies away. It is the words "a stone that looked like a piece of fat" that for some reason stick in his mind. Somewhere deep within himself he feels he has an elusive memory of such a stone, and as he gropes for it he falls into a kind of trance in which his consciousness becomes detached from his body.

In this trance state he finds himself reliving the life of one Athanasius Pernath, who then takes over as the "I" of the story. Pernath is an artist who cuts images in precious stones and lives in a dingy room high up in a house in the Jewish ghetto of Prague, sometime during the reign of Emperor Franz Josef. Pernath can remember nothing of his previous life, before he came to live in the ghetto, but learns that he was brought there by a doctor after undergoing a period of insanity.

From his friend Zwakh he hears about the golem. Zwakh explains that the golem, according to Jewish legend, is a man made out of clay by means of Kabbalistic magic and that one such golem is believed to haunt the Prague ghetto every thirty-three years, when he appears at the window of an inaccessible room high above the street. Here occurs a remarkable passage in which Zwakh puts forward the idea that the golem is really a manifestation of the collective soul of the ghetto, "an inner explosion that propels our dream consciousness into the daylight, . . . creating a phantom that, in expression, gait and behavior, must unfailingly reveal to everyone the symbol of the collective soul, provided one correctly understands the secret language of forms."[2]

Thus Meyrink presents the golem as a kind of egregore, a collective thoughtform representing all the hidden fears, tensions, anxieties, and dark emotions of the ghetto. This puts Meyrink ahead of his time in his understanding of group psychology.

There is, however, another aspect to the golem. He is not only a collective phenomenon but also represents the inner self of each individual. Hence certain people see him as a kind of doppelgänger of themselves. This happens to Pernath when he finds his way through a labyrinth of passages to the room where the golem lives. There he finds a pack of tarot cards from which he takes away the card known as the Magus, or Juggler, symbolizing the poised human will exercising mastery over its world. Pernath's finding of the card signifies the beginning of his discovery of his true will.

However, before his complete self-realization, he has many experiences and tribulations to undergo. Like Meyrink's other heroes he has a guru or initiator—namely, the Jewish archivist and holy man Schemajah Hillel, a pious and otherworldly individual who lives with his daughter Mirjam in extreme poverty in an apartment below Pernath's. Hillel helps Pernath to make sense of the strange things that happen to him. Speaking of the golem, Hillel says, "Our grandmothers said of him that he lives high up in a room without a door, only a window from which communication with the people is impossible. The person who knows how to hold him under a spell and refine him, that person will be a good friend to himself."[3]

In another scene, Pernath is walking alone in the streets near the Hradschin, the hilltop palace that towers over Prague, when he finds

Fig. 10.1 The golem of Prague, as depicted by Hugo Steiner-Prag in Gustav Meyrink's novel about the golem legend.

IMAGE COURTESY OF CENTER OF JEWISH HISTORY, NEW YORK, VIA WIKIMEDIA COMMONS.

himself in the so-called Street of the Alchemists. At the end of the street he comes to a house larger than the rest and shining out of the fog as though it had been newly whitewashed. He peers through a window and sees a room filled with dusty alchemical equipment. An old man appears in the room, carrying a candle, and turns toward the window but appears not to see Pernath, even when the latter knocks on the glass. Pernath knocks at the door but receives no reply and goes away. Later, in conversation with friends, he learns that what he had seen was the House of the Last Lantern, a ghost house that appears at certain times in a position where normally only a large, gray stone is visible. According to legend the stone conceals a great treasure that will remain buried until, at some distant time, the house will be occupied in great splendor by a hermaphrodite.

As we have seen, the figure of the hermaphrodite is an important motif in alchemy, representing the union of Sol and Luna, a theme that I have argued is a recurring Leitmotif running through the history of German culture. The importance of the hermaphrodite is underlined several times in *The Golem,* as, for instance, when Mirjam tells Pernath how she aspires to "a magical union of male and female to create a demigod."[4] She hopes to achieve this through union with a perfect soul mate. Eventually it is Pernath's love for her that brings about his own final transformation.

In 1915, the year in which *The Golem* was published, a film of the same title was released, apparently by coincidence or synchronicity. It was directed by Paul Wegener and Heinrich Galeen with Wegener in the role of the golem and was the first of a trilogy of golem films made in Berlin studios. Set in modern times, it told the story of an antique dealer who finds a golem in the ruins of a synagogue and reanimates him so that he can work as a servant. The second in the trilogy was *The Golem and the Dancing Girl* (1917), which mixed horror with comedy. It was followed in 1920 by *The Golem, How He Came into the World,* by far the most powerful of the three films. Like the other two, it was codirected by Wegener, who again played the title role. Wegener's golem, with his sinister, lumbering gait, grim expression, and distinctive helmetlike haircut, became for a time almost as familiar an icon as Boris Karloff's Frankenstein's monster did in the 1930s.

The 1920 golem film was set in sixteenth-century Prague, the era of the legendary Rabbi Judah Loew, whose grave can be seen in the cemetery of the Old New Synagogue. Loew is said to have created the golem at a time when the city's Jewish community was being harassed by fanatical elements in the Catholic Church and constantly accused of ritual murder and other crimes. The making of the golem is described in Chayim Bloch's *Mystical Tales from the Ghetto of Prague.* In a dream Loew was instructed to make a golem out of clay, who would come to the aid of the Jews in their struggle. The rabbi summoned his son-in-law Isaac and his pupil Jakob and explained to them that the four elements, *aysh, mayim, ruach,* and *aphar* (fire, water, air, and earth), would be necessary for the operation: "Thou, Isaac, art the element of fire; thou, Jakob, art the element of water; I myself am air; working together, we shall make out of the fourth element, earth, a Golem."[5]

Having gathered clay from the banks of the Moldau and formed it into the shape of a man, they then carried out an elaborate nocturnal ritual using Kabbalistic formulae to bring the figure to life. The golem then proceeded to help the Jewish community in various ways such as by going incognito among the Jew-baiters to listen to what they were plotting and report it to Rabbi Loew so that evasive action could be taken.

Against this background the film tells the story of how Rabbi Loew, with the help of the golem, persuades Emperor Leopold to withdraw an edict of expulsion against the Jews, and how a young nobleman called Florian falls in love with Miriam, the rabbi's daughter, arousing the jealousy of the rabbi's assistant. The latter activates the golem, who runs amok, killing Florian and setting the house on fire. In the fields outside the town, he finds a young girl at play, whom he picks up gently. Fascinated by a pentagram talisman fixed to his breast, she pulls it off, thereby causing him to fall down dead. The visual style of the film is characteristic of the expressionist movement, which emerged on the eve of the First World War and included many artists, writers, and filmmakers. It was marked by exaggeration, distortion, jarring images, and heavy symbolism. Typically the Prague of *The Golem* is a place of gloomy alleyways, houses leaning at crazy angles, cavernous interiors, and sharply contrasting light and shadow.

Although Meyrink's novel tells a completely different story from any of the three films, the popularity of the novel must have been enhanced by the films and vice versa. Meyrink went on to write other novels that, like *The Golem,* are in the German tradition of the *Bildungsroman,* the novel of education and character development. The fact that literary scholars commonly use the German term for this genre indicates that it is something characteristically German. The German individual's search for the authentic self is bound up with the wider national preoccupation with social, philosophical, religious, and ethical questions. Thus, in Wolfram von Eschenbach's *Parzival,* which could be considered a kind of medieval Bildungsroman, the hero's self-discovery is dependent on his acquiring knightly values and a knowledge of the role that he will assume when he replaces Amfortas as the Grail King. And in Goethe's great Bildungsroman, *Wilhelm Meister's Apprenticeship* (*Wilhelm Meisters Lehrjahre*), the eponymous hero learns over time how to conduct an ethical and responsible life. In this he is helped by an older man, Lotario, who introduces him to an initiatic circle, the Society of the Tower, somewhat resembling a Masonic order and reflecting Goethe's own membership in a Masonic lodge.

Another outstanding exponent of the Bildungsroman was Meyrink's near contemporary Hermann Hesse (1877–1962). He was born of Protestant missionary parents in the picturesque Swabian town of Calw (in what is now the state of Baden-Württemberg). Swabia was a region steeped in Pietism, an austere and purist form of Protestantism dating from the late seventeenth century, which had distinctly mystical and theosophical traits. From an early age, therefore, Hesse was confronted with profound religious and philosophical questions. He began to write poetry and short prose pieces while working as a bookseller and had his first literary success with his novel *Peter Camenzind,* published in 1904. In the same year, he married the Basel photographer Maria Bernoulli, with whom he had three sons. It was the first of his three marriages.

In 1911 he went for several months on a tour of the Far East in search of spiritual inspiration. Shortly afterward he moved with his family to Switzerland, where he lived for the rest of his life. In 1916 he suffered a psychological crisis through personal traumas and the events of the First World War. This led to his undergoing a psychological analysis with Carl Gustav Jung, who lived in a house that he had built on an idyllic spot on Lake Zürich.

As with Meyrink, most of Hesse's stories deal with a journey of self-discovery. He is not occult in the way that Meyrink is, but his work still has a mystical tinge. The influence of his analysis with Jung comes across in the symbols and archetypes that unfold in his narratives. This can be seen clearly in his novel *Demian* (1919), originally published under the name of Emil Sinclair, who is also the narrator. The title refers to his friend Max Demian, who, even as a schoolboy has an impressive, sage-like aura. Under the guidance of Demian and later of an organist called Pistorius, Sinclair grows to maturity. In the process he is confronted with certain symbols and motifs that are signposts for his inner development: a hermaphrodite, a bird of prey pecking its way out of an egg, and the mysterious god Abraxas. In one way or another the theme running through the book is the familiar one of the reconciliation of polarities: light versus dark, good versus evil, order versus chaos. Here is Sinclair reflecting on Demian's words about Abraxas:

> Demian had said that we had indeed a god whom we honoured but he represented only one half of the world . . . that is to say the official, authorized "world of light." But we ought to be able to honour the whole world and so we must have either *one* god who was also devil or side by side with the cult of God we should institute a cult of the Devil. So we had Abraxas the god who was both God and Devil.[6]

Here the influence of Jung is obvious if one knows Jung's visionary work *VII Sermones ad Mortuos* (*Seven Sermons to the Dead*), written under the pseudonym of Basilides of Alexandria. Published privately by Jung in 1916, it formed part of his *Red Book,* which was only published in full after his death. For example, the theme of Abraxas is writ large in the *VII Sermones:*

> There is a god whom ye knew not, for mankind forgot it. We name it by its name ABRAXAS. It is more indefinite still than god and devil.
>
> That god may be distinguished from it, we name god HELIOS or Sun.
>
> Abraxas is effect. Nothing standeth opposed to it but the ineffective . . . Abraxas standeth above the sun and above the devil. It is improbable probability, unreal reality. Had the pleroma a being, Abraxas would be its manifestation.[7]

Carl Gustav Jung himself (1875–1961) is of course part of this story. Although he was Swiss by nationality, he was of German ancestry on his father's side and German was his language, so he can be considered a German thinker in the broad sense that I have adopted. The son of a pastor, he studied medicine at Basel University, where he wrote a doctoral dissertation focusing on mediumistic phenomena. For a time he was a close disciple of Sigmund Freud but eventually broke away to found his own system, which he called analytical psychology.

Jung's enormous oeuvre cannot be done justice here, but there are three major planks of his psychology that should be mentioned: First there is the notion of the collective unconscious; that is, the deep level of ourselves that, as he claimed, we share with all of humanity. Second, there is his concept of the archetypes, which he saw as powerful motifs present in the collective unconscious but operating in a particular way in the individual. These include the anima or animus (male or female essence), the shadow, the sage, the jester, and the hero.

The third important doctrine is that of individuation; that is to say, the process whereby a person attains inner wholeness. As Thomas Hakl writes:

> In order for this to happen, however, it is necessary to put aside one's everyday mask, the persona, in order to become that which one truly is in one's most essential being. Jung saw the archetypal images as being all facets of the so-called self. . . . At the end of the process all these images would come together to form a wonderfully harmonious *mandala*.[8]

Hakl also draws attention to a fascinating fact, mentioned by the Jungian psychologist Marie-Louise von Franz:

> Jung, especially in his later works, allowed his unconscious to participate in the writing and thus work in accordance with the archetypes. In this way, his writings have the capacity not only to convince the reader logically but also to evoke a resonance within the soul. . . . And this perhaps makes it easier to understand the far-reaching and emotional impact of his work.[9]

Jung wrote a great deal about alchemy, in which he saw a symbolic representation of the individuation process—although in my view he unduly ignored the practical work of the alchemists with their furnaces, crucibles, and flasks. His book *Mysterium Coniunctionis* is subtitled *An inquiry into the separation and synthesis of psychic opposites in alchemy*.

Not surprisingly, he saw the figure of the hermaphrodite, often reproduced in alchemical books, as symbolic of the coming together of opposites into a peaceful coexistence in the human soul. Another theme to which he returns repeatedly is the polarity between good and evil and the problem of the existence of evil in the world. He came to believe the Gnostics had arrived at a convincing answer to the problem with their concept of a demiurge, a mischievous god who created the world as a place where human beings are trapped, cut off from the true divine world above.

Much more than a psychologist, Jung has for many people taken on the character of a great spiritual sage and master. Today there are Jungian astrologers, tarot readers, and practitioners of various forms of psychology. While he is in many ways controversial, there is no denying the enormous influence he has had. Christine Maillard, in her entry on Jung in the *Dictionary of Gnosis & Western Esotericism,* has written of him, "The scope of his work and the extent of his knowledge make Jung one of the greatest figures of western esotericism in the 20th century."[10]

VISIONARY ARTISTS

The movement of quest and reform, of which Hermann Hesse was part, also left its mark on the world of the visual arts. One significant example is the artist Hugo Höppener, better known under his nom de plume Fidus (1868–1948), whom Hesse knew and greatly admired. Fidus is fascinating for a number of reasons. He was a proto-hippie, a vegetarian, a Theosophist, a nudist, and an advocate of sexual freedom, but he was also someone who romanticized the Germanic spirit and the notions of nation and tribe. His artistic works are in some ways strikingly modern, with a psychedelic quality. At the same time many of them evince a nostalgia for a heroic Germany of the past. One theme that pervaded his work and outlook was that of light, especially sunlight, to the extent that he would sign his letters with the salutation *Lichtgruß* (light greeting) or *Lichtheil* (light hail). His images also exhibit the themes of polarity and synthesis that we encountered earlier.

To give a brief overview of his life, he was born in Lübeck in 1868, the son of a confectioner, and showed an early talent for drawing, which his parents encouraged. In due course he studied at the Munich Academy of Visual Arts and privately under the artist and back-to-nature messiah Karl von Diefenbach (1851–1913), one of the avatars of the Lebensreform (life reform) movement, of whom

Höppener became both a pupil and a disciple. It was Diefenbach who gave the young artist his new name as a result of an incident involving a clash with conventional mores. One day Diefenbach, together with his son Helios (named after the Greek sun god) and Höppener were sunbathing naked in a secluded quarry, unaware that they were being spied on by a policeman. The result was a charge of indecency and a prison sentence of eight days, which Höppener was able to serve in lieu of Diefenbach on account of the latter being ill. Out of gratitude Diefenbach dubbed his young pupil Fidus (the "Faithful One"). It was not long before Fidus rebelled against Diefenbach's authoritarian ways, but he retained a respect for his old teacher and remained faithful to the Lebensreform movement.[11]

By the turn of the twentieth century, Fidus was living in Berlin and had become one of the best-known artists in Germany. His works ranged from visionary landscapes bathed in an eerie northern light to images of sword-wielding heroes of Germanic legend, and from naked sun worshippers to delicate silhouettes of dancing children. He was in constant demand as a book and magazine illustrator and a designer of ex libris plates and the like. During this period his private life was unsettled. He had a three-year liaison with a schoolteacher that produced a daughter, then a marriage from which came a second daughter and a son and which ended with the death of his wife, and finally a second marriage, which lasted until his death. The Fidus house at Woltersdorf, built in 1908 to 1910 to Fidus's own design and located in a rustic setting close to Berlin, was constantly crowded with visiting artists, writers, Lebensreform activists, Theosophists, and all manner of proto–New Age types.

Meanwhile Fidus was engaged in various projects related to the arts, social reform, and the back-to-nature movement. One of his dreams was a new kind of nature religion with its own temples, for which he produced a series of designs. This led to a collaboration with a self-appointed prophet called Joshua Klein, who claimed to be the incarnation of the "Logos." Klein had a project to create a utopian community on a property by the Walensee lake in Switzerland, and in 1903 he persuaded Fidus to move there with his family and supervise the building of a temple. Unfortunately it all proved to be a pipe dream, and the community quickly broke up in disarray.[12] But Fidus's extraordinary temple designs remain.

A more durable initiative was the St. George Society (St. Georg-Bund), named after both the dragon-slaying saint and Georg Bauernfeind, a pastor's son and close friend of Fidus, who had died of anorexia while staying in the house at Woltersdorf in 1911. The aims of the society were stated in a publicity flier issued at the time of its foundation in 1912:

> The St. George Society is a creative union, founded by Fidus, Gertrud Prellwitz, Alwine von Keller, Jacob Feldner and various creative kindred spirits, with the aim of bringing their art . . . to their friends in a different and more direct way than that of the market. . . . Thereby will a healthier, more life-enhancing exchange take place between the creators and the recipients/collaborators so as to realize common cultural ideals and to activate that strong, joyful new spirit of life from which those ideals spring.[13]

Fidus's works display a number of contrasting moods. His naked, sun-worshipping athletes and embracing couples are all ecstasy and lightness, while other works have a darker quality, as in an image of glowering, black-winged Lucifer, intended for a stained-glass window in one of his unrealized temples. In a passionate essay titled "Tempelkunst" (Temple Art) he wrote:

> We shall again have a temple art! A great, sacred art, before which and with which the people will be reverent, indeed blessed!
>
> We need temples where the spirit of the time will be present in still meditation, where it will celebrate the sacred festivals, will experience its own beauty and grow beyond itself towards the eternal!

This will not happen just through acquiescence, talk, invention and discovery—we need deeds and life![14]

In his design for a Temple of the Earth, the colossal entrance portico is dominated by an enormous letter *T* inscribed with the word *TAT* (deed). If there had been a Shangri-La pavilion at the Paris Universal Exhibition of 1900 it might have looked something like this. The ground plan of the temple, shown in figure 10.3, is particularly interesting, as it brings together different elements representing the ethos of the nature religion that Fidus envisaged. There is a square main building incorporating a Hall of Devotion, a Hall of Will, and a Hall of Feeling, as well as four smaller halls of Love, Lust, Ambition, and Longing.

Fig. 10.2. Design by the artist Fidus for a Temple of the Earth.

Fig. 10.3. Ground plan of Fidus's Temple of the Earth.

Beyond the main building is a circular construction containing an inner sanctum with a solar cross and a radiating pattern in the floor. To enter the sanctum one would first have to pass through a Chamber of Silence and a small chamber labeled, simply "The Dark," an example of how Fidus combined light and dark motifs.

Fig. 10.4. *Shambhalah,* a visionary work by Melchior Lechter, painted in 1925, in the collection of the Meiningen City Museums, Thuringia. (See also color plate 7.)

Fidus was just one of a number of artist-prophets of the time. Some, like Ludwig Fahrenkrog and Michael Bossard, we have already encountered in the chapter on the old gods. Another visionary artist worth mentioning is Melchior Lechter, who was for a time a member of the Stefan George circle and who evinced the same homoerotic streak that is present in George. His entry into the Theosophical Society caused a rupture with George, who could tolerate no masters other than himself, let alone the Mahatmas of the Theosophists.[15] The influence of Theosophy in Lechter's work can be seen in his extraordinary painting *Shambhalah*. It depicts a circle of gold angels perched on roughhewn columns of rock rising above a mass of pink clouds and surrounding a circular temple surmounted by a sort of glittering monstrance with a solar disc sending out light rays.

Artists like Fidus and Lechter remind me of a present-day group of artists in Russia that I wrote about in my books *Beyond the North Wind* and *Occult Russia,* whose work is marked by a kind of visionary romanticism celebrating Russian legends and folk culture and portraying never-never lands like Byelovodye and Hyperborea. Unlike most contemporary artists in Western countries, these Russian artists believe that they have a sacred mission to create works of beauty that uplift, inspire, and enchant. In Germany the generation of Fidus, Lechter, Bossard, and Fahrenkrog was the last to have a mission of this kind. With the coming of the Third Reich and its philistine, propagandist approach to art, these artists generally found themselves left out in the cold. And after the Second World War a modernist, secular mentality took over the arts establishment, so that today students in art colleges are taught that art has nothing to do with beauty and the traditions of the past have no relevance. Just a few courageous artists are standing up against this bleak orthodoxy.

INTERBELLUM AND ARMAGEDDON

The Anglo-Polish writer Rom Landau, in his book *God Is My Adventure* (first published in 1935), said the following: "After the war of 1914–18, wherever I went . . . conversation was likely to turn to supernatural subjects. It looked as though many people were feeling that their daily lives were only an illusion, and that somehow there must somewhere be a greater reality."[1]

If this was true of the world it was especially true of Germany, which had gone almost overnight from being a leading power to being a defeated and impoverished nation, plagued by economic chaos and political turmoil. To quote Rom Landau again:

> In no country after the war could the desire for new ideals have been stronger than in Germany. Germany had become the melting pot of so many contradictory tendencies that some spectacular results were bound to follow. The Nazi Revolution fifteen years later was only one of them.[2]

One tendency was a surge of enthusiasm for modernity: the stark minimalism of the Bauhaus architectural movement; the epic theater of

Bertolt Brecht and Erwin Piscator with its didactic approach to social and political issues; the expressionist school in art, film, and literature. For many people these things represented a decisive break with the old order and the dawn of a new and better one. Others retreated into a decadence of which Berlin became a particular hotbed, as vividly portrayed in Christopher Isherwood's novels and the film *Cabaret,* based on his *Goodbye to Berlin.* Others again sought salvation in various extreme political movements of the left or the right.

GATEWAYS TO ILLUMINATION

Then there were those who were looking for something eternal beyond the daily struggle or the desperate pleasure of the moment. They were ready to turn to the nearest guru or charismatic spiritual teacher or to join an order offering admission to some inner sanctum of the mysteries. Many such organizations—fringe Masonic lodges, Rosicrucian circles, ritual magic orders, neo-pagan groups, and the like—had continued or resumed their activities after the war, while new ones sprang up. Theodor Reuss remained active in the esoteric scene until his death in 1923, and he sent out impulses that were felt far beyond Germany's borders. In about 1908 he had granted an OTO charter to Arnoldo Krumm-Heller (1876–1949), who had lived for a time in Latin America and retained strong ties there. In 1927, Krumm-Heller founded his own order, the Fraternitas Rosicruciana Antiqua (FRA), inspired by the OTO, and today the FRA is active in many Latin American countries. Reuss also corresponded with H. Spencer Lewis, who at that time was building up his Rosicrucian organization, the Ancient and Mystical Order Rosae Crucis (AMORC), in the United States. Later, under the auspices of AMORC, the German alchemist Albert Riedel, under the name Frater Albertus, founded the Paracelsus Research Society. By the time Reuss died in 1923, Aleister Crowley had become the main driving force in the OTO. After Crowley's death in 1947 the leadership of the OTO was taken over by his appointed heir Karl Germer

(1885–1962), a German who had emigrated to the United States. There were also some splinter groups such as the re-founded Swiss OTO of Hermann Jospeh Metzger (1918–1990).

One of Theodor Reuss's contacts during the last years of his life was with Heinrich Tränker (1880–1956), a Berlin antiquarian book dealer who led a network of initiatic groups operating under the name Pansophia (a word associated with the Rosicrucian movement of the seventeenth century). His circle of collaborators included Karl Germer and one Eugen Grosche (1888–1964), who used the order name Gregor Gregorius. Grosche, like Tränker, ran a bookshop in Berlin. It was Grosche who, in 1926, founded what Hans Thomas Hakl has called the "most important magical secret lodge of the 20th century in the German-Speaking world"[3]—namely, the Fraternitas Saturni (Fraternity of Saturn, FS). The FS accepted Aleister Crowley's revelation of a coming New Aeon and adopted his doctrine of "Do what thou wilt shall be the whole of the law. Love is the law, love under will" but changed and expanded the wording so that it became "Do what thou wilt is the whole of the law, there is no law beyond do what thou wilt. Love is the law, love under will, compassionless love."[4]

The early members of the FS included the film producer and artist Albin Grau, famous for two classic films: *Nosferatu,* based on the story of Dracula, and *Schatten* (English title *Warning Shadows*).[5] During the Nazi period the FS was banned, and Grosche served a term of imprisonment. After the war he found himself living in East Germany, where he also had problems with the authorities on account of his esoteric interests. In 1950 he moved to West Berlin and was effective in resurrecting the order. After his death in 1964 the FS underwent a power struggle leading to the formation of a number of splinter groups.[6]

As regards the teachings and ritual system of the FS, these have been searchingly investigated by Stephen Flowers in his book *The Fraternitas Saturni: History, Doctrine and Rituals of the Magical Order of the Brotherhood of Saturn,* and by Hans Thomas Hakl in an article on the FS in the *Dictionary of Gnosis & Western Esotericism.* The content of the system is a bricolage of elements from the grimoires, the works of Cornelius Agrippa, Kabbalism, witchcraft, Theosophy, Rosicrucianism, Golden Dawn magic, high-degree Freemasonry, Vedic elements, astrology, and various other ingredients. Sexuality is an important theme, but not an exclusive one. As Thomas Hakl writes:

> The phallus is regarded as the earthly manifestation of the divine power of will and imagination; the vagina is the symbol for chaos as the creative ground of being; and the male seed is the vehicle of the divine spirit. Tantric practices are also taught, which are supposed to lead to a transformation of the powers of generation into spiritual energy.[7]

The core of the FS belief system is a gnostic cosmology in which the figures of Lucifer and Saturn are writ large. In the beginning was a primal darkness in which light was concealed. Lucifer, the Light-Bringer, released the light, breaking the cosmic status quo and triggering a great war in heaven between Lucifer and the Solar Logos. To quote Hakl again:

> Lucifer is regarded as the "higher octave" of Saturn . . . the outermost planet and polar opposite of the Sun. Saturn . . . is the Guardian of the Threshold, or the gateway to transcendence. . . . His heavy, dark, leaden qualities must be transformed into gold by the magician.

The sphere of Saturn is the abode of the GOTOS, the spiritual head and egregore of the order—an egregore being a thoughtform on a higher plane, created by the collective mind of a group.[8]

The FS has a structure of thirty-three degrees, plus a threshold grade of Neophyte, numbered zero. As one passes up through the degrees one follows a rigorous curriculum of self-development, reinforced by an intensive program of private study. For example, the requirements for the 8th degree, that of Gradus Mercurii, are as follows:

The initiate must have been a member of the FS for at least three years. The conditions for the conferring of this degree are: (1) mastery of ritual, symbolism, and esoteric teachings of the apprentice grades; (2) knowledge of the Theosophical doctrines of karma, reincarnation, the seven principles, and the planes of existence; (3) mastery of basic astrology; (4) basics of symbolism; and (5) a written work on the elementary concepts of the R+C [the Rose Cross].[9]

Thomas Hakl writes of the FS that "even in its heyday it has probably never had more than 200 members. Nevertheless it has produced a comprehensive, original and varied literature, which in itself guarantees it an important place in the history of magical and occult orders."[10] The fraternity remains active today and has a presence on the internet.

The FS was only one of a number of esoteric groups active in the interwar years in the German-speaking lands. They formed an ever-changing kaleidoscope in which societies promising enlightenment were constantly appearing and disappearing. There was, for example, the Adonis Society (Adonistische Gesellschaft), founded in Vienna in 1925 by Franz Sättler (alias Dr. Musallam) (1884–1942), a many-faceted, widely traveled, multilingual man with more than a touch of the confidence trickster. Adonism, he claimed, was the primal religion of humankind into which he had been initiated while visiting the Middle East. He presented it as an anarchistic creed that advocated freedom from institutional constraints and prohibitions. Sexual magic was reportedly part of its program. The society acquired a scandalous reputation, and Sättler was charged with fraud. The organization was finally banned in the Nazi period. One of the people who was in contact with it was the Czech magician, author, and healing practitioner Franz Bardon (1909–1958).[11]

The theme of the Grail, which we have encountered already, is the focus of an organization called the International Grail Movement, founded in the 1920s by Oskar Ernst Bernhardt (1875–1941), who wrote under the name of Abd-ru-Shin (Persian for "Servant of the

Light"). Born in Bischofswerda, Saxony, he traveled widely as a young man and during the First World War was interned in Britain. Having pursued a career in business and then as a novelist and dramatist, he began in the 1920s to promulgate a Christian mystical teaching centered on the symbolism of the Grail. His book *The Grail Message* attracted a following in Germany and other European countries, and in 1928 he and a group of followers established a center at Vomperberg in the Austrian Tyrol. When the Nazis occupied Austria in 1938, the center was closed and Bernhardt was arrested. Released the same year, he was sent back to Germany and died in 1941. After the war, the center was reopened and the movement revived by Bernhardt's second wife, Maria, and her family. Soon a Brazilian branch split off as a result of a dispute over the succession; later, Maria's descendants also quarreled, and the main movement split into two. Today these factions plus some smaller splinter groups comprise a total international membership of about twenty thousand. The readership of Bernhardt's three-volume book, *In the Light of Truth: The Grail Message,* is considerably larger.[12]

While some seekers turned to the mystery traditions of the East or West, others looked to things that were closer to home. For them, light came from the Germanic past and the heritage of the *Volk*—a difficult word to render in English, meaning something approaching "tribe," "kindred people," or "native countrymen/women." Hence the word *völkisch* to characterize such movements. The word now has a pejorative connotation, because these movements have come to be seen as precursors of National Socialism, although in fact they were largely rejected and persecuted by the Nazi regime. I have already mentioned some of these movements in chapter 4 on the old gods, and the subject has been searchingly covered by authors such as Nicholas Goodrick-Clarke and, more recently, Stephen Flowers. They included groups such as the Germanic Order (Germanenorden) and the Thule Society (Thule Gesellschaft).

Some of these orders adopted a chivalric style, which appealed to those who had a penchant for knightly pageantry and the things that went with it: ceremonial robes, coats of arms, eques (knight) of this and that. One group that combined a chivalric style with a völkisch agenda was the Austrian New Templar Order (Ordo Novi Templi, ONT). It was founded by Jörg Lanz von Liebenfels (1874–1954), a former Cistercian monk and priest from the monastery of Heiligenkreuz, near Vienna, which he left at the age of twenty-four to follow the path of a völkisch writer, publicist, and activist. Having come under the influence of Guido von List and other völkisch writers, he became convinced that there was a perennial conflict going on in the world between two great forces of good and evil, which he identified with the superior and inferior races.

In 1907 he and a group of friends bought an old castle, Burg Werfenstein, perched on a cliff above the Danube, as the headquarters for the New Templar Order. As Nicholas Goodrick-Clarke writes:

> Lanz's first interest in the Templars stemmed from a reading of the medieval lays concerning Parsifal and the knights of the Grail. These epics were enjoying a contemporary vogue owing to their operatic treatment by Richard Wagner and the subsequent popularization of their mythology by such neo-romantic authors as Erwin Kolbenheyer and Friedrich Lienhard between 1900 and 1914. In their novels mystical pilgrimages and chivalrous heroism combined to create an emotional climate in which the figure of the Grail-knight denoted the spiritual man's search for eternal values in a modern trivialized world based on materialistic assumptions.[13]

After the First World War the ONT expanded its activities, and new branches were founded in Germany and in Hungary, where Lanz lived for many years from 1918. Having supported the Nazis, he was bitterly disappointed when he was scorned by Hitler and his order banned by the regime. After the Second World War he reactivated the order, which has been continued by his successors.

A GURU WHO SPOKE TO THE HEART

Bô Yin Râ is a fine-sounding name—one might suppose it to be Chinese or perhaps Indian—but at any rate an appropriate one for an author with a spiritual message and a cult following. In fact those who looked into the identity of Bô Yin Râ discovered that he was a German by the name of Joseph Schneiderfranken (1876–1943). In a pamphlet published in 1927, after he became famous, he explained why he used the name Bô Yin Râ:

> I wish to state here very clearly, once and for all, that this name is not a combination of three words from whose "significance" one might deduce hermetic secrets—even though they are root syllables of an ancient tongue. Rather, they represent my real spiritual name for the one and only reason that the resonances of their sounds are consonant with what I am—in the same way that, in musical notation, a group of notes expresses a specific chord.[14]

Fig. 11.1. Joseph Schneiderfranken, alias Bô Yin Râ (1876–1943), artist and guru. Drawing by Konrad Immanuel Böhringer, dated 1920.
WIKIMEDIA COMMONS.

Born of peasant ancestry in Aschaffenburg, near Frankfurt am Main, he was obliged, on account of family hardship, to leave school early and work at a lathe. Nevertheless, possessing artistic talent, he was able to study painting at an art school in Frankfurt and receive free instruction for a year and a half from the prominent romantic painter Hans Thoma. He continued his studies in Paris and Vienna, established a studio in Munich, and did much traveling, especially in Greece, where he began to write the works that became what he called the *Hortus Conclusus* (Secluded Garden) series, with titles such as *The Book of the Living God, The Secret,* and *The Book of Man.* In 1923 he and his family moved to Switzerland, where he remained until his death. He left behind more than thirty books and some two hundred paintings. The latter are striking, visionary works depicting weird, unearthly landscapes and abstract compositions, all in bright colors and bathed in a mystical light.[15]

There was much about Bô Yin Râ that was reminiscent of Theosophy. He claimed to receive his knowledge via spiritual communication from certain "Masters" who, like the Mahatmas of Blavatsky, resided somewhere in the East. Rom Landau summarizes his teaching as follows:

> Its main thesis was that we can find true and lasting happiness only within ourselves, and that we must abandon the search for it in the world without. The moment we begin to listen with greater attention to ourselves we uncover spiritual powers that create happiness. Although happiness was a definite command in Bô Yin Râ's doctrine, he did not base it on any asceticism or self-denial, but on a sensible and deliberate acceptance of life, on honest and decent living and on the absolute elimination of fear. . . . The style of his books was almost that of books for children; no religious or intellectual conversion was required; his kind of happiness could be achieved by the rich and the poor. Above all, he appealed to the emotions.

Landau adds:

> Even in his appearance Bô Yin Râ inspired confidence. He was big
> and heavy, rather rough cut, of peasant features and yet of gentle
> expression. One easily believed that he loved fewer things better
> than climbing high mountains, planting trees in his garden, or per-
> forming manual work.[16]

Bô Yin Râ still has a following today, and his books have been
translated into some fourteen languages. There are two foundations
devoted to preserving and promoting his legacy, one in Germany, the
other in Switzerland.

THE SAGE OF DARMSTADT

An almost exact contemporary of Bô Yin Râ, but a sage of a very different kind, was Count Hermann Keyserling (1880–1946). Born into an
aristocratic Baltic German family on their estate in Livonia, then part
of the Russian empire, Keyserling lost the property and the bulk of his
fortune during the Russian Revolution. Widely read and traveled, he
became a prolific writer of books such as his bestselling *Travel Diary of
a Philosopher*. Moreover, he had a mission—namely, the reorientation of
Germany away from a political and imperial role and toward its natural
role as a source from which spiritual and philosophical wisdom would
emanate. Under the patronage of the Grand Duke of Hesse he established a School of Wisdom in one of the ducal residences in Darmstadt.

Keyserling is one of the figures described by Rom Landau in *God Is
My Adventure*. Landau writes:

> Keyserling's fame spread over the spiritual horizon of Germany over-
> night. . . . People compared his narrow eyes and high cheekbones
> with those of Genghis Khan, and they talked of him as though he
> were an Eastern autocrat. His School of Wisdom was said to promise

the delivery of spiritual products that would enable pupils to climb
the ladder of a new human order. . . . Slowly a new civilization would
come into being, replacing one that was founded on scientific creeds
and that was purely materialistic.[17]

Landau describes how Keyserling's fans descended in large numbers
on Darmstadt, especially for the conferences that were held there every
year or two, packing the town's hotels and over breakfast dropping the
names of Buddha, Plato, and Laozi "as though they belonged to social
celebrities of the moment."[18]

Besides Keyserling himself, the speakers at these events included
distinguished figures such as the sinologist Richard Wilhelm, the psychologist Carl Gustav Jung, the Judaic scholar Rabbi Leo Baeck, and
the Indian poet Rabindranath Tagore.[19] However, many of the audience, as Landau reports, did not come for knowledge or enlightenment
but instead primarily to gossip and bask in the courtly atmosphere.
Among them were many aristocrats who felt adrift in a country where
they no longer had an official status. In Count Keyserling's vision of an
aristocracy of the spirit they found something with which they could
identify.[20]

Although the audiences did not always come with the most serious
intentions, the School of Wisdom nevertheless provided a rich feast of
scholarship, knowledge, and wisdom. It also had an important after-
math. It was there that a meeting took place between C. G. Jung and
an Anglo-Dutch woman named Olga Fröbe-Kapteyn. The latter, partly
inspired by the School of Wisdom and with Jung's help, went on to
found the Eranos seminars at Ascona in Switzerland, as already dis-
cussed in chapter 9.

BARD OF "SECRET GERMANY"

On July 21, 1944, when the leader of the failed plot to assassinate Hitler,
Claus von Stauffenberg, stood before a firing squad, the last words before

he fell are reported to have been, "Long live our secret Germany."[21]

The words *secret Germany* would have held a special meaning for Stauffenberg, as they are the title of a poem by Stefan George (1868–1933), who played a key role in Stauffenberg's life as a role model and spiritual mentor. Indeed for Stauffenberg and for many others of his generation, George was a kind of messiah.

Who was Stefan George? He was born in 1868 at Büdesheim, now part of Bingen on the Rhine, to prosperous parents—his father was an innkeeper and wine merchant. He received his schooling in Bingen and Darmstadt, independently acquiring a knowledge of many languages, both classical and modern, and beginning to discover his vocation as a poet. There followed several years of traveling throughout Europe, frequenting literary circles in London, Paris, and Vienna. Evidently his poetic vocation gave him the sense of belonging to an aristocracy of the mind and of being marked for a special mission to elevate German culture and values. The main raison d'être of his poetry and of his life was to uphold beauty and nobility against the ugliness and vulgarity of modern life. To this end while he was still in his midtwenties, he cofounded a periodical titled *Blätter für die Kunst* (Leaves for Art) and gathered a group of followers that came to be called the George Circle. Its members were expected to treat him with reverence and obedience, and in return they were encouraged to believe that they were an elite corps who were going to initiate a new Germany. The membership of the circle was almost entirely male, and there is an obvious current of homoeroticism in George, probably of a sublimated kind. Photographs of him in his mature years show a striking face framed in a mane of white hair, with hard, angular lines, tight lips, and a pair of steely, penetrating eyes. The severe expression suggests that he is about to reprimand one of his audience for making a frivolous remark.

In his whole style and persona George appeared to be acting out a dream of chivalry of the kind that we have already seen in Abd-ru-Shin and Lanz von Liebenfels. However, George differed from the latter in his attitude toward the Nazis, who came to power in the last year of

his life. When they tried to appropriate him for their cause, he held
aloof and remained strongly opposed to the Nazi regime. In his band
of followers there was something of the aura of the Grail Knights or
the Templars and something of the Rosicrucian Brotherhood with its
emissaries going out incognito into the world to perform good works.
Indeed in one of his poems, titled "Templer" (Templars), George invokes
the themes of both chivalry and Rosicrucianism. The first stanza reads:

> *We are one with all on the golden journey—*
> *For an inconceivable time our band has shunned the*
> > *horde*
> *We are the Rose: the youthful inner flame*
> *We are the Cross: the art of suffering with pride.*[22]

George's worldview is even more forcefully expressed in his long
poem "Geheimes Deutschland" (Secret Germany), written and read
aloud to his circle in 1928 and published the same year in a collection
of his poems. In the first two stanzas he lambastes the degeneracy of
his age:

> *Abyss, draw me to your verge*
> *But confuse me not!*
>
> *Where insatiable greed*
> *Has trampled over every inch*
> *From the pole to the equator*
> *Ruthless and garish*
> *Flinging its lightning bolts over*
> *Every nook and cranny of the world.*

He goes on to lament the passing of the golden age of classical
antiquity "when the twin brothers suckled at the wolf"—a reference
to Romulus and Remus, the legendary founder of Rome and his twin

brother. Then he hears a voice saying to him, "Go back to your sacred homeland" and find its "primordial ground." The final two stanzas read as follows:

> *And that which you deem to be of greatest worth*
> *Is decaying leaves in the autumn wind*
> *And belongs to finality and death.*
>
> *Only that which still slumbers*
> *Long protected and untouched*
> *In the deepest shaft*
> *Of the sacred earth—*
> *A marvel unfathomable—*
> *Only that can be a match for what is to come.*[23]

NIGHTFALL

One might say that the cataclysm of the Third Reich was an extreme example of what can happen when Sol and Luna are out of balance in the collective mind of a people. The solar aspect of National Socialism was evident in the festivals marking the equinoxes and solstices; in the swastika, found as a solar symbol all over the world; and in the martial character of the movement. But there was also a lunar side to which the Nazi establishment had an ambivalent attitude. Thus, even as occultists and neo-pagans were being persecuted and thrown into concentration camps, SS members were conducting pagan rituals in the crypt of the Wewelsburg and at sites such as the Sachsenhain, near Verden. And, even as Hitler and the Nazi top brass publicly poured scorn on occult beliefs and practices, a secret institute in Berlin was running an entire study program devoted to those very beliefs and practices. Apart from what I discovered about this institute, and despite the mountain of written material on Nazism and the occult, I have not found any further reference to it, no doubt because of its highly secret nature.

I came across the story while working on my book *Occult Russia,* in which I spoke about a fascinating Russian astrologer, occultist, and healing practitioner called Count Sergei Vronsky (1915–1998), who spent some years in Germany before and during the Second World War.[24] He arrived there in 1933 not long after Hitler had come to power. In a highly competitive selection process, he was chosen for enrollment at the secret Bioradiological Institute, sometimes referred to as *Lehranstalt* (teaching institute) No. 25, located in Berlin. Apart from a few articles in Russian about Vronsky and a video interview with him at his Moscow apartment,[25] I have not been able to find any information about this mysterious establishment. But if Vronsky's account is true—and I believe, at least in some of what he says, he can be given the benefit of the doubt—the story constitutes a fascinating piece in the jigsaw puzzle of occultism during the Nazi era.

According to Vronsky the syllabus of the institute was intended to provide the students with paranormal abilities, alternative healing skills, and the like, that could be used to support the higher echelons of the Nazi apparatus. The teaching faculty included Tibetan lamas, Indian yogis, Chinese acupuncturists, and Western doctors specializing in treatments such as the Kneipp water cure. There were also clairvoyants and astrologers. Among the latter was Elsbeth Ebertin (1880–1944), the first woman in Germany to achieve fame as a professional astrologer through her books and her annual predictive almanac.

In 1923 she had made an astonishingly accurate prediction concerning Adolf Hitler, then still a marginal political figure. After casting his horoscope, she wrote that he ran the risk of exposing himself "to personal danger by excessively uncautious action." She went on to say:

His constellations show that this man is to be taken very seriously indeed; he is destined to play a "Führer-role" in future battles. It seems that the man I have in mind . . . is destined *to sacrifice himself for the German nation,* also to face up to all circumstances with audacity and courage, even when it is a matter of *life and death.*"[26]

Hitler himself scoffed when shown the prediction, but a few months later, in November 1923, came the Nazis' abortive beer-hall putsch in Munich, which resulted in Hitler's imprisonment.[27] It would not be surprising if Hitler, in his comfortable prison quarters, remembered Elsbeth Ebertin's warning about the dangers of "uncautious action" and concluded that there was something in astrology after all. At any rate, according to Vronsky the institute in Berlin had Hitler's full support.

Vronsky remembered that among the other astrologers teaching at the institute were Karl Ernst Krafft (1900–1945) and Louis de Wohl (1903–1961). Krafft's extraordinary career is covered in Ellic Howe's book *Urania's Children*. A Swiss by birth, he grew up in Basel and suffered from domineering parents. Astrology was an obsession with him from an early age and offered an escape from the stifling atmosphere of his parental home. In 1937, after a period in Zürich working at various commercial jobs, he married and moved to Germany, where he hoped to find a greater appreciation for his talents as an astrologer. He soon established contact with prominent members of the Nazi hierarchy, including Robert Ley, Minister of Labor, and Hans Frank, the future governor of occupied Poland. In 1939 he caused a stir by predicting the unsuccessful attempt on Hitler's life when a bomb was placed in the Bürgerbräu beer house in Munich but exploded only after the führer had left. For a time, he was employed by the foreign intelligence department of Heinrich Himmler's Reich Security Office, writing predictions about economic, political, and military matters, and later he worked for Josef Goebbels's Propaganda Ministry, where he was involved in the use of Nostradamus's prophecies for war propaganda purposes. In the wake of Rudolf Hess's flight to Britain in 1941, which was believed to have been linked to astrological predictions, Krafft was arrested along with many other astrologers in what was called the Hess Operation. He died in Buchenwald concentration camp in 1945. The idea that he was Hitler's personal astrologer is mistaken, as Ellic Howe convincingly shows, but it led to British intelligence employing an astrologer to anticipate what Krafft was supposedly telling the führer. The astrologer in question was the above-mentioned Louis de Wohl, who fled to England in 1935 and was hired by British intelligence.

Nazi attitudes toward astrology varied greatly. Some, like Rudolf Hess, believed in it. Others saw it as decidedly false. And there were those, like Goebbels, who merely wished to exploit it for propaganda purposes. But whether true or false, it was seen as dangerous, as it could destabilize the masses. All the same, the existence of Teaching Institute 25 shows that astrology and other forms of occultism were taken seriously by a significant section of the Nazi hierarchy.

One other institute is worth mentioning here—namely, the so-called Pendulum Institute, founded in Berlin in 1942 with full official authorization and headed by Captain Hans Roeder of the German navy. The raison d'être of the institute was that the British navy had been destroying an inordinate number of German submarines, and Captain Roeder believed that the positions of the U-boats were being identified by dowsers using pendulums. Ellic Howe describes the theory as follows:

> Roughly speaking, the pendulum "operator" would be sitting in a room at the Admiralty in London with a map of the Atlantic Ocean in front of him. He would then "search" the map with his pendulum and at a given moment, if all went well, the pendulum would begin to move or swing in a prescribed manner. Eureka! Another German submarine found![28]

Roeder reasoned that two could play at that game. Hence the institute was founded to train German dowsers in the same technique, which could then be deployed against the British navy. Ironically, many of the people hired by the Pendulum Institute had spent time in prison after the Hess Operation.

Count Vronsky throws interesting light on the Hess mission to Britain. According to Vronsky's account, he and Hess became friends through the latter's occult interests, and Vronsky taught Hess how to cast astrological charts. Together they consulted a chart for the contemplated invasion of Russia and received a message that the result would be catastrophic for Germany. Possibly spurred on by this prognostication, Hess made his famous flight to Scotland in May 1941 in an attempt to bring about a peace agreement with Britain and thus avoid the risk of a two-front war. There followed a mass arrest of astrologers, which Vronsky somehow escaped. The invasion of Russia started just over a month later. There remain many unanswered questions about the whole affair, not least the question of whether the mission had been authorized by Hitler. If that were the case it is conceivable that, when the mission failed, Hitler used the astrologers as a scapegoat rather than admit having approved it himself. There is much conflicting evidence on this matter, and we shall probably never know the truth.

12

POSTWAR PERSPECTIVES

I first visited Germany as a schoolboy in 1960. The postwar austerities were over, and the Economic Miracle was in full swing—Coca-Cola, Volkswagen, the Adenauer government, the brand-new radio blaring out "Happy days are here again," and the voice of Chris Howland, a quirky British Forces radio announcer who had stayed on to become a star disc jockey, actor, and singer. "Happy days" meant full supermarket shelves, package holidays, and feel-good films with Romy Schneider as the empress "Sissi" of Austria. The New Age movement had not yet arrived, and materialism rather than spiritual quest was the prevailing mood of the day. Nevertheless, there were various less materialistic prewar movements that became active again after the war.

One such movement was Freemasonry, banned during the Nazi period when Masons had worn, as a sign of their secret affiliation, a buttonhole pin in the form of a tiny forget-me-not flower. With Nazism defeated, the Masons could make a new start, but this entailed some difficult decisions. For most of its history German Freemasonry had been a fragmented affair with many different systems and obediences vying with one another. The main division was between the lodges that were fundamentally Christian and those that were religiously neutral or demanded only a belief in a Great Architect of the Universe.

Organizationally the situation was complex, with a number of different Grand Lodges exerting jurisdiction over their constituent lodges. The picture grew even more complicated when it came to relations with foreign Masonic bodies. For example, recognition by the doctrinally secular Grand Orient of France meant nonrecognition by the Grand Lodge of England.

A series of difficult negotiations took place over many years, resulting finally in the creation in 1958 of the United Grand Lodges of Germany (Vereinigte Großlogen von Deutschland), an umbrella organization comprising five Grand Lodges counting as regular according to the Grand Lodge of England. There are also the higher-degree systems that regular Masons can join if they wish, such as the Ancient and Accepted, or Scottish Rite with its thirty-three degrees, which is also active in Germany. The Masonic community in Germany is served by a fine library and museum at Bayreuth, which was looted and shut down by the Nazis but reconstituted after the war. Outside the above-mentioned obediences there are numerous irregular Masonic and quasi-Masonic organizations. There are the lodges of mixed male and female membership, such as those belonging to the Droit Humain system, and there are women-only lodges.

The fate of Freemasonry in the Third Reich was shared by numerous other organizations classified as esoteric, secret, or subversive. A notable example was the Anthroposophical movement with its church (the Christian Community), its Waldorf schools, its holistic medicine, and its biodynamic agriculture. Bit by bit the various branches of Anthroposophy were closed down. For a while the movement was protected by Deputy Führer Rudolf Hess, but after Hess's flight to Britain in 1941 in an attempt to negotiate a peace, the fate of Anthroposophy was sealed. All its remaining institutions were banned, including the Christian Community, whose priests were imprisoned. After the war Anthroposophy set about reconstituting itself, and today it is flourishing in Germany as never before, with more than 200 Waldorf schools, more than 120 Christian Community congregations, the firms of

WALA and Weleda manufacturing Anthroposophic remedies, the Demeter wholefood products, the farms practicing biodynamic agriculture, and many more related activities such as the eurythmy dance method and the psychotherapeutic approach known as biography work.

Anthroposophy is part of the wider Rosicrucian/alchemical legacy that was explored in chapter 6 and includes Paracelsian medicine and homeopathy, pioneered by Samuel Hahnemann. Today the name of Paracelsus is perpetuated in numerous clinics and apothecaries bearing his name, and his spagyric medicine, thanks to the work of Alexander von Bernus and others, continues to be practiced today, as does homeopathy.

POLTERGEISTS AND PHANTOM VOICES

A territory that had been much explored in Germany in the late nineteenth and early twentieth centuries, and to some extent in the Third Reich, despite the ambivalence of the Nazis toward it, was parapsychology. In postwar Germany, with its materialistic and rationalistic ethos, there were few places where parapsychological phenomena were seriously studied, but there was and remains one famous exception, the Institute for Border Areas of Psychology, founded at Freiburg by Hans Bender (1907–1991).

Bender, who before the war had corresponded with the parapsychologist J. B. Rhine at Duke University in the United States, became involved in the investigation of some famous cases of the paranormal, such as that of the Rosenheim poltergeist. Rosenheim is a mid-sized, picturesque town in Bavaria where, in 1967, curious things began to happen in the offices of a law firm. Pictures moved, ceiling lamps swung to and fro, lightbulbs exploded, telephones rang with no one at the other end, and cables showed wild fluctuations in voltage. It was time to call in Professor Bender, who quickly linked the strange happenings to a nineteen-year-old typist in the office. When she was absent everything was calm, but as soon as she returned the disturbances started again. She turned out to be full of psychological and emotional tensions, fears, aggression, suppressed anger, and unresolved conflicts, all which caused her to give off psychokinetic energy (that is, energy that can move objects at a distance).[1]

A similar case concerned a fifteen-year-old apprentice who worked in a Bremen china shop where glasses and plates would inexplicably fall to the floor and smash. Another case involved the household of the mayor of Neudorf in Baden-Württemberg, where the phenomena included some nails materializing just below the ceiling of a bedroom and falling to the floor. In that case the happenings were attributed to the mayor's thirteen-year-old son. In all of these cases the individual causing the phenomena was psychologically disturbed.[2]

Even more astonishing were the cases of teleportation—when objects disappear in one place and reappear in another, like the characters in *Star Trek* ("Beam me up, Scotty"), even moving through walls and other obstacles. This happened in the house of a family in Nickelheim, Bavaria, where bottles and other household objects would move out of closed rooms. When Bender visited the house one winter day his own coat was teleported from a closet and found lying in the snow outside.[3]

Another phenomenon investigated by Bender, among others, was that of phantom voices that appeared on sound recordings. In 1959 this phenomenon came to the attention of the Swedish film producer Friedrich Jürgenson. When listening to tape recordings in his film studio he found that they contained sentences spoken by deceased individuals. Together with the Latvian psychologist Konstantin Raudive he collected about 100,000 samples of such voices. Their work was followed up by Bender and the physicist Friedbert Karger of the Max Planck Institute. They, too, collected a large number of recordings containing phantom voices. Bender's theory was that the voices came from the subconscious minds of the experimenters, but the psychologist Peter Bander of Cambridge, England, questioned this on the grounds that the voices often spoke in languages unknown to the experimenters. The phenomenon remains a mystery.[4]

On the subject of the paranormal, and backtracking a few years, it is worth mentioning the case of the Austrian physicist Wolfgang Pauli (1900–1958), who was notorious for the way in which laboratory equipment would break when he was present, without his even touching anything. This happened so often that it became known as the "Pauli effect." In one famous incident in the 1920s some equipment in a laboratory in Göttingen broke, and the personnel remarked with surprise that Pauli was not around. It later turned out that he had been on a train that had stopped at Göttingen when the breakage happened.

What is more significant about Pauli is his long friendship and association with the psychologist Carl Gustav Jung, with whom he shared a profound interest in the phenomenon of synchronicity (acausal connections between events) and the relationship between scientific theories and the inner world of the psyche with its archetypes and symbols. They conducted an intense correspondence from 1932 to 1958. In 1952, Pauli published an essay on archetypal ideas in the scientific theories of Johann Kepler, which appeared in a joint volume with Jung. In this essay Pauli shows that Kepler's view of the universe, while making use of reason and exact observation, was still imbued with Kepler's own deep religiosity:

> Kepler's archetypal concepts are hierarchically arranged in such a way that the trinitarian Christian Godhead . . . occupies the highest place, and each level is an image of the one above it. . . . Kepler invokes the authority of the *signatura rerum,* the signs of things. . . . According to this theory . . . things have a hidden meaning that is expressed in their external form, inasmuch as this form points to another, not directly visible level of reality.[5]

For Kepler, the most beautiful illustration of this truth is the form of the sphere. "The image of the triune God is . . . in the centre, the Son's in the outer surface, and the Holy Ghost's in the equality of relation between point and circumference."[6] Furthermore, the Earth is a living being with a soul with qualities comparable to those of the human soul and acting as a formative power.[7]

Here Pauli highlights an important point—namely, that a magical view of the universe need not be in conflict with science but can in fact nourish important scientific discoveries. A scientist who sees the world as ensouled and full of beauty and meaning is likely to have insights that will elude the purely rational scientist. Kepler was not the only example of a scientist with a foot in the magical universe. Other examples include Paracelsus; Francis Bacon; Isaac Newton; Samuel Hahnemann, the founder of homeopathy; and the electrical genius Nikola Tesla, who was reciting a passage from Goethe's *Faust* when he thought of the idea of alternating current.

In an ideal culture the magical and the rational worldviews, which overlap with the modalities of romanticism and realism, are held in balance, but in modern Western culture a wedge has been driven between them, as though separating the right and left brain. In Germany this dichotomy is particularly strongly marked. While the mainstream scientific establishment is staunchly rational and materialistic, the spirit-and-matter school of thought, of which I have given many examples, is still very much alive.

FACETS OF THE NEW AGE

In the 1970s, when I resumed my visits to Germany, the country was in a nervous mood. The student demonstrations of 1968 had brought reforms, but there were those who wanted full-scale revolution and were prepared, like the Red Army Faction (RAF), to bring it about by violent means. At the same time the New Age was in full swing. There were esoteric bookshops and magazines and a commensurately lively publishing industry. There were gurus, Eastern and Western, and all manner of cults and groups. Alongside older established movements like Theosophy and Anthroposophy, there were Gurdjieffians, Crowleyans, Scientologists, adherents of Bhagwan Rajneesh (later

Osho), Rosicrucians of various hues, pagans, and followers of the neo-witchcraft movement, which often overlapped with the burgeoning feminist movement.

In short, there was a large public interest in esotericism, occultism, and alternative spirituality in general. At the same time, among the keepers of intellectual culture—in the universities, the cultural establishment, and the mainstream media—there was a general disdain for things esoteric and often an outright hostility toward them. In Germany this attitude was particularly strong on account of the trauma left by the Nazi years. Because for many people National Socialism was associated with extreme irrationality, any form of irrational belief was liable to be tarred with the Nazi brush. The philosopher Theodor Adorno, doyen of the Frankfurt School, expressed a typical view among the intelligentsia when he said, "Occultism is the metaphysics of the blockheads."[8]

This state of affairs became more pronounced over subsequent years. From 1996 to 1998 an inquiry into "sects and psycho-groups" was conducted by a commission of the German parliament, which included representatives of the main churches. This resulted in a proposed law to place tight restrictions on astrologers, Reiki practitioners, yoga teachers, feng-shui advisors, clairvoyants, tarot readers, and the like.[9] In the end the law was abandoned, but hostility toward "the irrational" remained.

The resulting damage to the collective mind of Germany was observed by the Hungarian historian Lásló Földényi. In an article published in 1998 in the newspaper *Süddeutsche Zeitung,* he wrote:

In the present-day intellectual life of Germany receptiveness toward the transcendent . . . triggers a reaction of distrust, indeed scorn. This is of course a worldwide phenomenon. Nevertheless I experience it in a particularly painful way when I come to Germany and look instinctively for traces of the great cultural legacy of the country. Instead what I find is an obsessively political, sociological and ideological worldview, which ruthlessly dismisses anything that contradicts it . . . as "antiquated."[10]

This kind of extreme hostility toward anything transcendental is constantly voiced in the media. For example, in 1997 the weekly *Die Zeit* published a special extra volume titled *Beware Soul-Catchers! Sects, Gurus, Psycho-Freaks,* in which the introductory editorial stated:

> Only by confidently deploying reason as the (only) measure against naive or malicious forms of irrationality do we stand a chance of protecting weak and endangered people. . . . The tolerance of the Americans in matters of belief cannot hold for Germany. Too fresh in our minds is the memory of what happens when pure madness becomes systematic.[11]

In the same year in the magazine *Psychologie Heute* (Psychology Today) the science journalist Holger Plana wrote, "It is esotericism itself that, from the start and in its essential core, coincides with the basic concepts of right-wing extremist thinking."[12]

In pronouncements like this the whole mystical and esoteric heritage of Germany was thrown overboard—the visions of Hildegard of Bingen and Meister Eckhart, the Kabbalah of Reuchlin, the art of Albrecht Dürer, the holistic medicine of Paracelsus and Hahnemann, Mozart's *Magic Flute,* the novels of Gustav Meyrink and Hermann Hesse, and much more. Be that as it may, the New Age has taken hold in Germany as elsewhere, along with its gurus and occultists, its specialist publishers, bookshops, magazines, and websites.

The esoteric publishing scene, which had been so lively before the Second World War, began to pick up again after the war. Characteristic of the scene was the monthly magazine *Esotera,* which was for a time the leading esoteric magazine in Germany. Over the years it went through various incarnations, going back to 1949, when a small-circulation magazine titled *Okkulte Welt* (Occult World) appeared in Hannover covering "extra-sensory phenomena, spiritualism, magic, astrology, and border areas of occultism." A year later it was renamed *Okkulte Stimme* (Occult Voice) and widened its coverage to include not just occult phenomena but also topics relating to spiritual development and the search for deeper meaning. In 1958 the magazine was acquired by the occult publisher Hermann Bauer of Freiburg im Breisgau, who changed its name to *Die andere Welt* (The Other World). In 1970 the name was finally changed to *Esotera,* and the content settled down to a mixture of New Age thinking, parapsychology, holism, alternative science, and the like. After being a niche publication for many years it began to distribute through newsagents and achieved a print run of some sixty thousand. But success brought competition, financial difficulties arose, and the magazine as it was ceased publication in 2001, although it continued for a time to appear sporadically in a somewhat different form.

Another esoteric magazine, which has outlived *Esotera,* is *Tattva Viveka,* a quarterly periodical published since 1994 and now based in Berlin. Its editor and founder, Ronald Engert, described to me how the project started. Having broken off a university program in German literature and philosophy and being somewhat adrift, he happened to attend a workshop given by a Native American shaman, who confronted him with the question, "What is your path with heart?" To help him find the answer, he went on a vision quest during the workshop and decided that he wanted to publish a magazine. To acquire the necessary skills, he completed a two-year apprenticeship with a publisher and then launched the magazine with start-up capital provided by himself and a friend. Its aim was to provide a wide-ranging forum combining the spiritual and the scientific. The name chosen, *Tattva Viveka,* is taken from Sanskrit and means "distinguishing truth from illusion." The magazine took off quickly and is now distributed throughout the German-speaking world, with a print run of some 3,500 as well as a digital version. In total the magazine has 1,500 subscribers at the time of this writing. In addition there is a related program of workshops and lectures. The content ranges from alternative medicine to Germanic and Celtic mythology and from sacred architecture to techniques of meditation. Speaking about the German esoteric scene generally, Engert said that in recent years it had experienced a setback in its public image owing to the number of people who were prepared to believe in anything, including the wildest conspiracy theories. He admits that he would like to save the world, and he believes that spiritual knowledge is the best way to do that.

Meanwhile the German esoteric publishing scene has continued to change radically, largely on account of the effect of the internet. Hermann Bauer Verlag declared insolvency in 2001, and other esoteric publishers were taken over by large conglomerates. Ansata Verlag, which had been a household name in the esoteric field, was absorbed into the Penguin Random House group, as was the New Age imprint Arkana. Book publishers, like everyone else, have been forced to adapt to the world of the internet. When I first went to the Frankfurt Book Fair back in the 1990s most of the books on display were produced in a way that essentially had not changed since Gutenberg; that is, by a process of applying ink to a prepared surface and pressing the surface against a sheet of paper. Today, if Mr. Gutenberg were to visit the fair he would be bewildered by the world of digital publishing, print on demand, e-book readers, and multimedia. For esotericists, all of this has opened up tremendously exciting vistas, but at a price. With so much that was half hidden now openly and rapidly accessible, the world of the esoteric has lost something of its old magic.

ESOTERICISM MADE EASY

In the early 1980s, together with my friend Eva Loewe, I translated a book by Thorwald Dethlefsen (1946–2010), who at that time was probably the most famous esoteric guru in the German-speaking world. Born in Bavaria, he had studied psychology and been involved in the esoteric coterie of Oscar Schlag. Through his books, lectures, workshops, and charismatic personality he had built up a large following. In addition, he was one of the pioneers in Germany of reincarnation therapy, for which he had a practice in Munich. He also founded an Institute for Paranormal Psychology, which he later renamed Kawwana, Church of the New Aeon. The book in question, titled in English *The Challenge of Fate,* contains the essence of his teaching, which is a mixture of astrology, Kabbalah, the Hermetic tradition, gnosticism, and the doctrine of karma and reincarnation. Dethlefsen very skillfully created a combination of these elements and presented them in simplified form and in plain, accessible language. Here he is talking about fate:

> Fate, instead of being an anonymous force of blind coincidence that poses a threat to mankind, now gradually reveals to the seeker its innermost law: fate is the authority which ensures that the individual follows his prescribed path. Thus the supposed enemy becomes a partner whose task is to make sure that our own inertia does not prevent our evolution. The more a person refuses to resolve particular problems in a spirit of learning and the more he puts up a resistance against fate, the more he will attract the negative aspect of fate, namely suffering.[13]

Dethlefsen goes on to say:

> Suffering only becomes superfluous when we make the effort constantly to increase our understanding of our own path and voluntarily to conform to it. Only the person who knows how to subordinate himself to superior law will cease to experience that law as a form of compulsion.[14]

For Dethlefsen, a person's successive incarnations are stages on their path, and everything that happens to them, even misfortune, is fate attempting to steer them to act in accordance with their true essence. Divinatory methods such as astrology are ways of understanding that essence and identifying the deficits that need to be remedied. According to Dethlefsen, illness should be treated as a message from fate that holds an important lesson for the sick person. The foreword to the book *Krankheit als Weg* (republished as *The Healing Power of*

Illness), written together with the physician Rüdiger Dahlke, begins as follows: "This book is uncomfortable, for it deprives the individual of illness as an alibi for their unsolved problems. We wish to show that the sick person is not the victim of some imperfection in nature but is in fact the perpetrator."[15]

The same principle, according to Dethlefsen, applies to any unpleasant event in someone's life. At the time I was working on the translation of *The Challenge of Fate,* I was myself in a situation of crisis and was sufficiently impressed by Dethlefsen's arguments to take a drastic existential decision that had profound consequences for my life. Now I am unsure whether it was the right one, but, at any rate, I feel that Dethlefsen's philosophy at least needs to be treated with caution. It can lead to a passive acceptance of problems and misfortunes as lessons of fate, to the detriment of one's own judgment.

13

PAGAN PATHWAYS

Fortunately, outside the secular world of the intellectual establishment there are still plenty of places where magic can be found. I had the good luck to have one close to my place of work when I settled in Hamburg in 1994 to take up a position at what was then the UNESCO Institute for Education (now the UNESCO Institute for Lifelong Learning), located in the Feldbrunnenstrasse. A stone's throw away in the Rothenbaumchaussée stood, and still stands, a famous museum. Formerly called the Museum of Ethnology, it now bears the rather cumbersome name of the Museum at Rothenbaum: Cultures und Arts of the World.

The museum was founded in the 1870s at a time when Hamburg's shipping firms were carrying on an increasingly booming trade with countries and colonies in different parts of the world. From these voyages the vessels brought back not only industrial goods and raw materials but also indigenous cultural artifacts to add to museum collections and facilitate the study of the diverse history of humanity. Over the years Hamburg's Museum of Ethnology acquired a collection of many thousands of such objects, ranging from Benin bronzes to Polynesian canoes and from Siberian shamans' robes to masks of the Japanese No theater.

The museum also became famous for its Witchcraft Archive (Hexenarchiv). This was the legacy of Johann Kruse (1889–1983), a schoolteacher in Schleswig-Holstein and later in Hamburg, a man of socialist, rationalist, and anticlerical views who spent much of his life conducting a crusade against the belief in witchcraft. As a child growing up in a rural part of Schleswig-Holstein, Kruse became aware of the sufferings of women accused of being witches. He recalled how, at the age of twelve, he overheard an old woman talking to his mother in the kitchen and bemoaning how a neighboring farmer had just driven her out of his property, shaking his stick at her and shouting, "There's the witch! You bewitched my children and my cattle and made them sick." On the same day the farmer hired a local *Hexenbanner* (meaning, roughly, a "protector against witches"), who went through the farm carrying a pan full of hot coals on which he burned a resin called "devil's dung," made from the root of the asafoetida plant, which he had bought from the village chemist. By fumigating the property in this way, he supposedly protected it from bewitchment.[1]

The Kruse collection contains a variety of such "de-witching" potions, which were available from Hamburg chemists until well into the 1980s. Ingredients included palm resin and the dried remains of a lizard native to the Arabian desert. There were also amulets, talismans, and objects allegedly used in magical attacks, such as a doll pierced by a needle or nail.[2] Kruse found it astonishing and deplorable that even in the twentieth century the belief in witchcraft and the profession of the Hexenbanner could still exist. He was determined to do his best to combat such relics of the benighted past along with all associated superstitions such as belief in the devil. He encouraged his pupils to adopt a skeptical attitude to these things, and he traveled widely throughout northern Germany, collecting relevant material and supporting women accused of witchcraft. For these activities he came into conflict with various authorities and was threatened with dismissal from his teaching job. In 1923 he published a book titled *Witchcraft Delusion in the Present Day* (*Hexenwahn in der Gegenwart*). In the late 1940s, by which time he was living in Hamburg, he founded his Archive for Research into the Modern Witchcraft Delusion (Archiv zur Erforschung des neuzeitlichen Hexenwahns), and in 1951 he published a second book, *Witches Among Us?* (*Hexen unter uns?*). For mysterious reasons, nearly all copies of the work were pulped six months after its publication, an act that Kruse attributed to some shadowy conspiracy against him.

In the 1950s and early '60s there was a wave of what the press called "witch trials," largely in rural districts. Ostensibly these were cases of women accused of libel or slander, but in fact it became clear that the hidden accusation was that they were practicing witchcraft. For unclear reasons this series of trials came to an end in the mid-1960s, but, while it was in progress, Kruse's archive was much used and misused by the press. Some journalists irresponsibly published the names of accused women, and Kruse felt obliged to destroy his correspondence with the women involved.

By this time Kruse had widened his crusade to target all the institutions that he saw as perpetuating the stereotype of the witch, including the churches, the educational establishment, and the folklorists. For example, he wanted to ban fairy tales such as *Hänsel and Gretel,* because they fostered the stereotype. In fact, he opposed anything that encouraged superstition or belief in magical powers. One much-publicized campaign that he fought was against two publishers in Braunschweig who had issued a collection of spells and occult lore called the *Sixth and Seventh Books of Moses* (sometimes spelled *Mose* or *Mosis*), allegedly a continuation of the first five books attributed to Moses, constituting the Pentateuch in the Old Testament.

Works under this title had begun to appear in Germany around the sixteenth century. They vary somewhat in content but usually consist of a potpourri of spells, invocations, and magical formulae in the manner of the traditional grimoire. Typically the contents of these manuals include folk remedies as well as procedures for attracting love, obtaining beauty, promoting fertility, improving crop yields, and of course protecting house and home from witches. The Moses grimoire in its various forms was carried far and wide and was used by German emigrants to America, especially the Pietist communities of Pennsylvania and later among the farmers of German origin in the Midwest. A German language edition was published in Philadelphia in 1853, which was a reprint of an edition published in Stuttgart in 1849 by Johann Scheible. The influence of the grimoire can be seen in the Pennsylvania hex signs, talismanic images painted on houses and barns belonging to farmers of German descent to guard against bewitchment (*Hexe* being the German word for "witch"). After being translated into English the grimoire spread to the black populations of the United States, the Caribbean, and West Africa and even reached India, where a version was published in Bombay (Mumbai) titled *The Original Key to the Sixth and Seventh Books of Moses* (no publisher or date given). Today there are several versions in print from various different publishers, indicating that the procedures in the grimoire are still being used. There are even what purport to be the eighth, ninth, tenth, eleventh, and twelfth books of Moses.

When Kruse heard about the Braunschweig edition of the Moses grimoire he brought a court case against the two publishers, arguing that these books should be banned, as they exerted a harmful influence by propagating the belief in witches. In what became a cause célèbre he was supported by the forensic doctor Otto Prokop and opposed by the distinguished historian Will-Erich Peuckert, who could see no danger in the book and said that it would not be possible to ban all publications that could conceivably nourish a belief in witches.[3] The trial lasted more than eight years, 1953 to 1961, and ended in the case against the publishers being dropped.

For many years, the professional ethnologists and folklorists were dismissive of Kruse's work, but that situation began to change in the 1970s with a new generation of experts in those fields. In particular, the Museum of Ethnology in Hamburg developed a cordial relationship with Kruse, as a result of which he donated his collection to the museum in 1978. In a letter to the museum Kruse wrote:

I am firmly convinced that the time is near when in the Federal Republic of Germany no woman and mother will be persecuted as a witch or driven to madness or suicide, and that within the next hundred years the belief in witches will be eliminated in all parts of the world.[4]

A year after the transfer of the archive the museum opened a special exhibition titled *Hexen* (Witches), dealing with the history of the witch persecutions and making use of the Kruse collection, which rapidly became a much-used resource for people studying the subject. After Kruse's death in 1983 the archive, with its associated program of lectures and introductions to the collection, increasingly attracted neo-pagans and members of the neo-witchcraft movement, which must surely have made Kruse turn in his grave, especially when, in 2003, the museum organized a series of events connected with the theme of witchcraft, including rituals and a symposium comprising both practitioners of witchcraft and scholars, including myself and my wife-to-be, Dr. Donate Pahnke, who conducted a series of rituals and delivered lectures on the witchcraft movement and its recent history. The whole program generated enormous interest, and at times there was a line of visitors waiting to enter that stretched far up the street.

The exhibition and symposium were a huge public success but attracted heavy criticism from a number of academics and curators of other museums, who accused the Hamburg museum of "going native." A dozen or so years later the museum underwent a modernization process, and the Kruse archive, which had evidently become something of an embarrassment, was closed to the public and its book collection largely incorporated into the main library of the museum.

PAGANISM IN GERMANY TODAY

Fast-forward to August 2015. We are in the leafy district of Prenzlauer Berg, Berlin, where the German branch of the Pagan Federation

International has taken over the premises of a family social and advisory center to hold a gathering. Many different neo-pagan and alternative religious groups are represented: Druids, Asatru, Wicca, Reclaiming, and the Crowleyan Ordo Templi Orientis. Their stalls are selling books, craft work, and ritual equipment. The program begins with a welcoming ceremony in the garden, opened by a priestess dressed in a white robe. Then two other priestesses go around the circle. One carries a censer containing burning charcoal onto which the other drops aromatic gum. Each participant receives a purifying puff of smoke and a blessing. The proceedings continue with an Asatru ceremony, a lecture on herbs in the Nordic tradition, a talk on runes, a Reclaiming ritual, and a workshop on shamanism given by Phoenix, a prominent German shaman. The day's activities end in a party atmosphere with much drumming and dancing around a fire.

This gathering is part of a larger annual event called the Long Night of the Religions, held at various locations throughout Berlin and bringing together representatives of many different faiths in an ecumenical spirit, including Jews, Muslims, Hindus, Buddhists, Catholics, Protestants, Orthodox Christians . . . and Pagans, whose presence at this inter-religious event shows that neo-paganism is now gaining ground in Germany as a religious community in its own right.

The pagan movement is a river into which many tributaries flow. The Austrian authors Eduard Gugenberger and Roman Schweidlenka, quoting the French sociologist Michel Maffesoli, have spoken of the return of Dionysus, positing what is essentially a variation of Nietzsche's Apollo/Dionysus polarity, except that they substitute Apollo with Prometheus. They speak of a primitive, visceral, irrational, orgiastic stratum in humanity that periodically breaks through the crust of civilization like a volcanic magma. They see this as having happened in the second half of the twentieth century with various alternative-culture movements emerging in reaction to the prevailing ethos of materialism.[5] Certainly dramatic things began to happen in Germany from about the 1970s, disturbing the prosperous but prosaic atmosphere of the Economic Miracle as though Dionysus, half naked, crowned with a grapevine, and flanked by his maenads had burst into the solemnity of a board meeting at the Bundesbank. But Dionysus is only one of many gods who have gained followers in the German lands.

A major influence came from the British organization the Pagan Federation (PF), founded in its present form in 1981, which has played a key role in establishing paganism as an accepted religion in Britain. The PF publishes the magazine *Pagan Dawn,* which appears every three months. In due course the PF created an international branch, the Pagan Federation International (PFI), which in turn spawned national branches, including one for Germany, the Pagan Federation International Deutschland. A leaflet issued by this organization describes its mission as follows:

> The term *Paganism*—or Heathenism, as it is more commonly called in Germany—encompasses a multiplicity of religious currents, independent of each other, that regard themselves as rooted in the old nature religions of the world. . . . Many groups feel connected with the pre-Christian religious traditions of Europe, whether they be those of our Germanic, Slavic, Roman, Greek, or other ancestors. Some attach great importance to indigenous traditions from farther afield such as those of the ancient Egyptians, the Native Americans, or the people of West Africa and the Caribbean. Common to many of these groups is that they conceive nature as permeated by the divine and the entire world as animated and sacred.[6]

The leaflet goes on to describe what the organization offers, including meetings in pubs (*Stammtische,* as they are called in Germany), an online community, regular conferences, and participation in events such as the Long Night of Religions.

A word about terminology: Outside Germany the word *heathen* tends to imply a follower of the Nordic path, so here, in speaking specifically about that path, I use the adjective *heathen* or the noun *Asatru.* When being less specific I employ the term *pagan.*

MOONRISE

The Germany of the Economic Miracle was a rather solar place—materialistic, male-dominated, competitive, fixated on order and efficiency. But a ray of moonlight came with the pagan movement. The logo of the Pagan Federation International depicts a sun and a crescent moon superimposed on a tree, with the moon placed horizontally so that it looks like a cup receiving the sun's rays, echoing the notion I mentioned earlier of the solar and lunar forces merging in the Grail. History has a habit from time to time of emphasizing certain symbols that express the collective mind of an age or a movement. Thus the moon came to be associated with paganism and in particular the neo-witchcraft movement, or Wicca. Charles Godfrey Leland's *Aradia,* one of the source books of the movement, contains a passage commanding the witches to eat "cakes of meal, wine, salt and honey in the shape of a crescent or horned moon."[7]

The theme of the moon was also addressed by my wife, Dr. Donate McIntosh (then Donate Pahnke), in an article of 2001:

> The moon is perhaps the most important symbol of the witchcraft religion, and because she is the personification of the Goddess, who reveals herself in the moonlight, there are often protests against the fact that the moon has a masculine gender in German grammar. . . . In the witchcraft religion the moon is above all the planet of women. In tune with her rhythms they menstruate and complete in the womb the magical cycle of three times three to create new life. In the classical form of the witch religion the priestess, at the opening of the ritual, draws down the lunar power into herself and the circle, so that it is active in all present.[8]

Modern witchcraft was an idea whose time had come, and it came from various sources. One was the above-mentioned book *Aradia, or the Gospel of the Witches of Italy,* written by the American antiquarian and folklorist Charles Godfrey Leland and published in 1899. Another was a work titled *The Witch Cult in Western Europe* by the English archaeologist Margaret Murray (1921). But the person who turned witchcraft from an idea into a system of practice was a retired English colonial civil servant named Gerald Gardner (1884–1964), author of a work titled *Witchcraft Today* and founder of a witches' coven that soon turned into a wider movement. Gardnerian witchcraft, or Wicca as it is usually called, is a bricolage of elements taken from Freemasonry, Golden Dawn magic, Leland's *Aradia,* and other sources. It has three grades of initiation and worships two deities: the Goddess of the Moon and the Horned God of the Sun. The Goddess is the most important of the two, and in a coven the leading role is played by a High Priestess, although the Wicca membership is drawn from both sexes.

Because of its emphasis on the Goddess and privileging of the female principle, witchcraft soon attracted members of the women's movement on both sides of the Atlantic. My friend the late Frederic Lamond, who had been in Wicca for most of his life, told me how American feminists were struck by a special kind of self-confidence and inner strength evinced by women who had participated in British covens. Soon there was a thriving American witchcraft movement and a commensurate flurry of books such as Margot Adler's *Drawing Down the Moon* (1979) and Starhawk's *The Spiral Dance* (1979). Starhawk (Miriam Simos) went on to cofound a movement called Reclaiming, which practices a universal, Goddess-oriented type of spirituality combined with a pacifist and ecological agenda.

In Germany the witchcraft movement fell on ripe soil among feminists, as shown by the enormous success of the Hamburg exhibition and conference. They began to practice their own form of witchcraft, independently from the Gardnerian Wicca movement transmitted from England. The horrific witch persecutions of the fifteenth to seventeenth centuries were part of the German collective memory, the traditionally patriarchal order in the country was only slowly changing, and many women were tired of the authoritarian male God of the established churches. To many it came as a life-changing revelation that there was a great Goddess who could speak to them at a deep level. Various groups, large and small, were formed to celebrate the Goddess and perform rituals. American practitioners such as Starhawk and Z. Budapest visited Germany to hold workshops and spread the word. Starhawk's Reclaiming movement was an important influence in these developments. Typically, in the early days its meetings and camps were restricted to women, but later, like many similar initiatives, it was opened up to both sexes. Meanwhile the Gardnerian movement, Wicca, which had always been androgynous, gathered its own following and established covens and pub moots throughout the country.

CLOSER TO HOME

So far in dealing with neo-paganism, I have talked much about ideas and movements imported from abroad. But what about homegrown pre-Christian traditions and the gods of the old Germanic pantheon? Here once again we come up against the Nazi elephant in the room. Removing an elephant from the mind—especially the mind of a nation—is a mighty labor, and I shall not try to do so but merely to keep the elephant in its correct perspective:

> *Tausend Jahre mussten wir schweigen,*
> *Durften Göttertreu' nicht zeigen.*
> *Tausendfach erklingt der Ruf erneut:*
> *Kommt zurück, wir sind bereit!*

> *(For a thousand years we had to be silent,*
> *Forbidden to show our loyalty to the gods.*
> *A thousandfold the call resounds:*
> *Come back, we are ready!)*

This is one of the songs that is often sung around the bonfire at gatherings of the Asatru religion; that is, the religion that honors the old Germanic gods. The name Asatru was adopted by the nascent Nordic pagan movement in Iceland in the 1970s (it means "loyalty to the Aesir," one of the two groups of gods in the Norse mythology, the Aesir and the Vanir) and quickly spread to other countries. In Germany there was a small postwar survival of some of the Germanic pagan groups from before the war, but essentially it was a new wave that carried the movement forward along with the New Age, the esoteric boom, and the pagan revival in general. While some people joined witchcraft groups or followed Eastern gurus, others felt a yearning to reconnect with the pre-Christian traditions of the Germanic world.

The mainstream media often convey a crude stereotype of the Germanic pagan—a Thor-hammer-swinging, mead-swilling barbarian, like a caricature of a Viking from the Asterix or Hagar comics. But this type of person is not characteristic. Over the years, I have known numerous Asatru followers, and they include as many people of high intelligence and education as in any religious community. Some years ago I became friendly with a married couple, both doctors, who had come to Asatru after a long search. Helmut (name altered) was born in Leipzig in the German Democratic Republic, lived for a time in a rural part of Brandenburg, then went to Berlin, where he studied physics and later medicine. His wife, Astrid (name altered), also grew up in the GDR and studied medicine at Magdeburg. After the reunification of Germany they moved to the west, but eventually settled back in the former GDR, where they continued to practice medicine and also embarked on a spiritual search.

"At some point in life," Helmut explained to me, "one feels the need to orient oneself spiritually. Our search took us far and wide—to India, Indonesia, and other places. We explored Hinduism, Buddhism, and other religions. Then we felt it was time to look closer to home. As the poet Goethe put it: '*Willst du immer weiter schweifen? Sieh, das Gute liegt so nah*' [Do you really wish to roam ever further afield?

Just look, the good is so near at hand]. We heard that an event called the International Asatru Summer Camp was going to take place in Denmark, and we signed up for it. The camp made a very positive impression on us, and we decided that this was going to be our path."

This led to their becoming active members of one of the German Asatru organizations. If you ask a cross-section of people of the Asatru persuasion why they chose to follow that particular path you will be given a variety of answers, of which the following are, in my experience, some of the most common:

- The need to connect or reconnect with one's ancient ancestral and regional traditions as opposed to those that have been imported from elsewhere. One comment that I have often heard from newcomers to Asatru or other forms of paganism, when speaking of their first experience of a ritual, is that "it was like coming home."
- The heathen conception of the gods. Instead of the single, authoritarian God of monotheism, the heathen religion posits many gods and goddesses. These do not reside in some remote heavenly realm but are present in the world, in nature, and in ourselves in the form of the different facets of our being. Heathens do not prostrate themselves humbly before the gods but instead treat them as old friends, family members, and wise elders who are there to give inspiration and guidance.
- The primacy of experience over belief. Asatru, like paganism generally, is not a religion of belief but of experience. One experiences certain forces and qualities in one's daily life and identifies them with different deities—courage and self-sacrifice with Tyr, forcefulness and strength with Thor, wisdom and eloquence with Odin.
- There are no dogmas and no claim to a unique truth, only an inherited body of tradition, mythology, and practice.
- The heathen has direct access to the gods and therefore needs no ordained priest as an intermediary. A person may have a leading

role in a ritual by virtue of seniority or experience, but they do not thereby have any claim to superiority.

Having said that, there are some groups that have their dominant personalities and their self-appointed guru figures who claim special authority in interpreting dharma, but they do not reflect the general spirit of the religion; nor do the few groups with far-right leanings, although sections of the popular media are always eager to perceive a fascist behind every heathen bush.

PROSPECTS FOR GERMAN PAGANISM

One of my most helpful interlocutors for this book was Gudrun Pannier, an information technology specialist living in Berlin who is prominent in the pagan scene and has been active in outreach to other religious communities. Gudrun gave me a highly interesting account of her journey to paganism and her views on its prospects in Germany.

She was born in 1965 in Bitterfeld, Saxony-Anhalt, in the German Democratic Republic, where her father was a technician in a factory making film for cameras, and her mother had a private practice as a ballroom dancing teacher—an anomaly in the GDR. The area was heavily polluted by the chemical industry and brown coal extraction. There was acid rainfall, smog hanging over the meadows, and the rivers were stained a sickly yellow. Even as a teenager she was upset by these conditions and felt sympathy for the nature that was being so abused all around her. She began to look for some source of meaning in life but did not find it in the official communist ideology, which she found utterly empty and lacking in any depth or substance.

At the age of sixteen she became a member of the Evangelical Church and joined an environmental group under its auspices. She became friendly with the pastor, and, being an avid reader, she was able to make full use of his enormous library. At his house she took part in lively and fascinating discussions on theology, philosophy, and much else. She also volunteered to give conducted tours of the church, explaining its various symbols to the visitors.

She duly graduated from high school but was refused a university place in the state system because of her nonconformity to the official norms. However, there were three independent theological colleges run by the church where she could study, provided she obtained a stipendium. After working for a year in a mission to the homeless (who officially did not exist in the GDR), she obtained the necessary stipendium and embarked on a theology degree at a church college in Berlin. She looks back on her time there as a thrilling experience. There were only 140 students, divided into small groups, so the atmosphere was intimate. The college had a wonderful library where she often used to read until it closed at midnight, and there she came into contact with books on the occult. The first one she remembers reading was Éliphas Lévi's *History of Magic*. She went on to read about Greek mythology, numerology, witchcraft, and the like, and through the Jewish library of the Oranienburg synagogue she had access to books on the Kabbalah. She recalls having great teachers, many of them very devout, and all of them decent and upright people.

When she was twenty-four the Berlin Wall fell. Shortly after that she graduated, left the church, and moved to West Berlin, where she found a job in information technology and studied psychology part time. In search of a belief system that honored a female deity and not simply the male God of monotheism, she looked for kindred spirits and discovered the Berlin pagan scene. She attended meetings and pub moots (*Stammtische* in German) where she met shamans, Wiccans, Druids, people from the Asatru heathen movement, and those who worshiped the Celtic pantheon, and she began to participate in the rituals of various groups. At first nothing very dramatic happened at these gatherings. Then, one day, she took part in an Asatru ritual in a forest, where she invoked the Nordic god Thor and a young Norwegian invoked the goddess Freya. She vividly recalls that the moment she spoke the invocation "something went *zing!*" There was a massive thunderstorm and torrential rain that soaked them to the skin. As she put it, "The Nordic gods had contacted me!"

She went on to join the Pagan Federation International and for a time was on its executive group. She has often been a spokesperson for the pagan movement and has interacted with other religious communities through events such as the Long Night of Religions in Berlin. She has friendly relations with members of a body called the Evangelische Zentralstelle für Weltanschauungsfragen (Evangelical Central Office for Questions of Worldview). They welcome interlocutors from other religious communities, but at the present time the German Pagans are too disunited for anyone to able to be able to speak for the community as a whole. Looking to the future, Gudrun hopes that Pagans will develop more mutual tolerance and more cooperation. "By working together," she says, "we can achieve much."

14

SPIRIT AND MATTER

In optics, my Brother, inconceivable things still lie hidden,
undreamt of by our physicists. Just think of the concave
mirror! But all this is only a hint that ought to lead the
researcher to higher truths.

KARL VON ECKARTSHAUSEN, *MYSTISCHE NÄCHTE*
(MYSTICAL NIGHTS), 1791

What is the connection between concave mirrors, shamanism, quantum
physics, telepathy, and the Rosicrucians? To find the answer one must
follow the history of the characteristically German strain of thought
that I have already drawn attention to—namely, the worldview that
perceives the sacred within physical matter, in contrast to the common
Christian tendency to separate spirit and matter and privilege the former, or the modern scientific tendency to perceive only the latter. As I
have shown earlier, this strain is present in Hildegard of Bingen and the
alchemists and continues through Goethe and Steiner right up to the
present day. It is a strain that is found particularly strongly in Germany,
Russia, and, to some extent, Britain, and surely constitutes one of the
most important benefits that these countries can offer to the world.

My "book angel" drew my attention to the above remark by the

Bavarian mystic Karl von Eckartshausen just as I was researching a device called the Kozyrev mirror, which was named after the Russian physicist Nikolai Kozyrev (1908–1983) but developed by two research scientists, Vlail Kaznacheev and Alexander Trofimov, at the International Institute for Scientific Research in Cosmo-Planetary Anthropoecology (ISRICA) in Akademgorodok, Siberia.[1] It continues to arouse great interest there and among certain scientists in Germany. The properties of concave mirrors for concentrating sunlight and for other purposes have been known for many centuries, and the Rosicrucian text called the *Fama Fraternitatis* mentions "mirrors of various good properties" that were discovered among other objects in the burial vault of Christian Rosenkreuz.[2] Possibly, therefore, the Russian scientists accessed an ancient technology and took it a stage further.

The mirror usually consists of a cylinder of polished aluminum large enough for a person to stand in, or lie in if the cylinder is placed horizontally. These mirrors appear to have extraordinary properties, including enabling thought transference between two people in different locations, each ensconced in a Kozyrev mirror. The mirrors can apparently heal sickness, create time warps, and induce something akin to the altered states of consciousness known to shamans, in which the user can access information from the past and predict future events. They can also have the effect of triggering strange physical phenomena such as lights that swirl and flicker across the sky.

As to how these mirrors function, each individual evidently has the innate capacity to attain cosmic consciousness, but this capacity is inhibited by the Earth's electromagnetic field. The mirror has the effect of weakening the field, thus enabling an expansion of consciousness to take place. Similarly there appear to be certain places on the planet, such as the Altai region of Siberia, where the electromagnetic field is weaker, which might account for the prevalence of shamanism in those regions.

The Kozyrev mirror features in an article on morphogenetic fields by the German scientist Waltraud Wagner, published in the magazine

Tattva Viveka in 2000.[3] Waltraud Wagner writes that the notion of morphogenetic fields is normally associated with the British scientist Rupert Sheldrake, but in fact the concept is older and was investigated by the German biologist Hans Driesch and the Russian Alexander Gurwitsch. Sheldrake apparently relied on a 1922 work by Gurwitsch, but the latter went on to discover what he called mitogenetic radiation, which then became the basis of research into biophotons (units of light emitted from living organisms) by the German biophysicist Fritz-Albert Popp (1938–2018). Popp is considered one of the pioneers of a holistic approach to biophysics. In a tribute to Popp on the occasion of his seventieth birthday, his fellow scientist Marco Bischoff wrote of Popp's approach:

> It is based, as one of the most fundamental aspects, on a field-oriented picture of the organism. This acts as a corrective to the . . . disconnected fragmentation of the biosciences by the dominating trend of molecular biology, and provides again a chance for developing a unifying picture of life and holistic life sciences. Together with many other recent developments in the biosciences, the results of biophoton research constitute one of the major contributions to an emerging new, holistic and comprehensive picture of life based on quantum physics.[4]

Popp's work was complemented in England by the German Jewish emigré Herbert Fröhlich (1905–1991) and his collaborator, Cyril Smith (1930–2022). The insight that all of the above-mentioned scientists shared was that objects in the physical world are not simply collections of molecules and atoms but possess fields of energy that give them their properties and interact with other energy fields. Not only living organisms but all objects have such fields. Once you take this field-based approach to the world it becomes clear why dowsing and homeopathy work, why certain sites like Stonehenge or the Externsteine can have a spiritual and psychological influence. It also explains how the outcome of an alchemical operation is affected by the state of mind of the alchemist.

The action of invisible fields has been known under different names for a very long time. It is the "animal magnetism" of Franz Anton Mesmer, who used it for healing purposes. Another person who hit on it was the German industrialist and inventor Karl von Reichenbach (1788–1869). After building up a highly successful career in industry he began in his late fifties, under the influence of the nature philosophy movement of the eighteenth century, to research what we would now call energy fields. He identified a radiation emitted by humans and animals as well as plants and mineral substances that could be perceived in the dark like an aura by people with the necessary sensitivity. He named this the "od" or "odic force," probably adopting the old Germanic word *od* or *ad,* meaning "happiness" or "blessing" (in northern Germany the dialect word for *stork,* "the bringer of children," is *Adebar,* "carrier of happiness," but possibly also means "bearer of the life force"). It may also be related to the old German word *Odem,* meaning "breath." This force, Reichenbach said, permeates the entire universe and explains phenomena such as telepathy and hypnosis. Unfortunately the science of his time had not yet developed the sensors that are available today, and most of the scientific establishment rejected Reichenbach's findings, much to his deep disappointment, although he found much support in the Spiritualist movement.

An even harsher treatment was experienced by the physician Wilhelm Reich (1897–1957). Born in a province of Austria-Hungary, he studied medicine in Vienna and started to practice psychoanalysis according to the system newly developed by Sigmund Freud. Soon he developed his own approach, focusing on how blockages of sexual energy could cause physical ailments. He conceived the sexual force, which he called orgone energy, as a radiation. In other words, he was essentially talking about the same thing as Mesmer and Reichenbach but focusing specifically on the sexual aspect of it. Nevertheless, he can be considered as following in the same German tradition of holistic thought. After practicing in Vienna and Berlin, he left Germany after the Nazi seizure of power in 1933 and, after spending time in Denmark and Norway, moved to the United States, where he experimented with orgone energy and invented what he called an orgone accumulator. The usual design is a heavily insulated cabin about the size of a telephone booth. The idea is that when someone sits inside the cabin they experience a vitalizing and healing effect from the accumulated orgone energy. Tragically, Reich was prosecuted for fraud by the American Food and Drug Administration and sentenced to two years in a federal prison, where he died of a heart attack. His work, however, is continued by his followers all over the world. His orgone accumulator can perhaps be seen as sort of cousin to the Kozyrev mirror.

Today there are various different systems of treatment based on the notion of omnipresent fields of radiation. Some commonly used terms are quantum healing, energy medicine, and information medicine. The alternative medicine community in Germany and internationally has eagerly embraced this general approach. One of its proponents in Germany is Marcus Schmieke (born 1966), author of many books, developer of a diagnostic system called Time-Waver, and founder of the Veden Academy, a center for training courses, seminars, and lectures, located in a splendid country house in the state of Brandenburg.

Meanwhile alchemy remains alive and well in Germany. As mentioned earlier, there are a number of firms producing spagyric (alchemical) medicines. Long ridiculed by scientists, the ancient knowledge of the alchemists and their remedies is coming into its own again. Doctors and healing practitioners are reporting astonishing successes with chronic conditions that even orthodox medicine considers difficult to heal.

What the alchemists and the above-mentioned scientists have in common is the view that we are part of a greater whole, in which everything is connected, so that a change to any part means that everything else changes as well, not only on the physical level but also on the mental level. This view runs counter to the prevailing social and economic system. To adopt it would mean rejecting experimentation on animals, factory farming, gene manipulation, pesticides, and pollution of the environment.

"In Germany and the Western world in general field theory has been pushed aside by particle physics and molecular biology Why? . . . because it is not in the interests of large-scale industry." Furthermore, scientists are accustomed to seeing a dichotomy between the particle theory and the wave theory of matter and do not realize that particles and waves are two sides of all physical phenomena.[5]

15

SOUL OF THE LANDSCAPE

In the summer of 1998, I visited friends in the village of Trabenig in Carinthia, Austria, and we spent a day exploring the nearby town of Villach, where the great alchemist Paracelsus spent his childhood in a house that bears a plaque in his honor. In a square in the town center there was a stone pillar with an intriguing carved motif: a circular recess in which was a stylized bird above a triangle between what looked like two leaves or petals. I learned that this is one of twelve similar works in the town, created by the Slovenian artist and geomancer Marko Pogačnik (born 1944). What Pogačnik practices is a kind of Earth acupuncture that he calls lithopuncture (from the Greek *lithos,* meaning "stone"). It works on the principle that the Earth has lines of energy like the acupuncture meridians in the human body. These Earth meridians are often referred to as ley lines, the term used by the British researcher Alfred Watkins (1855–1935). Lithopuncture involves placing megaliths at critical points on these lines on the same principle that the acupuncturist inserts needles into the skin. The purpose in both cases is to bring about a harmonious flow of energy. Each of Pogačnik's megaliths is carved with an image that he calls a cosmogram, a visual and tactile design intended to resonate with the energies of the spot where it is placed.

Pogačnik's lithopuncture has evidently produced some impressive results. A year after the completion of his project in Villach, the mayor of the town called a meeting to get reactions to the project from the citizens, who overwhelmingly responded positively. Apparently at one dangerous crossing in the town the number of traffic accidents had been significantly reduced. Equally remarkable were the results of a project carried out by Pogačnik at Türnich Castle, an imposing moated property in the Rhineland. By the 1980s the estate had fallen into a sorry condition through neglect, vandalism, and falling groundwater levels. Trees were dying, and birds and other wildlife were much reduced. As part of a comprehensive restoration project, Pogačnik was commissioned by the owner to carry out his lithopuncture treatment, and within a year or so the results were apparent. Trees and other vegetation were recovering, wildlife was increasing, and vandalism had mysteriously decreased.[1]

Pogačnik's work in the German-speaking world is symptomatic of a general upsurge of interest in geomancy there. Of course, geomancy under different names has been practiced since prehistoric times, when megalith builders aligned their constructions with the movements of the heavenly bodies and with lines of force running through the Earth. Over time, these practices died out in Europe, save for a few scattered remnants here and there, but in China geomancy, or feng shui as it is called there (meaning "wind and water"), remained alive and well, and eventually word of it began to find its way to Europe. At the same time, European researchers began to discover their own native versions of feng shui.

In Germany it has taken some time to come to terms with the memory of the way in which geomancy was pursued in the Third Reich and the period leading up to it. But today feng shui and geomancy are thriving in Germany, as the following examples will illustrate.

GEOMANCY IN AN ARTISTS' COLONY

Worpswede is a name to conjure with—a beautiful little town in Lower Saxony that came to fame in the late nineteenth and early twentieth century as an artists' colony whose members included painters like Fritz Mackensen, Otto Modersohn, Paula Modersohn-Becker, and Heinrich Vogeler. Something about the landscape fascinated them—flat, rather sleepy moorland, stretching to the end of the world, little clusters of silver birches, old thatched farmhouses, canals that were dug long ago to make the land suitable for cultivation. It all has a sort of agreeable melancholy, like a bittersweet tune. The town lies between the moorland and a hill called the Weyerberg, the only one for many miles, which rises gently to the splendid height of 54.4 meters (172 feet). Today Worpswede still has a thriving artists' community.

One of the paths up the Weyerberg brings you to a clearing in the trees where suddenly a strange and forbidding monument looms up against the sky—a vast eagle made of red brick, crouching with wings folded and shoulders raised. This is the Niedersachsenstein (Stone of the Lower Saxons), a war memorial of the 1920s designed by the sculptor and architect Bernhard Hoetger. The geomancer, the late Harald Jordan, who lived in Worpswede, saw this monument as preserving an equilibrium between dark and light, positive and negative:

> Every high-energy point needs an opposite pole. In Asia they used to take this into account in the building of every temple by including a small temple specially for the great adversary. . . . In our Western culture we do not have this wise practice. So, in order to create a balance of forces, such a point will often appear of its own accord or through human agency, albeit unconsciously.[2]

This, he writes, is what happened in Worpswede with the Niedersachsenstein. Until it was built, the spot was energetically neutral. Through the building of the monument, a dynamic was introduced on a subtle level. During the planning phase there was a fierce quarrel about the project, and the tension was projected on to the site. It is not

Fig. 15.1. The Niedersachsenstein (Stone of the Lower Saxons) at Worpswede, designed by Bernhard Hoetger and built in 1922 as a war memorial.
WIKIMEDIA COMMONS. PHOTOGRAPH BY C. LÖSER.

a place that invites one to sit down and have a jolly picnic. Nevertheless, as Harald Jordan writes, "This spot, precisely because it partakes of the 'shadow side,' is part of the vital balance of the surrounding area and the breath of the landscape."[3]

Harald Jordan saw Worpswede as a place full of polarities: the hill emphasizing the surrounding wide horizons, the dark moor and the bright silver birches, the quiet wilderness and the noisy streets. All of these things and more are what give the place its special energy, and Harald Jordan's specialty was studying such energies and working with them.

Harald lived in a picturesque, half-timbered former farm building on the edge of Worpswede, where a number of artists have their studios. He came to geomancy by a roundabout route. After training as a builder and then earning an engineering degree, he set up his own business as an engineer, prospered, and made a good income. After going through a personal crisis, he spent a period in retreat in the Tyrol and began to develop an interest in geomancy and radiesthesia (dowsing), which he learned from the architect, author, and geomancer Eicke Hensch. After a period as an engineer specializing in the care and restoration of historic monuments, he focused increasingly on developing his own approach to geomancy and on transmitting his knowledge through books, lectures, and seminars.

In his book *Räume der Kraft schaffen* (Creating Spaces of Power), he writes:

> For our forebears building was a spiritual act. If we wish to learn from them—and it is time that we reconnected with their knowledge—then we need to project ourselves into their worldview . . . how they identified directly with the elements and honored the earth; and how they regarded the building of a house as a creative act, a repetition of the divine creation. Not a single stone was laid without tuning in to the divine, for every place of true healing power is a godly place.[4]

Harald adopts what he calls an "analogical" approach to geomancy; that is to say, one based on analogies or correspondences between different levels of reality—between the cosmos and the individual, above and below, inner and outer. These correspondences are expressed in images and symbols. A good example is the classical concept of the four elements: earth, water, air, and fire, which correspond to four states of matter (solid, liquid, gaseous, and plasmic) and four temperaments in human beings (melancholic, phlegmatic, sanguine, and choleric). Harald writes:

The strengthening and harmonizing of the elements is the key factor for healthy and wholesome living and building. Here the input of the individual consciousness is important, for all elements influence each other or offset each other like water and fire. Through the power of the individual soul the elements in the human body are held in place and made vital.[5]

Astrology, sacred geometry, and dowsing are some of the other systems that Harald Jordan used in his geomantic work. An important stage in his career was his participation in Hagia Chora, a teaching initiative in the field of geomancy and sacred landscape architecture, cofounded in the mid-1990s by Marko Pogačnik and others. For some years there was a related journal, also under the name *Hagia Chora* (Sacred Landscape), which unfortunately ceased publication after about a decade and a half, but the back copies remain a goldmine of information about geomancy and related matters.

Christiane Fink, a landscape architect who devotes part of her time to giving courses and workshops with Hagia Chora, told me how she came to geomancy. While studying landscape architecture she began to feel restricted by the way the course focused solely on form and function and left out the subtler levels of reality. After completing her studies, she took a course with Hagia Chora and eventually became a member of the teaching team. She observes a strong increase of interest in geomancy and related things, shown by the growing demand for the regional workshops given by members of the Hagia Chora team. When dealing with mainstream landscape architects she often finds that they are prejudiced against her geomantic work, but sometimes she is able to open their minds a little.

DANCING NATURE SPIRITS

In 2004 my wife and I moved into a 1960s terrace house in Bremen with a tiny front garden and a back garden measuring about forty feet by twenty feet. When we took it over, the garden was basically a rectangle with straight flower beds on either side, so the energy simply shot through it in a straight line. In the middle was a rectangular lawn in very bad condition, which we almost never used. We replaced the lawn with a paved area, enlarged the beds, and rounded off the borders, immediately causing the energy to flow in curves rather than in a straight line. Symbolically the garden revolved around the sun, moon, compass directions, and elements. The focal point was a sundial that we had made as a wedding present by the stonemason Frank Graupner, with symbols for the elements and compass directions carved in relief on the sides. On the south side of the garden we placed a stone obelisk—in Roman tradition symbolizing a solidified ray of sunlight. Other features were introduced for earth, water, and air. The curving flower beds gave the garden the shape of a crescent moon to complement the solar-lunar theme.

At that time I ran a small folk-dancing group in Bremen, and one afternoon we held a session in the garden, performing English and German folk dances, much to the delight of the neighbors, who remarked how beautiful they found the folk music. I believe the spirits of place were also pleased that the garden was being used for something other than a grill party. If they were listening, they must have found the music more congenial than hard rock or heavy metal, and maybe they were dancing along with us.

That might sound far-fetched, but something similar is reported by the ethnobotanist and anthropologist Wolf-Dieter Storl in his book *Pflanzendevas* (Plant Devas). He recalls working for a time in the gardens of the Aigues Vertes village in Switzerland, a community set up under the Anthroposophical movement to work with mentally handicapped people and assist their integration into society. Storl writes:

> The gardeners often held spontaneous festivities in the garden arbour . . . with live music and swirling dances of a kind that one doesn't learn in dancing schools. These parties were often so wild

and abandoned that it was as though Pan himself were playing his magic flute. Only later did I realize that it was not only the gardeners who were dancing and singing. The nature spirits and elemental beings always took part as well. . . . Mild nights of bright moonlight were what they liked best.[6]

16

OCCULT GERMANY TODAY

In the first chapter I looked at Heidelberg, where famous avatars of learning like Max Weber used to rub shoulders with poets and alchemists as well as anthropologists and theologians. Can that kind of rich interchange still be found today in the Germanic world of learning? Before attempting an answer, let me take a look at the treatment of occult and esoteric subjects in the wider academic world.

Where the occultists, magicians, alchemists, New Age followers, and neo-pagans boldly went, the scholars eventually followed like explorers cautiously entering a jungle, protected by pith helmets and armed with binoculars to observe the natives at a safe distance—that is, except for those explorers who had "gone native," to the disapproval of their colleagues. At first there were only a few daring pioneers like Frances Yates at the Warburg Institute in London and Antoine Faivre at the Sorbonne in Paris, as well as some dedicated scholars outside academe. Then gradually other universities and colleges began to establish courses and programs in Western esotericism, to use the now widely accepted term for the field. I, myself, was part of such a program at the University of Exeter, led by Professor Nicholas Goodrick-Clarke, which ended in 2012 following Nicholas's untimely death. Another such program, founded around the same time, is in the History of Hermetic Philosophy and Related Currents at the University of Amsterdam under Professor Wouter Hanegraaff. Scholarly associations were also founded, such as the European Society for the Study of Western Esotericism and the American Society for the Study of Esotericism.

Curiously, the German-speaking world, despite its rich esoteric history, has been slow to follow suit. This is partly because of the Nazi elephant in the room and its association with irrationality. Many German scholars shy away from anything they deem to be irrational and regard themselves as having a mission to defend the Enlightenment principles of rationality and progress and are unwilling even to consider esotericism as a legitimate field of study. This situation is now gradually changing and a number of excellent scholars have entered the field, but there is still a long way to go.

One person who, although outside official academe, has made a towering contribution to the study of Western esotericism is the Austrian Hans Thomas Hakl (born 1947), who has played an important role in my own esoteric adventure. I first met Thomas at the Frankfurt Book Fair in the 1990s. We became friends and subsequently I visited him several times at his home in Graz, where he had constructed a purpose-built library, the Octagon, housing his remarkable book collection focusing on esoterica, one of the largest such private collections in the world. I also translated into English the bulk of his definitive book on the Eranos meetings at Ascona, *Eranos an Alternative Intellectual History of the Twentieth Century,* and I contributed to the collection of essays commemorating the library, which was published in four volumes in 2015–2018 under the title *Octagon*. His own contribution to the collection is an autobiographical essay in which he reflects on his life and the creation of his library.

He recalls how even as a teenager he was an avid reader of works like Lobsang Rampa's *The Third Eye*. Later he graduated to Emil Dürkheim, Alan Watts, D. T. Suzuki. C. G. Jung, and Mircea Eliade. As a student he became acquainted with Professor Adolf Hemberger (alias Dr. Klingsor), whose book *Experimentalmagie* aroused in him a fascination with magical orders, and he set out to acquire all the works cited there, assisted by Hemberger himself. His search led him on to other collectors and occultists like Oskar Schlag of Zürich and Hermann Metzger, head of the Swiss OTO (Ordo Templi Orientis) with its large library at Stein in the Appenzell Canton. He cast his net wider, to booksellers and auction houses in England, France, Italy, and the United States. He recalls that "the most important auction in the field of alchemy and occultism in Germany took place in autumn of 1998 at Ziska and Kistner in Munich. Half the world gathered there and incredibly high prices were fetched."[1] At the same time he was building up a highly successful import-export business, which he eventually sold, enabling him to build an annex to his house to accommodate the library. The building itself is full of symbolism. The design is based on Castel del Monte, a mysterious fortress in Apulia, southern Italy, built in octagonal form by the Hohenstaufen emperor Frederick II, eight being the number of resurrection, heavenly perfection, and the super-planetary sphere. To quote his own description of the building:

> Characteristic of this library are the high, narrow windows in every part of the octagon. Not only do they increase the incident light, they also lend the entire room a certain sacral "touch." A view onto the "heavens" is opened up by a small glass cupola, which corresponds to a gilded disc on the floor: thus whoever glances down into the reflective disc looks up into "heaven." As above, so below.[2]

Arrangements have been made for the library eventually to be taken under the wing of the Giorgio Cini Foundation with premises on an island in the Venice lagoon.

Thomas has also been involved in various esoteric publishing firms, and in 1995, together with Hildegard and Wolfram

Fig. 16.1. Entrance to the Octagon, the esoteric library
created by Thomas Hakl in Graz, Austria. (See also color plate 8.)

PHOTOGRAPH BY THE AUTHOR.

Frietsch, he founded a German-language publishing enterprise called Archiv für Altes Gedankengut und Wissen (AAGW) (Archive for Ancient Thought and Knowledge). Its output includes the journal *Gnostika,* a highly unusual periodical in that it encompasses the world of the scholar as well as that of the practitioner. Also for a time, AAGW published finely produced reprints of rare esoteric texts. This became no longer viable with the advent of the internet.

Like Thomas Hakl, I am the sort of bibliophile who appreciates books both for their content and for their aesthetic quality. My researches have taken me to wonderful libraries and bookshops in London, Paris, Munich, Vienna, and other cities. Those were the days when I was willing to travel halfway across Europe to consult books that I can now read online and usually gratis. For me, as a writer on esotericism, my visits to those libraries and bookshops were themselves part of an esoteric quest. Sometimes I had the feeling of stepping in to one of those novels where the hero wanders into an occult secondhand bookshop and has a life-changing encounter. Although such shops still exist here and there, since the arrival of the internet, book hunting is not what it was.

THE INTERNET AS
A MINIATURE WORLD

Sometimes I like to playfully suggest that the *minutus mundus,* the miniature world that the Rosicrucian brethren discovered in the burial vault of Christian Rosenkreuz, was in fact a computer connected to the internet. I made this idea the subject of a short story called *The Meyerbeck Manuscript,* set in the seventeenth century and narrated by one of the brethren who comes into possession of the object.[3] Another story, titled "Tlön, Uqbar, Orbis Tertius," by one of my favorite writers, the Argentinian Jorge Luis Borges, describes a group of people, clearly based on the Rosicrucians, who decide to create an imaginary world that they call Tlön. They proceed to circulate descriptions of this world and artifacts seemingly made there, so that people become more and more fascinated by Tlön, and gradually the real world starts to imitate the imaginary one.[4] Supposing for a moment that the internet is indeed a Rosicrucian invention, I wonder what those original brothers would think if they were to be reincarnated in the present age and witness what the internet has become. I believe they would see both negative and positive aspects.

On the negative side, apart from the obvious dangers of criminality, fraud, and dissemination of lies, there is, as I have said, the loss of the feeling of adventure and quest that the book seeker used to experience. And there is a loss of a sense of mystery and secrecy when you can enter a magical temple online, watch a video of a ritual, and even take part in one. There is also a tendency toward trivialization and superficiality in the domain of social media. When people's attention span is the length of a sound bite, they are apt to lose the ability to read in depth, which is called for when dealing with esoteric material. With English being the standard medium on the internet there is a danger of the erosion and corruption of languages like German, which is such a key medium for esoteric studies. Even the notion of nationality is becoming eroded. When I am sitting at my computer there is a sense in which I am not in a specific country called Germany but rather in the "Nowhere Land" of cyberspace or in any one of a number of virtual worlds that I can access. On the positive side, the internet has enabled one, however obscure one's interests may be, to interact with kindred spirits all over the world, whether on a personal level or through the specialized groups on social media platforms or in online conferences. Furthermore, one has access to an unlimited quantity of material—books, images, films, podcasts—and one can attend distance-learning courses on an almost endless variety of subjects.

Borges ends his story by saying that "a scattered dynasty of solitary men has changed the face of the world."[5] If we replace Tlön with the internet, then the story becomes curiously prescient.

"OCCULTURE" IN GERMANY

Turning to the question of the interface between culture and the occult or esoteric domain in Germany, how much remains today of the rich heritage that I have described in earlier chapters? In the field of the visual arts, one looks in vain for the present-day counterparts of Albrecht Dürer, Caspar David Friedrich, or Friedrich Otto Runge. One reason for this is what I would call the "progressivist" paradigm, which says that the artist should not refer back to tradition but should always try to move forward and break new ground. Provoke, startle, challenge—these are the watchwords of the present-day arts establishment in Germany and elsewhere.

Some German artists have attempted to combine this approach with esoteric themes. For example, in 1969 the artist Sigmar Poppe (1941–2010) created a work consisting of a large white rectangle with the top right-hand corner filled by a black triangle and with a typewritten sentence across the lower part of the picture saying, *"Höhere Wesen befahlen: rechte obere Ecke schwarz malen"* (Higher beings commanded: paint the upper right-hand corner black).[6] Another German artist, Joseph Beuys (1921–1986), was influenced by Rudolf Steiner and incorporated some Anthroposophical motifs into his art, but these are exceptions to the mainly secular nature of the German arts establishment. By contrast, in the domain of popular and commercial art it is possible to find much exciting and imaginative work featuring esoteric themes—comics, posters, book covers, CD covers, website designs, and multimedia creations such as virtual worlds and settings for interactive computer games.

In the sphere of music, we do not find the modern equivalents of Mozart's *Magic Flute* or Wagner's *Ring*. As for the world of popular music, there are many bands that like to épater les bourgeois by flaunting a "satanic" image or filling their performances with references to Aleister Crowley's Thelema and the like. What I find more interesting is the music that is being produced by bands of the pagan folk genre, such as the remarkable Bavarian group Faun, founded in 1998, which has created an inimitable sound by combining time-honored instruments—Celtic harp, lute, bagpipes, and others—with modern electronic amplification. The songs are sometimes soft and wistful, sometimes loud and percussive but always hypnotic. They are sung in a variety of languages, including modern German, medieval German, Old Norse, Latin, Hungarian, and Finnish, and they reflect the group's pagan, nature-oriented form of spirituality, which draws heavily on the *Edda* and Northern mythology. The same spirit is evident in their beautifully filmed videos. In a similar genre is Heilung (Healing), a German-Danish-Norwegian group founded in 2014. Their video performances, which are like shamanic rituals, are carried out in forest clearings or amid ancient megaliths, and the music has a haunting, incantatory quality. Altogether heavier in style is Skaldenmet, a group of the "Viking metal" category, founded in Hamburg in 2015. The name of the group means "mead of poetry" and refers to a story in the *Edda* about how the mead was created.

These groups answer to a longing that many Germans feel for the mythic and the epic, a longing that has led to the enormous popularity of the stories of J. K. Rowling and J. R. R. Tolkien. Sadly, it is hard to find equivalents of these in modern German literature, although one outstanding exception is Michael Ende's brilliant novel *The Neverending Story* about a boy who starts to read a fairy tale and finds that he himself is a character in the story and can influence events in the narrative.

GERMANY, WHAT OF THE NIGHT?

These words appear in Algernon Charles Swinburne's poem *A Watch in the Night,* published in 1871. The poet asks Germany "What of the night?" and Germany replies:

Long has it lulled me with dreams;
Now at midwatch, as it seems,
Light is brought back to mine eyes,
And the mastery of old and the might
Lives in the joints of mine hands,
Steadies my limbs as they rise,
Strengthens my foot as it stands.[7]

This was the time when Bismarck's new German Reich was founded and Germany was on the up and up. Since then, Germany has been through other long nights and a period of prosperity followed by new crises. Now it is struggling to rediscover itself and its true role in the world.

As I have argued in this book, the key achievement of Germany on the spiritual level lies in the interface between spirit and matter. The effort to combine the two is what lies at the heart of the Rosicrucian movement and is central to the alchemical tradition, which survived in Germany long after it had declined elsewhere. The furor that followed the appearance of the Rosicrucian manifestos was symptomatic of a clash of worldviews. On the one hand were the followers of the Rosicrucian–Hermetic–alchemical–neo-platonic tradition, which taught the principle of "as above, so below"; that is to say, that heaven and earth are linked by myriad correspondences and that God's truth is written in physical matter and in nature as well as in the scriptures. On the opposite side there were those who insisted on a complete separation between religion and science. The latter was for them a legitimate way of learning about the workings of the mundane realm, but only the scriptures could reveal divine truths.

The moment of choice between these worldviews could be described as a Rosicrucian moment. If the Rosicrucian path had been chosen, mainstream science might have developed in a much more holistic way, but certain influential theologians were determined that it should be otherwise. Wouter Hanegraaff, in his book *Esotericism and the Academy,* has shown how figures like the Evangelical pastor Ehregott Daniel Colberg (1659–1698) were intent on condemning all the esoteric traditions as heretical. In a work titled *Platonisch-Hermetisches Christenthum* (Platonic-Hermetic Christianity) he wrote:

> The greatest—I would almost say: the only—danger for theology comes from the scandalous *mixing of philosophical teachings and the word of God.* For although the philosophical arts and sciences are . . . a wonderful gift of God . . . they create much confusion if they are applied to the divine mysteries of revelation and transcend their natural boundaries of reason.[8]

In other words, what he was saying was, religion is religion and science is science, and never the twain shall meet. The result of this attitude was that, as scientific thinking developed, divinity was taken out of the material world (Weber's "disenchantment of the world"). Then, when religion declined, it was taken out of the heaven as well, so that we were left with a godless universe, devoid of meaning and created by blind coincidence.

But that is not quite the end of the story, because the esoteric-Hermetic-alchemical worldview has remained as alive in Germany as elsewhere, indeed perhaps to a greater extent than elsewhere. I sense the arrival of a new Rosicrucian moment. The traditions I have described are present in spagyric medicine and the work of enterprises like Soluna and Phylak. The same combination is found in the achievements of Rudolf Steiner, his Anthroposophical medicine, his biodynamic agriculture, and his system of body movements called eurythmy. We can see a similar integration of spirit and matter in the research of Viktor Schauberger and Theodor Schwenk into the properties of water as a substance full of cosmic meaning. It is also found in the work of geomancers like Harald Jordan and in that of botanists like Wolf-Dieter Storl, who work, in the spirit of Goethe, with the subtle forces in the plant world. Common to all these people and movements is the perception that the world of nature, and indeed the whole universe, is ensouled. That is a message that speaks urgently to our age.

NOTES

PREFACE

1. Dorn and Wagner, *Die deutsche Seele,* 7.

INTRODUCTION: SKY-GOD LAND

1. Staël, *De l'Allemagne,* 9 (my translation).
2. Belloc, *Short Talks with the Devil and Others,* 9.
3. Menghira and Schauer, *Der Goldkegel von Egelsdorf.*
4. Eliade, *Shamanism,* 379.

I. HEIDELBERG: AN ENCHANTED GATEWAY

1. Caus, *Le Jardin Palatin.*
2. Patterson, "The 'Hortus Palatinus'"
3. French, *Disenchanting and Re-Enchanting German Modernity.*
4. French, *Disenchanting and Re-Enchanting German Modernity,* 139.
5. Baigent and Leigh, *Secret Germany.*

2. PLACES OF POWER

1. Website of the Infozentrum Externsteine (Externsteine Information Center).
2. Teudt, *Germanische Heiligtümer,* 22.
3. Flowers, *The Occult in National Socialism,* 276.
4. Goodrick-Clarke, *The Occult Roots of Nazism,* 186–87.
5. *New English Bible,* 335.

6. Luczyn, *Magische Reisen Deutschland,* 275–78.

7. Luczyn, *Magische Reisen Deutschland,* 275–78.

8. Luczyn, *Magische Reisen Deutschland,* 336.

9. Luczyn, *Magische Reisen Deutschland,* 336–37.

10. C. McIntosh, *The Swan King,* 184–85.

11. Petzet, "Die Gralswelt König Ludwigs II," 63.

3. FOLLOWING ANCIENT FOOTPRINTS

1. Gugenberger and Schweidlenka, *Die Fäden der Nornen,* 41 (my translation).

2. Pahnke *"Schweig nicht, Völva,"* 13.

3. Bächtold-Stäubli, *Handbuch des deutschen Aberglaubens,* 1:954.

4. Tacitus, *Germania,* section 9.

5. Kaplan, "The Sacred Mushroom in Scandinavia," 72–79.

6. Olsen, "Odin's Well of Remembrance."

7. Rätsch, *Der Heilige Hain,* 57–58.

8. Rätsch, "Sacred Plants of Our Ancestors," 165–79.

9. Kantilli, *Natur Heiligtümer in Europa,* 182.

10. Hensch, *Geomantische Reisen,* 145.

11. Löns, "Das Osterfeuer," 156–57.

12. Grimm, *Deutsche Mythologie,* 524.

13. Eliade, *Shamanism,* 69–70.

14. Eliade, *Shamanism,* 43.

15. Bächtold-Stäubli, *Handbuch des deutschen Aberglaubens,* 8:498–507.

16. Grimm, *Deutsche Mythologie,* 207 (my translation).

17. Branston, *Gods of the North,* 131–32.

18. Storl, *Pflanzendevas,* 134 (my translation).

4. FALL AND RISE OF THE OLD GODS

1. *Die Sage vom Wilden Mann.* On website of the town of Wildemann, accessed December 10, 2021.

2. Goethe, *Faust II,* 56 (my translation).

3. Graichen, *Das Kultplatz Buch,* 251–53.

4. Roselius, *Reden und Schriften,* 97–105 (my translation).

5. Bahn, "The Friedrich Hielscher Legend," 243–62.

5. MYSTICS, MAGICIANS, AND WITCHES

1. Strehlow and Hertzka, *Hildegard of Bingen's Medicine,* xviii.
2. Strehlow and Hertzka, *Hildegard of Bingen's Medicine,* 127–28.
3. Eschenbach, *Parzival,* 244.
4. Eschenbach, *Parzival,* 251–52.
5. Jung and Franz, *The Grail Legend,* 34.
6. Eckhart, *Meister Eckharts mystische Schriften,* 14–15 (my translation).
7. Eckhart, *Meister Eckharts mystische Schriften,* 43 (my translation).
8. Eckhart, *Meister Eckharts mystische Schriften,* 61.
9. Eckhart, *Meister Eckharts mystische Schriften,* foreword, 5–12.
10. Eckhart, *Meister Eckharts mystische Schriften,* foreword, 5–12.
11. Joseph Dan, "Reuchlin," in Hanegraaff et al., *Dictionary of Gnosis,* 2:990–93.
12. Gershman, "Dürer's Enigma."
13. Michaela Valente, "Agrippa," in Hanegraaff et al., *Dictionary of Gnosis,* 1:4–8.
14. Valente, "Agrippa," in Hanegraaff et al., *Dictionary of Gnosis,* 1:4–8.
15. Butler, *Ritual Magic;* and Sandy Schulman, "Faust," in Cavendish, *Man, Myth and Magic,* no. 33, 922–27.
16. Benzenhöfer and Gantenbein, "Paracelsus," in Hanegraaff, *Dictionary of Gnosis,* 2:922–31.

6. ROSICRUCIANS, FREEMASONS, AND ALCHEMISTS

1. McIntosh and McIntosh, *Fama Fraternitatis,* 19.
2. McIntosh and McIntosh, *Fama Fraternitatis,* 47.
3. C. McIntosh, *The Rose Cross and the Age of Reason,* 73.
4. Patai, *The Jewish Alchemists,* 465.
5. Danciger, *The Emergence of Homoeopathy,* 20.
6. Safranski, *Goethe,* 73.
7. Goethe, *Die Metamorphose der Pflanzen.*
8. Chailley, *The Magic Flute Unveiled,* 294.
9. Steiner, introduction to Goethe, *Die Metamorphose der Pflanzen,* 5.
10. Arndt, "Das große Werk des spagyrischen Heilens."
11. Website of Phylak Sachsen GmbH.

12. Hauschka, *The Nature of Substance,* 44.

13. Hauschka, *The Nature of Substance,* 56–57.

7. SYMBOL-STREWN SPACES

1. Waitz von Eschen, *Parkwege als Wissenswege.*

2. Rode, *Beschreibung des Fürstlichen Anhalt-Dessauischen Landhauses,* 128–29 (my translation).

3. Rode, *Beschreibung des Fürstlichen Anhalt-Dessauischen Landhauses,* 130 (my translation).

4. C. McIntosh, *Gardens of the Gods,* 110.

8. SEERS AND SOMNAMBULISTS

1. Caroutch, *Gustav Meyrink,* 14.

2. Lennhoff and Posner, *Internationales Freimaurer-Lexikon,* 875.

3. Kolb, *Die Wiedergeburt.*

4. Kerning, *Wege zur Unsterblichkeit,* 93 (my translation).

5. Lennhoff and Posner, *Internationales Freimaurer-Lexikon,* 1363.

6. Quoted by Andrew Weeks in an article on Boehme, in Hanegraaff et al., *Dictionary of Gnosis & Western Esotericism,* 1:185.

7. Novalis, *Die Lehrlinge zu Saïs,* 1 (my translation).

8. Hanegraaff, article on Kerner, in *Dictionary of Gnosis & Western Esotericism,* 2:660–62.

9. Hanegraaff et al., article on Kerner, in *Dictionary of Gnosis & Western Esotericism,* 2:661.

10. Hanegraaff et al., article on Kerner, in *Dictionary of Gnosis & Western Esotericism,* 2:661.

11. Howe, *Urania's Children,* 78.

9. SEEKERS OF THE LIGHT

1. Baumstark and Koch, *Der Gral,* 100 (my translation).

2. Baumstark and Koch, *Der Gral,* 100 (my translation).

3. Nicholas Goodrick-Clarke, article on Hartmann, in Hanegraaff et al., *Dictionary of Gnosis & Western Esotericism,* 1:458–59.

4. Howe, *Urania's Children*, 78–85.

5. Marco Pasi, article on the Ordo Templi Orientis, in Hanegraaff et al., *Dictionary of Gnosis & Western Esotericism*, 2:898–906.

6. Marco Pasi, article on the Ordo Templi Orientis, in Hanegraaff et al., *Dictionary of Gnosis & Western Esotericism*, 2:898–906.

7. Kennedy, "Children of the *Sonne*," 197.

8. Kennedy, "Children of the *Sonne*," 197.

9. Kennedy, "Children of the *Sonne*," 201.

10. Hakl, *Eranos*, 93.

11. Antoine Faivre, article on Oskar Schlag, in Hanegraaff et al., *Dictionary of Gnosis & Western Esotericism*, 2:1041.

12. Hakl, *Eranos*, 92.

13. Hakl, *Eranos*, 139, quoting Portmann's book *Probleme des Lebens* (Problems of Life).

14. Hakl, *Eranos*, 44.

10. JOURNEY TO THE SELF

1. Eduard Frank, "L'Esotériste Gustav Meyrink," in Caroutch, *Gustav Meyrink*, 130.

2. Meyrink, *Der Golem*, 55 (my translation).

3. Meyrink, *Der Golem*, 141 (my translation).

4. Meyrink, *Der Golem*, 217–18 (my translation).

5. Bloch, *Mystical Tales from the Ghetto of Prague*, 66.

6. Hesse, *Demian*, 88.

7. Jung, *VII Sermones ad Mortuos*, 17.

8. Hakl, *Eranos*, 49.

9. Hakl, *Eranos*, 49.

10. Christine Maillard, article on Jung, in Hanegraaff et al., *Dictionary of Gnosis & Western Esotericism*, 2:648.

11. Ute Wermer, "Fidus: Künstler alles Lichtbaren," in De Bruyn, *Fidus*, 20–103.

12. Ute Wermer, "Fidus: Künstler alles Lichtbaren," in De Bruyn, *Fidus*, 46–47.

13. Ute Wermer, "Fidus: Künstler alles Lichtbaren," in De Bruyn, *Fidus*, 65 (my translation).

14. Rentsch, *Fiduswerk*, 134 (my translation).

15. Wouter J. Hanegraaff, "Theosophy in Secret Germany," 2015. Posted on Hanegraaff's Creative Reading blogspot and on the Academia.edu website.

II. INTERBELLUM AND ARMAGEDDON

1. Landau, *God Is My Adventure,* 18.
2. Landau, *God Is My Adventure,* 23.
3. Thomas Hakl, article on the Fraternitas Saturni, in Hanegraaff et al., *Dictionary of Gnosis & Western Esotericism,* 1:379.
4. Flowers, *The Fraternitas Saturni,* 73.
5. Flowers, *The Fraternitas Saturni,* 25–26.
6. Hakl, article on the Fraternitas Saturni, in Hanegraaff et al., *Dictionary of Gnosis & Western Esotericism,* 1:380.
7. Hakl, article on the Fraternitas Saturni, in Hanegraaff et al., *Dictionary of Gnosis & Western Esotericism,* 1:381.
8. Hakl, article on the Fraternitas Saturni, in Hanegraaff et al., *Dictionary of Gnosis & Western Esotericism,* 1:381.
9. Flowers, *The Fraternitas Saturni,* 80.
10. Hakl, article on the Fraternitas Saturni, in Hanegraaff et al., *Dictionary of Gnosis & Western Esotericism,* 1:382.
11. Hakl, "Franz Sättler (Dr. Musallam) and the Twentieth-Century Cult of Adonism."
12. Massimo Introvigne, article on the Grail, in Hanegraaff et al., *Dictionary of Gnosis and Western Esotericism,* 1:436–38.
13. Goodrick-Clarke, *The Occult Roots of Nazism,* 108.
14. Bô Yin Râ, "Why I Use My Name," posted on website of the Kober Press, founded to promote the spiritual legacy of Bô Yin Râ, accessed September 21, 2022.
15. "Bô Yin Râ—Brief Biography," posted on website of the Bô Yin Râ Organization, accessed September 21, 2022.
16. Landau, *God Is My Adventure,* 44–45.
17. Landau, *God Is My Adventure,* 25.
18. Landau, *God Is My Adventure,* 30.
19. Landau, *God Is My Adventure,* 30, 36; Hakl, *Eranos,* 39.
20. Landau, *God Is My Adventure,* 33.
21. Baigent and Leigh, *Secret Germany,* 67.
22. George, "Templer," in *Der siebte Ring,* 52 (my translation).
23. George, "Geheimes Deutschland," in *Das neue Reich,* 59–65 (my translation).
24. C. McIntosh, *Occult Russia,* 72–75.
25. "Sergei Vronsky—The Last Soviet Astrologer." Recorded in 1990 by

Christian Borup with Farida Assadulina as interpreter, available on Vimeo and YouTube.

26. Howe, *Urania's Children,* 90–91.
27. Howe, *Urania's Children,* 90–91.
28. Howe, *Urania's Children,* 238.

12. POSTWAR PERSPECTIVES

1. Cavendish and Rhine, *Encyclopedia of the Unexplained,* 198.
2. Cavendish and Rhine, *Encyclopedia of the Unexplained,* 198.
3. Cavendish and Rhine, *Encyclopedia of the Unexplained,* 198.
4. Cavendish and Rhine, *Encyclopedia of the Unexplained,* 267.
5. Jung and Pauli, *The Interpretation of Nature and the Psyche,* 159.
6. Jung and Pauli, *The Interpretation of Nature and the Psyche,* 160.
7. Jung and Pauli, *The Interpretation of Nature and the Psyche,* 176–77.
8. Adorno, *Minima Moralia,* 468 (my translation).
9. Schmidt-Reinicke, "Die Angst vor dem Transrationalen," 36–37.
10. Schmidt-Reinicke, "Die Angst vor dem Transrationalen," 36–37 (my translation).
11. Schmidt-Reinicke, "Die Angst vor dem Transrationalen," 37 (my translation).
12. Schmidt-Reinicke, "Die Angst vor dem Transrationalen," 37 (my translation).
13. Dethlefsen, *The Challenge of Fate,* 205.
14. Dethlefsen, *The Challenge of Fate,* 205.
15. Dethlefsen and Dahlke, *Krankheit als Weg,* 7 (my translation).

13. PAGAN PATHWAYS

1. Maren Tomforde, "Das Hexenarchiv im Hamburgischen Museum für Völkerkunde," in Schmelz, ed., *Hexerei, Magie und Volksmedizin,* 7–8.
2. Maren Tomforde, "Das Hexenarchiv im Hamburgischen Museum für Völkerkunde," in Schmetz, *Hexerei, Magie und Vilksmedizin,* 23.
3. Maren Tomforde, "Das Hexenarchiv im Hamburgischen Museum für Völkerkunde," in Schmetz, *Hexerei, Magie und Vilksmedizin,* 14–15.
4. Maren Tomforde, "Das Hexenarchiv im Hamburgischen Museum für Völkerkunde," in Schmetz, *Hexerei, Magie und Vilksmedizin,* 18 (my translation).

5. Gugenberger and Schweidlenka, *Die Fäden der Nornen,* 36–39.

6. Information leaflet issued for the 2017 conference of the Pagan Federation Deutschland (my translation).

7. Leland, *Aradia,* 13.

8. Pahnke, "Mondlicht auf dem Buch der Schatten," 167 (my translation).

14. SPIRIT AND MATTER

1. C. McIntosh, *Occult Russia,* 223–25.

2. McIntosh and McIntosh, *Fama Fraternitatis,* 40.

3. Wagner, "Energie, Information und Form," 20–27.

4. Bischoff, "A tribute to Fritz-Albert Popp," 267–72.

5. Wagner, "Energie, Information und Form," 22.

15. SOUL OF THE LANDSCAPE

1. Pogačnik, *Die Erde heilen.*

2. Jordan, *Worpswede,* 46 (my translation).

3. Jordan, *Worpswede,* 46 (my translation).

4. Jordan, *Räume der Kraft schaffen,* 17 (my translation).

5. Jordan, *Räume der Kraft schaffen,* 117 (my translation).

6. Storl, *Pflanzendevas,* 142 (my translation).

16. OCCULT GERMANY TODAY

1. Hakl, *Octagon,* 2:15.

2. Hakl, *Octagon,* 2:20.

3. C. McIntosh, "The Meyerbeck Manuscript," in *The Sorceress of Agartha,* 28–43.

4. Borges, "Tlön, Uqbar, Orbis Tertius," in *Labyrinths,* 27–43.

5. Borges, "Tlön, Uqbar, Orbis Tertius," in *Labyrinths,* 43.

6. Tessel M. Bauduin, "The Occult and the Visual Arts," in Partridge, *The Occult World,* 429–30.

7. Swinburne, *Songs before Sunrise,* 27–33.

8. Hanegraaff, *Esotericism and the Academy,* 108.

BIBLIOGRAPHY

Adler, Margot. *Drawing Down the Moon*. 2nd ed. Boston: Beacon, 1986.

Adorno, Theodor. *Minima Moralia*. Frankfurt am Main: Suhrkamp, 1951.

Albertus, Frater [Albert Riedel]. *The Alchemist's Handbook*. Rev. ed. London: Routledge and Kegan Paul, 1976.

Arndt, Ulrich. "Das große Werk des spagyrischen Heilens." *Esotera,* no. 10 (October 1997): 50–60.

Bächtold-Stäubli, Hanns, ed. *Handbuch des deutschen Aberglaubens*. 10 vols. New York: Walter de Gruyter, 1987.

Bahn, Peter. "The Friedrich Hielscher Legend." *TYR* 2 (2004): 243–62.

Baigent, Michael, and Richard Leigh. *Secret Germany: Stauffenberg and the Mystical Crusade against Hitler*. London: Penguin, 1995.

Baumstark, Reinhold, and Michael Koch, eds. *Der Gral: Artusromantik in der Kunst des 19. Jahnhunderts*. Munich: Bavarian National Museum, 1995.

Belloc, Hilaire. *Short Talks with the Devil and Others*. London: Cayme Press, 1926.

Bischoff, Marco. "A Tribute to Fritz-Albert Popp on the Occasion of His 70th Birthday." *Indian Journal of Experimental Biology* 46 (May 2008): 267–72.

Bloch, Chayim. *Mystical Tales from the Ghetto of Prague*. Blauvelt, N.Y.: Rudolf Steiner Publications, 1972.

Borges, Jorge Luis. *Labyrinths: Selected Stories and Other Writings*. Harmondsworth, UK: Penguin, 1979.

Branston, Brian. *Gods of the North*. London: Thames and Hudson, 1955.

Butler, E. M. *Ritual Magic*. Cambridge: Cambridge University Press, 1949.

Caroutch, Yvonne, ed. *Gustav Meyrink*. L'Herne series. Paris: Editions de l'Herne, 1976.

Caus, Salomon de. *Le Jardin Palatin*. With afterword by Michel Conan. Paris: Editions du Moniteur, 1981.

Cavendish, Richard, ed. *Man, Myth and Magic*. Originally published as a magazine in 112 issues. London: BPC Publishing, 1970–1971.

Cavendish, Richard, and J. B. Rhine, eds. *Encyclopedia of the Unexplained*. London: Routledge & Kegan Paul, 1974.

Chailley, Jacques. *The Magic Flute Unveiled*. Rochester, Vt.: Inner Traditions, 1992.

Danciger, Elizabeth. *The Emergence of Homoeopathy*. London: Century Hutchinson, 1987.

De Bruyn, Wolfgang, ed. *Fidus: Künstler alles Lichtbaren*. Berlin: Schelsky und Jeep, 1998.

Derolez, R. L. M. *Götter und Mythen der Germanen*. Wiesbaden: VMA-Verlag, 1963.

Dethlefsen, Thorwald. *The Challenge of Fate*. Translated by Christopher McIntosh and Eva Loewe. London: Coventure, 1984.

Dethlefsen, Thorwald, and Rüdiger Dahlke. *Krankheit als Weg*. Munich: Bertelsmann, 1983.

Dorn, Thea, and Richard Wagner. *Die deutsche Seele*. Munich: Knaus Verlag, 2011.

Eckartshausen, Karl von. *Mystische Nächte*. Munich: Joseph Lentner, 1791.

Eckhart, Meister. *Meister Eckharts mystische Schriften*. Edited and introduced by Gustav Landauer. Berlin: Karl Schnabel, 1903.

Eliade, Mircea. *Shamanism*. London: Arkana, 1989.

Ende, Michael. *The Neverending Story*. Translated by Ralph Manheim. New York: Firebird, 2005.

Eschenbach, Wolfram von. *Parzival*. Translated and with an introduction by Helen M. Mustard and Charles E. Passage. New York: Vintage, 1961.

Flowers, Stephen E. *The Fraternitas Saturni*. Rev. ed. Rochester, Vt.: Inner Traditions, 2018.

———. *The Occult in National Socialism*. Rochester, Vt.: Inner Traditions, 2022.

French, Aaron. *Disenchanting and Re-Enchanting German Modernity with Max Weber and Rudolf Steiner*. Ph.D. dissertation, University of California at Davis, 2021.

Gardner, Gerald. *Witchcraft Today*. London: Rider, 1954.

George, Stefan. *Das neue Reich*. Berlin: Georg Bondi, 1928.

———. *Der siebte Ring*. Berlin: Blätter für die Kunst, 1907.

Gershman, Zhenya. "Dürer's Enigma: A Kabbalistic Revelation in Melencolia." Lecture to the Philosophical Research Society, Los Angeles, April 4, 2019.

Goethe, Johann Wolfgang von. *Faust II*. Stuttgart & Tübingen: Cotta, 1832.

———. *Die Metamorphose der Pflanzen*. Annotated and with introduction by Rudolf Steiner. Stuttgart: Verlag Freies Geistesleben, 1992.

———. *Wilhelm Meisters Lehrjahre*. Munich: Deutscher Taschenbuch Verlag, 1984.

Goodrick-Clarke, Nicholas. *The Occult Roots of Nazism*. Wellingborough, UK: Aquarian Press, 1985.

Graichen, Gisela. *Das Kultplatz Buch*. Augsburg: Verlagsgruppe Weltbild, 2004.

Grimm, Jacob. *Deutsche Mythologie,* Vol. 1. Facsimile reprint. Wiesbaden: Fourier, 2003.

Gugenberger, Eduard, and Roman Schweidlenka. *Die Fäden der Nornen*. Vienna: Verlag für Gesellschaftskritik, 1993.

Hakl, Hans Thomas. *Eranos: An Alternative Intellectual History of the Twentieth Century*. Translated by Christopher McIntosh with Hereward Tilton. Sheffield, UK: Equinox Publishing, 2013.

———. "Franz Sättler (Dr. Musallam) and the Twentieth-Century Cult of Adonism." *Pomegranate: The International Journal of Pagan Studies* 12, no. 1 (January 1, 2010).

———, ed. *Octagon,* Vol. 2, *The Quest for Wholeness*. Gaggenau, Germany: Scientia Nova, 2015–2018.

Hanegraaff, Wouter. *Esotericism and the Academy*. Cambridge, UK: Cambridge University Press, 2012.

Hanegraaff, Wouter J., et al., eds., *Dictionary of Gnosis & Western Esotericism*. 2 Vols. Leiden: Brill, 2005.

Hauschka, Rudolf. *The Nature of Substance*. English translation. London: Vincent Stuart, 1966.

Hensch, Eike. *Geomantische Reisen*. Nienburg: Eike Hensch Verlag, 2001.

Hesse, Hermann. *Demian*. Translated by W. J. Strachen. London: Panther, 1969.

Howe, Ellic. *Urania's Children*. London: William Kimber, 1967.

Jordan, Harald. *Räume der Kraft schaffen*. Freiburg im Breisgau: Hermann Bauer, 1997.

———. *Worpswede—ein Ort der Kraft?!* Nienburg, Germany: Eike Hensch, 2011.

Jung, C. G. *Mysterium Conjunctionis*. Translated by R.F.C. Hull. Princeton, N.J.: Princeton University Press, 1970.

———. *VII Sermones ad Mortuos. The Seven Sermons to the Dead Written by Basilides of Alexandria the City Where the East Toucheth the West*. Translated by H. G. Baynes. London: Watkins, 1967

Jung, C. G., and Wolfgang Pauli. *The Interpretation of Nature and the Psyche*. London: Routledge & Kegan Paul, 1955. Originally published in German as *Naturerklärung und Psyche*. Zürich: Rascher Verlag, 1952.

Jung, Emma, and Marie-Louise von Franz. *The Grail Legend*. New York: Putnam, 1970.

Kantilli, Günter. *Natur Heiligtümer in Europa*. Freistadt, Austria: Plöchl, 2010.

Kaplan, Reid. "The Sacred Mushroom in Scandinavia." *Man* 10, no. 1 (March 1975): 72–79.

Kennedy, Gordon. "Children of the *Sonne*." *TYR,* no. 3 (2007–2008): 197.

Kerning, Johann Baptist. *Wege zur Unsterblichkeit*. Lorch, Germany: Renatus-Verlag, 1936.

Kolb, Karl. *Die Wiedergeburt, das innere wahrhaftige Leben. Das sogenannte Buchstabenbuch*. 1908. Republished. Lorch: Renatus-Verlag, 1935.

Landau, Rom. *God Is My Adventure*. London: Faber and Faber, 1953.

Leland, Charles Godfrey. *Aradia, or the Gospel of the Witches*. London: David Nutt, 1899.

Lennhoff, Eugen, and Oskar Posner. *Internationales Freimaurer-Lexikon*. Reprint of 1932 edition. Vienna: Amalthea-Verlag, 1980.

Löns, Hermann. "Das Osterfeuer." 1912. Tr. Markus Wolff. *TYR,* no. 1 (2002).

Luczyn, David. *Magische Reisen Deutschland*. Rottenburg, Germany: Kopp Verlag, 2001.

Maffesoli, Michel. *The Shadow of Dionysus*. Translated by C. Linse and M. K. Palmquist. Albany: State University of New York Press, 1992.

McIntosh, Christopher. *Gardens of the Gods*. London: I. B. Tauris, 2005.

——. *Occult Russia*. Rochester, Vt.: Inner Traditions, 2023.

——. *The Rose Cross and the Age of Reason*. Albany: State University of New York Press, 1992.

——. *The Sorceress of Agartha*. Lilienthal, Germany: Vanadis Texts, 2017.

——. *The Swan King: Ludwig II of Bavaria*. Rev. ed. London: I. B. Tauris, 2016.

McIntosh, Christopher, and Donate Pahnke McIntosh, trans. *Fama Fraternitatis: Manifesto of the Most Praiseworthy Order of the Rosy Cross*. English version, with introduction by Christopher McIntosh. Bremen: Vanadis Texts, 2014.

McIntosh, Donate Pahnke, trans. *Fama Fraternitatis: Manifest des hochlöblichen Ordens des Rosenkreuzes*. Modern German version with introduction by Christopher McIntosh. Bremen: Vanadis Texts, 2014.

Menghira, Wilfried, and Peter Schauer. *Der Goldkegel von Egelsdorf*. Stuttgart: Theiß, 1983.

Meyrink, Gustav. *Der Golem*. Leipzig: Kurt Wolff, 1915.

Murray, Margaret. *The Witch Cult in Western Europe*. Oxford: Clarendon Press, 1921.

New English Bible. Oxford: Oxford University Press/Cambridge, UK: Cambridge University Press, 1970.

Nietzsche, Friedrich. *Die Geburt der Tragödie aus dem Geiste der Musik*. Leipzig: Fritzsch, 1872.

Novalis [Friedrich von Hardenberg]. *Die Lehrlinge zu Saïs*. 1798–1799. Online at Projekt Gutenberg.

Olsen, Scott. "Odin's Well of Remembrance." Lecture delivered at the Esoteric Quest conference of the New York Open Center, Iceland, 2016.

Pahnke, Donate. "Mondlicht auf dem Buch der Schatten." *Hexenwelten* 31 (2001): 165–71.

——. "Schweig nicht, Völva, ich will dich fragen, bis ich alles weiß!" In *Schlangenbrut* no. 57 (1997), 13–16.

Partridge, Christopher, ed. *The Occult World*. Abingdon, UK: Routledge, 2015.

Patai, Raphael. *The Jewish Alchemists*. Princeton, N.J.: Princeton University Press, 1994.

Patterson, Richard. "The 'Hortus Palatinus' at Heidelberg and the Reformation of the World." *Journal of Garden History* 1, nos. 1/2 (1981): 67–104, 179–202.

Petzet, Michael. "Die Gralswelt König Ludwigs II.: Neuschwanstein als Gralsburg und die Idee des Gralstempels." In Baumstark and Koch, *Der Gral: Artusromantik in der Kunst des 19. Jahhunderts*, 63–86.

Pogačnik, Marko. *Die Erde heilen: Das Modell Türnich*. Munich: Eugen Diederichs, 1989.

Portmann, Adolf. *Probleme des Lebens*. Basel: Friedrich Reinhardt, 1949.

Rätsch, Christian. *Der Heilige Hain*. Munich: AT Verlag, 2005.

———. "Sacred Plants of Our Ancestors." *TYR*, no. 2 (2003–2004): 165–79.

Rentsch, Arno. *Fiduswerk*. Dresden: Verlag der Schönheit, 1925.

Rode, August von. *Beschreibung des Fürstlichen Anhalt-Dessauischen Landhauses und Englischen Gartens zu Wörlitz*. Dessau: Heinrich Tänzer, 1814. Facsimile reprint. Wörlitz: Kettmann-Verlag, 1996.

Roselius, Ludwig. *Reden und Schriften zur Böttcherstraße in Bremen*. Bremen: G. A. von Halem, 1932.

Safranski, Rüdiger. *Goethe: Kunstwerk des Lebens*. Munich: Carl Hanser Verlag, 2013.

Schlag, Oskar R. *Von alten und neuen Mysterien: Die Lehren des A*. Edited by Antoine Faivre and Erhart Kahle. 14 vols. Stäfa, Switzerland: Rothenhäusler, and Würzburg, Germany: Ergon, 1995–2011.

Schmelz, Bernd, ed. *Hexerei, Magie und Volksmedizin*. Bonn: Holos Verlag, 1997.

Schmidt-Reinicke, Wolfgang. "Die Angst vor dem Transrationalen." *Tattva Viveka*, no. 14 (July 2000): 36–37.

Staël, Madame de. *De l'Allemagne*. Paris: Librairie de Firmin Diderot Frères, 1852.

Starhawk [Miriam Simos]. *The Spiral Dance*. San Francisco: Harper and Row, 1989.

Storl, Wolf-Dieter. *Pflanzendevas*. Aarau, Switzerland: AT Verlag, 2004.

Strehlow, Wighard, and Gottfried Hertzka. *Hildegard of Bingen's Medicine*. Santa Fe, N.Mex.: Bear & Company, 1988.

Swinburne, Algernon Charles. *Songs before Sunrise*. London: F. S. Ellis, 1871.

Tacitus, *Germania*. Translated by Alfred John Church and William Jackson Brodribb. London: Macmillan, 1868.

Teudt, Wilhelm. *Germanische Heiligtümer*. Jena: Eugen Diederichs, 1931.

Ungewitter, Richard. *Die Nackheit*. Stuttgart: self-published, 1907.

Wagner, Waltraud. "Energie, Information und Form." *Tattva Viveka,* no. 14 (July 2000): 20–27.

Waitz von Eschen, Baron Friedrich. *Parkwege als Wissenswege: Der Bergpark Wilhelmshöhe als naturwissenschaftliches Forschungsfeld der Aufklärung*. Kassel: Verein für Hessische Geschichte und Landeskunde Kassel, 2012.

Wohlleben, Peter. *The Hidden Life of Trees*. Berkeley, Calif.: David Suzuki Institute, 2016. Originally published in German as *Das geheime Leben der Bäume*. Munich: Ludwig Verlag, 2016.

INDEX

Aachen Cathedral, 29–30

Abraxas, 138–39

Adonis Society, 152

Adorno, Theodor, 172

Agrippa, Heinrich Cornelius, 72–74

air, 45–46

alchemical symbolism, 12, 20, 69, 81

alchemy
  about, 18–20
  Golden and Rosy Cross order and, 81–82, 101
  hermaphrodite in, 135, 140
  Jung and, 140
  landgraves and, 97
  marginalization of, 84
  Paracelsus and, 75–76, 91
  the sacred and, 68
  symbols, 19

alternative medicine, 197

Amanita muscaria, 40

American Society for the Study of Esotericism, 208

Ancient and Mystical Order Rosae Crucis (AMORC), 93, 149

animal magnetism, 110, 196

Anthroposophical medicine, 85, 91–92, 167–68

Anthroposophical Society, 87

Antonia, Princess, 79, 80, *pl. 2*

aphrodisiacs, 41

Apollo and Dionysus, 11–12

archetypes, 139–40, 170

Archiv für Altes Gedankengut and Wissen (AAGW), 211

Arminius Monument, 58

Arp, Hans, 122

Asatru religion, 188–90

Atma, 127–28

Baader, Franz von, 109, 111

Barbarossa, 30–31

Bauer, Hermann, 174

Belloc, Hilaire, 1

Bender, Hans, 168–69

Bernhardt, Oskar Ernst, 152–53

Bernus, Alexander von, 22, 87–89, 92

Besant, Annie, 118, 132

Beuys, Joseph, 213

Beyond the North Wind, 147

Bioradiological Institute, 162

black henbane, 41

Blavatsky, Madame, 7–9, 112, 117, 132

Boehme, Jakob, 6, 20, 108–9

Boniface, 37
Borges, Jorge Luis, 211–13
Bossard, Michael, 62–63
Böttcherstrasse, 61–63
Bô Yin Râ, 155–57
Brandler-Pracht, Karl, 118–19
Bremerhaven (Thieles Garden), 103–5
Bronze Age findings, 4
Brunnen (spring or fountain), 41
Buttmandeln, 50–51

cannabis, 40–41
carbon, 92–93
channeled wisdom, 127–29
Charlemagne, 5, 13, 27, 29–30
Christianity, 5–6, 12, 27, 35, 51, 193
Christmas tree, 36
Colberg, Ehregott Daniel, 216
Crowley, Aleister, 121, 149–50, 214

Dada movement, 122
dancing nature spirits, 204–6
de Caus, Salomon, 17
Der Morgen (The Morning), pl. 1
Dethlefsen, Thorwald, 175–77
"de-witching," 179
Diefenbach, Karl von, 141–42
Die Zeit, 173
Dionysus, 11–12, 183, 184
divinatory methods, 176
Drachenfels (Dragons Cliff), 60
Dürer, Albrecht, 70–72, 74, 173
dwarfs, 46–47

earth, 46–47
Easter fire, 43–44

Ebertin, Elsbeth, 162, 163
Ecclesiastica Gnostica Catholica (EGC), 121
Eckhart, Meister, 6, 69, 173
Economic Miracle, 184, 185
Edda, 35, 36, 55, 57–58, 214
Egyptian pyramid, 100–101
Eliade, Mircea, 5, 208
Engert, Ronald, 174–75
Enlightenment principles, 208
Eranos Circle, 22
Eranos seminars, 22, 128–29, 158, 208
Eschenbach, Wolfram von, 6, 33, 67–68
Esotera, 174
esotericism, 10, 127, 141, 173, 175–77, 207–8
European Society for the Study of Western Esotericism, 208
eurythmy, 216
Evangelische Zentralstelle für Weltanschauungsfragen, 192
Externsteine cliffs, 25–27

Fahrenkrog, Ludwig, 60
Fama Fraternitatis, 77–79, 194
Faust (Goethe), 50, 54, 85–86
Faust, Dr. Johann, 6, 73–74
Fidus
    about, 141
    ground plan of Temple of the Earth, 145
    Klein collaboration, 142–43
    life overview, 141–42
    light and dark and, 143, 146

St. George Society and, 143
"Tempelkunst," 143–44
Temple of the Earth, 144–46
Walensee lake property, 143
Woltersdorf house, 142
field theory, 198
Fink, Christiane, 204
fire
  Easter, 43–44
  pyromancy and, 44–45
  St. John's, 44
Flowers, Stephen, 150, 153
Földényi, Lásló, 172
Foster, Johann Georg, 97
Fox sisters, 111–12
Frankenstein's monster, 136
Frankfurt Book Fair, 175
Fraternitas Saturni, 6, 150–52
Frederick II, 30–31, 95, 97
Frederick William II, 100–101
Freemasonry
  about, 6
  gardens and, 95
  Grand Lodges, 167
  post-World War II and, 166–67
  symbolic death in, 21
Freikörperkultur (FKK), 125
Freud, Sigmund, 121, 139, 196
Frey, Max, 125–26
Fröhlich, Herbert, 195

gardens
  about, 94
  Aigues Vertes village, 205–6
  Freemasonry and, 95
  Heidelberg, 94–95
  Louisenlund, 102–3

nature spirits and, 204–5
  New Garden, 100–102
  Thieles Garden, 103–5
  Weimar, 100
  Wilhelmshöhe Park, 95–97
  Wörlitz, 97–100
Gardens of the Gods, 105
"Geheimes Deutschland" (George), 160–61
geomancy
  about, 200
  "analogical" approach to, 203
  as feng shui, 200
  Hagia Chora and, 204
  Harald Jordan and, 201–4
  practice of, 200
  Worpswede and, 200–204
George, Stefan, 10, 22, 147, 159–61
George Circle, 22, 147, 159
German Democratic Republic (GDR), 188, 190–91
German Faith Community, 60
Germany
  historical/mythical heritage, 1, 14, 46
  ley lines and, 3–4
  mystics and, xi
  "occulture" in, 213–14
  origins of, 2–3
  paganism in, 182–84
  Romans and, 4–5
  Russia versus, x
  secret life of, 159
  Third Reich and, x
  after World War II, 10, 166–67
Gershman, Zhenya, 70–72
gnosticism, 82, 140–41, 176

Goddess, 185–87
Goebbels, Joseph, 24
Goethe, Wolfgang von, 85, 92, 100
Golden and Rosy Cross order
  about, 6, 81
  aim of, 82
  alchemy and, 82, 101
  circles, 81
  initiation into, 9, 82, 101
Golden Dawn (Goldene
  Dämmerung), 9, 81, 132, 151, 186
the golem, 133, 134, 135–36
The Golem (Meyrink), 106, 130, 132,
  135, 137
Goodrick-Clarke, Nicholas, 207–8
GOTOS, 150–51
Grail castle, 31
The Grail Castle, 116
Grau, Albin, 150
Grimm, Jacob, 45, 46, 58
Grimm, Wilhelm, 58
Grombach, Magdalena, 111

Habsburgs, 18
Hagia Chora, 204
Hahnemann, Samuel, 84–85, 92, 173
Hakl, Thomas, 127–28, 140, 150,
  151, 152, 208–11, *pl. 8*
Hanegraaff, Wouter, 216
Hardenberg, Friedrich von, 109
Hartmann, Franz, 116–18, 120
Hauschka, Rudolf, 92–93
heathen (term), 184
Heidelberg
  about, 15
  Cautes and Cautopates and, 21
  Eranos, 22

garden, 94
Heiligenberg (Holy Hill), 23
Max Weber House, 21, 23
monastery of Saint Michael, 23–24
Museum of Pharmacy, 18, 20
Museum of the Palatinate, 21–22,
  23
Philosopher's Way, 23
Romanticism and, 20
Heidelberg Castle, 16–18
Hendrich, Hermann, 54–55, 59
Hercules statues (Wilhelmshöhe
  Park), 95–97
Hermann (Arminius) Monument,
  27, 28
hermaphrodite, 135, 140
hermetic-alchemical worldview,
  215–16
Hermetic Society, 127–28
Hermetism, 85
Hertzka, Gottfried, 66–67
Hess, Rudolf, 163–65
Hesse, Hermann, 10, 122, 130,
  137–38, 173
Hessen-Kassel, Karl von, 83–84, 95,
  102
Hess Operation, 163, 164
Hexen (Witches) exhibition, 182
Hexentanzplatz (Witches' Dance
  Arena), 51–52
The Hidden Life of Trees
  (Wohlleben), 39–40
Hielscher, Friedrich, 63–64
Hildegard of Bingen, 6, 65–67, 68,
  173, 193
History of Hermetic Philosophy and
  Related Currents, 208

History of Magic, 191
Hitler, Adolf, 60–62, 162–63, 165
Hoetger, Bernhard, 60–61
Hohle Fels (Hollow Cliff), 3
Holy Grail
  absent, 32–33
  Germany and, 7
  International Grail Movement and,
    152–53
  Parsifal (Wagner) and, 114–16
  quest for, 67–68
  symbolism and Germany and, 7,
    12–13
  theme, 114–29
Holy Roman Empire, 2, 30
homeopathy, 84–85, 90
Höppener, Hugo, 141. *See also* Fidus
horses, 55–56
House Atlantis, 61
House of the Holy Spirit, 77–78

Icehouse (Rosicrucian park), 102, *pl. 5*
illumination gateways, 149–54
Imperial Throne (Kaiserthron), 30
Independent Free Church, 63
Innerlichkeit ("indwelling spirit"),
  129
Institute for Paranormal Psychology,
  175–76
Institute of Flow Sciences, 43
International Grail Movement,
  152–53
International Institute for Scientific
  Research in Cosmo-Planetary
  Anthropoecology (ISIRCA),
  194
Internet, 211–13

Jordan, Harald, 201–4
Jung, Carl Gustav, 127, 129, 138–41,
  158, 170
Jünger, Ernst, 63

Kabbalah, 6, 70, 73, 81, 136, 173
Kabbalistic Instruction Tableau, 79,
  80, *pl. 2*
Kassel park, 95, 97
Kawwana, Church of the New Aeon,
  175–76
Kellner, Karl, 120–21
Kepler, Johann, 170–71
Kerner, Justinus, 110–11
Kerning, Johann Baptist, 106–8
Keyserling, Count Hermann,
  157–58
King Wilhelm of Prussia, 31
Klein, Joshua, 142–43
Konrad of Marburg, 67
Kozyrev, Nikolai, 194–95
Kozyrev mirror, 194–95, 197
Krafft, Karl Ernst, 163
Krampus, 50, 51
Krumm-Heller, Arnoldo, 149
Kruse, Johann, 179–82

Laban, Rudolf, 122–24
Labyrinth (Wörlitz park), 99, *pl. 4*
Landau, Rom, 148, 156–58
landgraves, 95–97
Lebensreform, 124–25
Lechter, Melchior, 146, 147, *pl. 7*
Lehrtafel (instruction tableau), 79, 80
Leitmotiv, 15
Lévi, Éliphas, 112, 191
ley lines, 3–4, 24, 199

Liebenfels, Jörg Lanz von, 154
Der Lichtbringer (The Lightbringer), 61–62
linden tree, 37, 38
Linnaeus, 85
lithopuncture, 199–200
Logos, 22
Lohengrin (Wagner), 58
Long Night of the Religions, 183, 192
Löns, Hermann, 44
Louisenlund park, 102–3
Luczyn, David, 32
Ludwig II of Bavaria, 31–33

The Magic Flute (Mozart), 86–87, 101, 107, 173, 213
Malleus Maleficarum, 72
Marble Palace, 101
Masonic gardens, 95
Matronae, 57
Max Weber House, 21, 23
medicine
    alchemical, 197
    alternative, 197
    Anthroposophical, 85, 91–92
    Hildegard of Bingen and, 66–67
    Paracelsus and, 74–76, 168
Melencolia I, 70, 71
Merseburg Spells, 55
Mesmer, Franz Anton, 110, 196
Metz, Dr. Johann Friedrich, 85
The Meyerbeck Manuscript, 211–12
Meyrink (Meyer), Gustav, 10, 106, 107–8, 130–32, 133–34, 137–38, 173
mind-body practice, 107
Mirandola, Pico della, 70

mirrors, 194–95
Mithraism, 20–21
Monte Vertà colony, 23, 122, 124
moon, 185–87
The Morning (Der Morgen), 7, 8
Moses grimoire, 180–81
Museum of Ethnology, 178–79, 181–82
Mythical Way, 52, 53
myths, 2, 10, 14, 34, 46, 55

National Socialism, 153, 161, 172
nature philosophy, 42, 66, 196
nature spirits, 204–6
Nazism, 10, 14, 153, 161, 164
Nebra Sky Disk, 4
Neuschwanstein castle, 32–33
The Neverending Story (Ende), 214
New Age, 23, 27, 119–21, 142, 166, 171–75, 188, 207
New Garden, 100–102
New Temple Order, 154
Nibelungenhalle (Hall of the Nibelungs), 54–55, 59
Niedersachsenstein, 201, 202
Nietzsche, Friedrich, 11–12, 21
"Nightside of Nature," 110–11
Novalis, 109–10

Oberstdorf Dance of the Wild Men, 48–50
De Occulta Philosophia (Of Occult Philosophy), 73
occultism, 10, 131, 162–64, 172–73, 209
Occult Russia, x, 147
"occulture," 213–14

Octagon, 208, 210, *pl. 8*
Odin, 31, 35, 36, 45, 52, 54–55, 61, 189
Okkulte Welt (Occult World), 173–74
Ordo Novi Templi (ONT), 154
Ordo Templi Orientis (OTO), 121–22, 149–50, 209
orgone accumulator, 197
orgone energy, 196
The Original Key to the Sixth and Seventh Books of Moses, 181

Pagan Federation (PF), 184
Pagan Federation International (PFI), 182–83, 184, 185, 192
paganism, German, 182–84, 185, 188, 190–92
Pahnke, Elisabeth, 91–92
Pannier, Gudrun, 190–92
Paracelsus, 6, 18, 74–76, 78, 84, 91, 168
Paracelsus Research Society, 149
Parsifal (Wagner), 114–16, 120
Patai, Raphael, 83
Pauli, Wolfgang, 170–71
Perchts, 50–51
Pernath, Athanasius, 133–35
philosophy, 17, 69, 78, 108–9, 111–12, 174. *See also* nature philosophy
Phylak Laboratory, 90
Pogacnik, Marko, 199–200, 204
Popp, Fritz-Albert, 195
Poppe, Sigmar, 213
postwar perspectives, 166–77
Prana, 118
"primal plant," 85
psychedelic plants, 40–41

psychokinetic energy, 169
Psychologie Heute, 173
pyromancy, 44–45

quantum healing, 197

Rätsch, Christian, 40–41
Reclaiming movement, 186, 187
Reich, Wilhelm, 196–97
Reichenbach, Karl von, 196
Reuchlin, Johannes, 70, 74
Reuss, Theodor, 119–23, 149, 173
Riedel, Albert, 93
Ring cycle (Wagner), 7, 59, 213
Rode, August von, 97–98
Roeder, Hans, 164
Romanticism, 7, 20, 147, 171
Rorschach, Hermann, 111
Roselius, Ludwig, 60–62
Rosenkreuz, Christian, 77–78, 194, 211
Rosicrucian manifesto, 77–78
Rosicrucian tradition
    about, 6, 16
    Germany as wellspring of, 9
    holistic vision, 16–17, 35, 94
    spirit of, 79
    symbolism, 81, 82–83
    Tlön and, 211–12
    worldviews and, 215

Sabbith Grade, 107
Saint-Germain, Comte de, 6, 83–84, 102
Saint Nicholas Day, 51
Sättler, Franz, 152
Scharfenberg, Albrecht von, 33
Schauberger, Viktor, 42, 216

Schelling, F. J. W. von, 109, 111
Schlag, Oskar, 127, 175
Schmieke, Marcus, 197
Schneiderfranken, Joseph, 155. *See also* Bô Yin Râ
School of Wisdom, 157–58
Schwenk, Theodor, 42–43, 216
secret Germany, 159
Secret Symbols of the Rosicrucians, 12, 13
"sects and psycho-groups," 209
seidh, 35
seidhkona, 35
shamanism
    about, 5–6
    birds and, 45
    prevalence of, 194
    seidh, 35
    World Tree, 36
Shambhalah (Lechter), 146, 147, *pl. 7*
Sheldrake, Rupert, 195
Sinclair, Emil, 138
Sixth and Seventh Books of Moses, 180
sky god (Teut), 2
Smith, Cyril, 195
Snake Stone, 100
Sokka Gakkai movement, 65
Sol and Luna, 11–12, 86, 135, 161
Soluna Laboratory, 87–89, *pl. 3*
spagyric, 89, 197
spirit and matter, 193–98, 215, 216–17
Spiritualism, 112, 117
springs, 42, 43
Starhawk, 186, 187
Stauffenberg, Claus von, 158–59
Steiner, Rudolf, 9, 85, 87, 91–92, 132, 216
St. John's fire, 44

Stone of Good Fortune, 100
stork, 45–46
Storl, Wolf-Dieter, 47, 205–6, 217
Street of the Alchemists, 135
Strehlow, Wighard, 66–67
sun and moon. *See* Sol and Luna
Swedenborg, Emanuel, 91
Swinburne, Algernon Charles, 214–15

Tacitus, 36, 46, 55
Tattva Viveka, 174
Templars, 154, 160
Temple of the Earth, 144–46
"Templer" (poem), 160
Tesla, Nikola, 171
Teudt, Wilhelm, 26–27
Teut (sky god), 2
Theosophical Society, 108, 112–13, 117–19, 120–24
Thieles, Grete, 103–5
Thieles Garden, 103–5
Thule Society, 153
Time-Waver, 197
Tlön, 212–13
topping-out wreath, 39
trees
    Christian worship of, 37
    Christmas, 36
    groves as worship, 36
    kinship with, 37
    linden, 37
    secret life of, 39–40
    topping-out wreath and, 39
    veneration of, 36
    village linden or oak, 37, 38
    World Tree, 36
Triple Goddess, 57

UNESCO Institute for Lifelong
   Learning, 178

Venus Temple, 97–98, 100
Verdandi-Bund, 55
visionary artists, 141–47
Vogelweide, Walter von der, 67
Vollrath, Hugo, 118–29
Vronsky, Count Sergei, 162, 164–65

Wachler, Ernst, 55
Wagner, Richard, x–xi, 12, 31–33,
   54–55, 58–59, 114–16
Waldorf schools, 167–68
Walpurgishalle (Walpurgis Hall), 52,
   54
Walpurgis Night celebration, 51–52
Wandervögel (Birds of Passage),
   125–26, *pl. 6*
Wasserschöpfen (collecting water), 42
water
   collection, 41–42
   extraordinary properties of, 42

flow of, 42–43
quality, testing, 43
veneration of, 41
Weber, Max, 21–23, 207
Weimar, 100
Weisthor (Wise Fool), 29
Wessel, Wilhelm, 77, 78
Wewelsburg Castle, 29
Wicca, 185–87
Wild Men, 48–50
William II, Frederick, 82–83
Wionfurter, Karl, 107–8
witchcraft, 185–87
Witchcraft Archive, 179
"witch trials," 180
Wohl, Louis de, 163–64
Wohlleben, Peter, 39–40
worldviews, choice between, 215–16
Wörlitz park, 97–100, *pl. 4*
Worpswede, 201–4
Wotan, 40, 45, 51–52, 54, 55, 59

Zimpel, Carl-Friedrich, 89–91

BOOKS OF RELATED INTEREST

Occult Russia
Pagan, Esoteric, and Mystical Traditions
by Christopher McIntosh

The Return of Holy Russia
Apocalyptic History, Mystical Awakening, and the
Struggle for the Soul of the World
by Gary Lachman

Occulture
The Unseen Forces That Drive Culture Forward
by Carl Abrahamsson
Foreword by Gary Lachman

The Occult in National Socialism
The Symbolic, Scientific, and Magical Influences on the Third Reich
by Stephen E. Flowers, Ph.D.

**Encyclopedia of Norse and Germanic Folklore,
Mythology, and Magic**
by Claude Lecouteux

Nightside of the Runes
Uthark, Adulruna, and the Gothic Cabbala
by Thomas Karlsson, Ph.D.

Hildegard von Bingen's Physica
The Complete English Translation of Her Classic Work
on Health and Healing
Translated by Priscilla Throop

John Dee and the Empire of Angels
Enochian Magick and the Occult Roots of the Modern World
by Jason Louv

INNER TRADITIONS • BEAR & COMPANY
P.O. Box 388 • Rochester, VT 05767
1-800-246-8648 • www.InnerTraditions.com

Or contact your local bookseller